Your other favourite authors love this gripping gut-punch of a thriller!

'A toxic, twisty, intelligent and emotional read'   Roz Watkins

'Creepy and unsettling . . . a tense, toxic read that will wrong-foot you at every turn'   Charlotte Duckworth

'A terrifying, compulsive read, deeply psychological with wonderfully drawn characters'   Lisa Ballantyne

'Ticking every single box for me . . . a fantastic one-sitting read'   Caz Frear

'Intensely unsettling'   Emma Christie

'A deeply accomplished novel that combines razor-sharp characterisation with perfectly-pitched suspense. A fantastic, slow-burn thriller'   Philippa East

'I loved it'   Chris Whitaker

'I barely took a breath between the first page and the last!'   Jessica Ryn

'Bravo Nikki Smith on this brilliant, addictive thriller'   Louise Fein

'Evocative and brilliantly written. I loved the clever observations of the complexity of human relationships and emotions which makes this such a gripping read'   Karen Hamilton

T0299459

'An absolutely cracking read'   Jo Jakeman

'Fantastic – what Nikki's really good at is keeping the reader on the edge of her seat'   Emma Curtis

'Another smart and emotional thriller – I devoured it in three sittings'   Louise Beech

'You have no idea who to believe'   Araminta Hall

'Bloody hell! Going to have to lie down in a dark room to stop my heart pounding and catch up on the sleep I've lost desperately racing to the end'   Trevor Wood

'So tense and twisty! I barely breathed!'   Laura Pearson

'Engrossing with heaps of suspense. A must-read for psychological thriller fans'   Olivia Kiernan

Nikki Smith studied English Literature at Birmingham University, before pursuing a career in finance. Following a 'now or never' moment, she applied for a Curtis Brown Creative course where she started writing her first novel, *All In Her Head*. She lives near Guildford with her husband, two daughters and a cat who thinks she's a dog.

Also by Nikki Smith
All In Her Head

LOOK WHAT YOU MADE ME DO

NIKKI SMITH

ORION

An Orion paperback
First published in Great Britain in 2021 by Orion Fiction,
an imprint of The Orion Publishing Group Ltd.,
Carmelite House, 50 Victoria Embankment
London EC4Y 0DZ

An Hachette UK Company

The authorised representative in the EEA is Hachette Ireland,
8 Castlecourt Centre, Dublin 15, D15 XTP3, Ireland (email: info@hbgi.ie)

3 5 7 9 10 8 6 4

A CIP catalogue record for this book is
available from the British Library.

ISBN (Mass Market Paperback) 978 1 4091 9304 3
ISBN (eBook) 978 1 4091 9305 0

Typeset by Input Data Services Ltd, Somerset

Printed and bound in Great Britain by Clays Ltd, Elcograf S.p.A.

www.orionbooks.co.uk

For my parents

'Hell is empty and all the devils are here.'

William Shakespeare, *The Tempest*

Prologue
July 2018

Paul notices it first. I'm too busy darting from one room to another trying to find her, anxiety expanding in my chest like a balloon, making it hard to breathe. She isn't in the kitchen or the lounge. Or behind the sofa in the snug, although, with the various toys lying discarded on the floor and felt-tip pens and colouring books littering every surface, I have to look twice to double check. I run upstairs, two at a time, my heart pumping, and throw open her bedroom door. The room is empty. Dropping down on my hands and knees, I peer under her bed.

'Livvi?' My voice wavers and I clear my throat. There's no answer and nothing to see on the cream carpet apart from a thin layer of dust, the grey fluff forming thick circles round the bottom of each wooden leg, as if attracted by a magnet. I stand up and wince, biting my lip as a burning pain shoots through my toe. I've caught it on the edge of her chest of drawers. Cursing, I hobble into Grace's room, pulling open her white-painted wardrobe doors covered in half-torn Disney *Frozen* stickers that she's tried to peel off now she's outgrown them. The rows of clothes hang motionless, no pairs of small legs protruding underneath.

'Livvi? It's Mummy,' I shout into the silence, trying to ignore the throbbing in my foot. 'You need to come out if you're hiding. I promise I won't be cross.' I listen intently, praying for the sound of a creaking floorboard, a muffled giggle, footsteps scuttling across the carpet. Nothing.

Our bedroom is at the other end of the hall where our duck-egg-blue throw lies undisturbed on top of the duvet, in exactly the same position I'd left it this morning. There's no sign of any obvious tell-tale lumps that I pretend not to spot during one of our games of hide-and-seek. Oh God, where is she? Our wardrobe is locked. The bathroom's empty. I wince as I swallow the metallic taste where I've bitten the inside of my cheek, running back down the stairs to the kitchen.

'She's not upstairs. I've searched everywhere,' I say. Paul glances over my shoulder whilst I'm speaking, staring out through the patio doors across our lawn. He's not listening to me. I grab his arm to get his attention, wondering if he can feel the same ice-cold fingers that are squeezing my lungs, the same weight that has sunk to the bottom of my stomach like an anchor, preventing me from moving. 'What are you looking at?' I ask, trying not to shout. 'We've already checked outside.' I can't keep the edge of hysteria out of my voice as I pull on the sleeve of his shirt, urging him to do something, anything, to find her. He shakes my hand off roughly, pushing me aside as he twists the door handle and realises it's locked, his gaze still fixed on the bottom of the garden.

'What? What is it?' I screw up my eyes against the brightness and blink away the tears that blur my vision. 'She's not out there, Paul.' Two swings dangle limply beneath a metal frame and the trampoline is empty, the canvas mat stretched tight, waiting expectantly for the next jumper.

'Get out of the way,' he yells. I stagger backwards, shocked by his unexpected aggression. 'Are you blind, Jo?' He jabs his finger repeatedly towards the end of the garden as he struggles to get the key off its hook on the wall and into the lock. I can't see what he's pointing at. 'There!' he shouts. 'Look!' I can hear the panic in his voice as he fights to open the door. At first all I can discern through the faint patterns of small handprints smeared on the pane of glass is his office at the end of the garden, the timber structure silhouetted against the evening sun. He finally manages to turn the key before I notice the faint haze around the bottom of the building that is spreading slowly across the grass. It drifts in swirls and the smell hits me the moment Paul flings open the patio door. Smoke.

'Have you searched in there?' He glances at me and I don't need to answer. He sprints across the lawn, screaming her name, as I sink down onto the tiled floor, unable to move as I watch the flames appear. Their red and orange tongues are initially hesitant, contemplating the taste, but once they realise it's a meal to be savoured, they rise up and devour the whole building in a matter of minutes.

One Month Earlier

FRIDAY

Jo

I stand up in the front pew of the crematorium for my father's funeral, one hand using the Order of Service as a fan, the other by my side holding a damp, screwed-up tissue. The rest of the congregation copy me; a hundred pieces of white card flapping ineffectually in the heat like faded butterflies' wings. I stuff the tissue in my pocket, focusing on the hymn my mother has chosen, the organ playing in time with the beats of air against my face, anything to distract me from the stares of the people in the pew behind that attach themselves to the back of my head. They hang heavily in my hair and I run my fingers through it in the hope it will disentangle them, the knots catching at the ends of the brown strands. I wish they'd find someone else to look at; I don't deserve their sympathy.

My mother is sandwiched on my right between my sister Caroline and me, her lips pursed, staring dry-eyed at my father's coffin. Paul stands awkwardly to my left, his new, one-size-too-large black suit jacket that he purchased specially for the occasion making him seem even paler than he already is. I'm glad we didn't bring the girls. I don't want them to see me like this, fragile with grief, the mask I'm wearing threatening to crack at any moment. We'd said Livvi, not yet eight, was too young and although Grace is three years older and we'd asked her if she'd wanted to come, she'd refused, saying she didn't want to see the coffin. Part of me wondered if that had just been an excuse. She's been avoiding Caroline ever since Dad died and I can't blame her after their last encounter. I reach for Paul's hand as the hymn finishes but he moves it away, wiping a few beads of sweat off his face. A small shiver runs across my skin, despite the temperature.

Paul takes a deep breath and follows Rob out of the pew to stand at the lectern. My mother had asked them both to speak; she hadn't trusted Caroline or myself not to break-down mid-sentence. I'd agreed; I know how much she hates displays of emotion. She had insisted my brother-in-law go first and I hadn't objected. My sister isn't holding any balls of sodden tissues; she's not at all flustered. Her hands are folded gently on top of her delicately crossed knees and after glancing down at her skirt, I make a futile effort to smooth the creases out of mine, the thin fabric sticking to my legs in the heat. Her lips move imperceptibly as Rob begins to talk and I realise she's mouthing his speech. I wonder if she wrote it. I doubt it. Rob is a natural orator, playing with words like a teacher handing out sweets to a class; offering them up to the congregation who swallow them greedily, their eyes fixed on him. Caroline nods in agreement as he finishes and I feel a flash of envy at the ease with which he completes the task. Her smile fades as she looks at Paul. She knows it's his turn next.

I pick at a small piece of skin next to my thumbnail, willing him to get through it. His face is chalk-white as he steps forward to take the microphone, Rob standing obtusely in his way. He hates having to speak in public, but I wonder if that's the only reason for his nerves. He's been distracted recently and I can't blame him; so have I. He coughs and the sound reverberates loudly in the silence, making a few of the mourners jump. My mother's eyes close briefly, failing to hide her disappointment and, for a moment, I wish he'd refused to do it, that he'd left it to Rob. Caroline's lips twitch. Don't mess this up, please don't mess this up. I repeat the words in my head like a mantra.

He fumbles in his pocket and for one horrible second, I think he's forgotten to bring it, but then he takes out a piece of paper which rustles as he unfolds it, the sound echoing uncomfortably in the silence as he stares out over the sea of pale faces in front of him. Caroline raises an eyebrow. Rob hadn't needed any notes to read from. Paul glances at me and I nod, hoping the movement will propel him into action. He looks down at what he's written, takes a deep breath, and begins his eulogy. It's not long, certainly nothing like the monologue Rob delivered, but he manages to get through it and I sense a ripple of support, or perhaps relief, amongst the other mourners as he follows Rob back to our pew. My mother looks at me, her expression unreadable. Her eyes linger on my creased skirt and I hold in my stomach; a long-held habit I can't seem to break. I smooth out the material again, the perspiration from my hand leaving a damp patch on the silk. She's still watching. I wonder if she can see straight through my skin to the writhing ball of guilt that is growing multiple shoots, each one making a desperate bid to reach the surface where they'll be visible to everyone.

Paul sits back down next to me with a jolt, tripping over Caroline's bag, which is lying on the floor in front of her seat.

'You did great,' I whisper. He smiles, but his hands tremble as he holds the Order of Service. My mother notices it too. I put my fingers over his to shield him from her gaze and this time he doesn't move away.

Caroline walks next to me as we head out of the crematorium after the service. I take a deep breath of fresh air, needing to push the lifelessness of the room we've been sitting in out of my body, squinting as I look upwards. My father had adored days like this. A clear blue sky with no clouds to spoil the view; a mini heatwave for June. He was only sixty-nine.

'At least now things can start getting back to normal,' Caroline says, fishing in her bag for her sunglasses. I can't bring myself to reply as I watch my mother, her smile un-wavering, greet the mourners as they leave the building. 'It was a nice service,' she continues, putting the shades over her eyes. 'The flowers were beautiful. I ordered them from that new shop near the office. They do great hand-tied bouquets if you ever need one.'

I nod, biting back my desire to tell her I don't give a shit about the bloody flowers.

'Rob's speech was impressive,' I say in an effort to change the subject.

'It was, wasn't it?' she says. 'We wanted to try and make it memorable.'

I nod again, watching my mother embrace the owner of the local golf club for a fraction longer than necessary. If Caroline had helped to write it, she'd managed to include a list of all Dad's achievements but the words hadn't encompassed the personality of the man who had spent his last few weeks attached to various items of medical paraphernalia, making my daughters giggle right up until his final few days. I remind myself she didn't know him like I did. Four years older than me, she was already a teenager, desperate to get out of the house, when he'd started to spend more time in it.

The last trickle of mourners dries up and Rob shakes the vicar's hand to say goodbye, grasping it firmly between his own, pumping it forcefully up and down. The movement sparks a distant memory and I'm conscious of a tingling sensation on my skin.

Rob ushers my mother down the path. 'Ready?' Caroline asks her.

She nods. 'Let's get this over with.' I wish we didn't have to go with them but we don't have a choice. I hesitate instinctively, waiting for my mother to walk ahead, resuming our natural family order as we file towards the waiting car, my mother next to Caroline at the front, me at the back. When I'd been growing up, I'd used to wonder whether I'd been adopted as she'd always favoured my sister over me. I'd found baby photos of us both in a drawer along with our birth certificates which had discounted this theory, but there had been something in her eyes when she'd been holding Caroline that had been missing in the pictures with me. A brightness in her face, as if she had been lit up from the inside. I had flicked through all the pages in the album, twice, desperate to find one of me with her where she'd looked like that, but there hadn't been a single one.

As the driver pulls out of the car park, Rob stares at my sister.

'What is it?' she asks.

'Your mascara's smudged.'

She pulls her compact out of her bag and examines herself in the mirror, wiping underneath one eye with a tissue. 'Better?'

He nods, barely glancing at her as she snaps the lid shut and puts it away. His fingers tap his knee impatiently. For once, he doesn't seem to know what to say.

'I hope they've switched the air conditioning on at the hotel,' my mother says. 'I couldn't breathe in the crematorium.'

I can't bring myself to look at her, glancing at my watch instead. Three o'clock. The girls will be finishing school. I'm overwhelmed by a sudden urge to hear their voices and touch their skin, to bury myself in their warmth and push death away into the distance. I get out my phone and type a message to Anna.

Hope you're still on for pickup and girls are OK. Should be home by 7ish. xx

It vibrates on my lap a few seconds later.

All good and no need to rush. Girls will be fine here, don't worry. Hope it all goes as well as these things can. A xx

Caroline looks at me. 'Everything OK?'

'Yes, just checking a friend is collecting the girls from school for me.'

She smiles. 'It's tricky to manage all the logistics, isn't it?' I force myself to smile back. As if she'd know. She'd never had to juggle work and childcare when Adam had been growing up; my mother had acted as her full-time Nanny. The same role had been available when I'd had Grace, but my mother had refused, citing the travelling distance to our old house as impractical. She was right, but still only ever visited for short occasions, never staying over, claiming she didn't want to interrupt my routine.

Caroline opens the window and Rob frowns and shuts it again, his knuckles white as he presses the button, and I feel a stab of guilt. This isn't her fault. I just want this day to be over. We sit together in an awkward silence, the rhythmic ticking of the taxi indicator counting down the seconds until we can get out. I contemplate reaching for Paul's hand again and then change my mind, unsure whether I'm offering comfort, or taking it; knowing I don't warrant the latter.

The car pulls up outside the hotel; apparently an old coaching inn that once provided the stage for Lady Hamilton and Lord Nelson's affair, the old red bricks now barely visible, covered in ivy. The concierge ushers us into the private room my mother booked for the occasion. I head for the table where the drinks have been laid out, pick up a flute of champagne and swallow it down in a couple of large mouthfuls, desperate for the alcohol to hit my bloodstream. Paul comes over, noting my empty glass as he opens a bottle of beer.

'At least you ordered a lot of booze,' he says.

I nod, picking up another drink, raising it towards the bottle in his hand. 'Yes. We're going to need it. The crematorium was packed. Here's to Dad.'

He smiles. 'To your dad.' He leans down, murmuring quietly in my ear, 'Who'd have hated that service, and would know how much I need this beer.'

I press my cheek against his, a brief moment of connection that has been lacking in our lives recently. 'I'd better go and thank people for coming,' I say, trying to fit one of the canapés into my mouth without spilling any of it down my top, gathering up the courage to mingle. I catch my mother watching me from the other side of the room and feel every centimetre of progress the smoked salmon and cucumber makes as it slides slowly down my throat, sitting like a stone in the bottom of my stomach.

The noise of a glass being repeatedly tapped with a spoon provides a welcome interruption to conversations I find exhausting. Caroline is standing in the middle of the room and a hush descends as everyone looks in her direction.

'I wanted to say a big thank-you to all of you for making the effort to come today. I know how much Dad would have appreciated it. He was an amazing husband to my mum, a wonderful father to me and Jo, and we were lucky to have him.'

And grandfather, I mutter to myself. I notice she doesn't mention that.

'I'm sure he'd be delighted if he could see us all here, and I can assure you he wouldn't want any of this food to go to waste, so please make sure you don't hold back, and I'd like everyone to raise a toast. To my father, Thomas. We'll miss you.'

I glance around. I can't see Paul, but then I notice the door opening and he comes back into the room. Caroline has made her speech without him even being here. She walks over, holding her glass of orange juice.

'We're going to make a move soon,' she says.

'Already?' I ask.

'Yes. Rob's ordered a cab. You can stay on,' she adds. I bite back a retort that I'm not asking for her permission. I'm not sure why she wants to rush off, it's not as if she's got anything to get back for. Adam's away. He'd only left to go travelling a couple of weeks ago, delaying his trip as long as he could until after Dad had died. Caroline had told me he was in Bali but she hasn't mentioned him today and it's always difficult to get any information about Adam out of Rob. He hadn't even gone to the airport to see him off.

'Mum said she's arranged a meeting next week with the solicitor,' Caroline says.

'What for?' I reply.

'Something about Dad's will, I think. I thought you knew.'

I stare at her. 'She hasn't mentioned it.'

'Hasn't she?' Caroline's cheeks are flushed. Up until a few weeks ago, we'd been getting on better than we had done for years, taking tiny steps to rebuild the relationship my mother had taken pleasure in driving apart; one that had remained firmly at arm's length, consisting of polite Christmas and birthday cards until I'd moved back here from Bristol three years ago following Dad's request to help with the business. But the last time we'd spoken properly had been when Dad was still alive – the fragile threads we'd hesitantly woven together had ripped apart, and now I feel like I did as a teenager; having to pretend she's not lying to me, when we both know differently. She scans the room, waiting for Rob to notice her and he inclines his head towards the door. He can't wait to get away.

Perhaps I'm being too harsh. None of us want to be here and everyone deals with grief in different ways – I know that better than anyone. Rob had only visited Dad once in those final days, stumbling out of the makeshift bedroom we'd constructed in the sitting room, his face an ashen-grey colour, walking straight past Paul and me without a word. No doctor's warning can prepare you for the sight of someone dying when you're confronted with it face to face. The waxy pallor of translucent skin stretched tightly over a heap of bones. Rob's probably still in denial. Looking at him now, as he ushers Caroline out of the room, I wouldn't be able to tell he's just lost his father-in-law. But then I know how difficult it is to be sure what Rob's really thinking.

I listen to a few of the guests swapping anecdotes about Dad, the three glasses of champagne I've drunk helping me to pretend they aren't talking about my father, burying my grief temporarily behind a hazy fog, almost bearable, thinking about how we need to get back to let Buddy out or he'll end up chewing the furniture. I put my empty glass down on the table, shaking my head as a waitress holds out a plate full of sausage rolls, and head out of the room to find the concierge.

Rob and Caroline are waiting at the entrance to reception. Rob has his back to me but it looks like they're arguing. He's leaning towards her, his face a couple of inches away from hers. She spots me approaching and steps backwards, her features rearranging themselves into the composed expression I'm more familiar with.

'Everything OK?' I ask, staring at her.

'Fine,' Rob replies, smiling. 'Our taxi's just a bit late.'

'It should be here any minute though,' Caroline says quickly.

'I'll let Mum know you're leaving, shall I?' I ask, hoping it'll prick her conscience.

'She already knows,' my sister replies. 'We're taking her with us – she's just nipped to the Ladies'.'

I wonder if my mother had asked to stay at theirs. She hadn't taken me up on my offer to come back with Paul and me. She appears out of the cloakroom and I can see she's reapplied her lipstick, the bright red colour bleeding into the fine lines along her top lip. The fact she hasn't outlined them in pencil first is the only sign that everything isn't exactly as it should be, the one oversight in her otherwise immaculate appearance. Rob reaches for Caroline's hand as I turn to go. I can't be sure if I imagine a momentary hesitation before she takes it, but there's no mistaking the look he gives me as I walk off down the corridor.

It makes my skin prickle; a reminder of what he's capable of.

SATURDAY

Caroline

Cleaning the kitchen takes me the entire afternoon. I remove all the jars from the cupboard very carefully, lining them up on the side of the counter so I can remember their original order, before wiping the rings of sticky residue off the wood and putting them all back. One centimetre too far the left or right could result in an immeasurably different outcome to my evening. My hands shake as I move the mint sauce, trying not to think about the significance of every decision or I won't do anything at all and he'll come home before I've finished. And I know how much Rob hates it if I leave anything unfinished.

I make sure I get the cloth into every crevice, into all the tight corners and plastic trays of the fridge door. The water in the sink turns an unpleasant brown colour as I wring out the damp material over and over again. I've done everywhere; the tops of the picture frames, the edge of the cupboard door that houses the bin, behind the pot we use to hold the washing-up brushes on the kitchen windowsill.

It helps keep my mind off the funeral. Off my sister. It hadn't been enough for her to have had Dad's almost undivided attention at the office for the past few years since moving back from Bristol. In the last couple of weeks she'd barely moved from the chair beside his bed, as if her presence at the critical moment would in some way erase all the years she hadn't been there. I'd felt like an intruder when I'd gone around to visit, my attempts at conversation stilted. I'd desperately wanted him to say something so I knew he understood. That he cared as much for me as he did for her. But he hadn't. She hadn't given him the chance. And now he's gone.

I'm sweating once I've finished and open the window to let in some air as I watch the dirty water drain away down the plughole, wiping round the inside of the whole sink with kitchen roll to make sure there aren't any smears left.

The house is always so quiet without Rob here. A silence that descends the moment he walks out of the front door, as if the whole building has let out its breath in a sigh of relief. I sink into its softness, knowing it won't last. As the length of his absence increases, the atmosphere gradually tightens with expectation, until I feel it as a physical pain that squeezes my head, making it throb in anticipation.

Once the radio pips beep for the hourly news, the time he's due back, my level of adrenaline is so high that my hands shake and I have to stop myself retching at the inevitable sound of his footsteps outside the front door. I have eleven seconds to compose myself whilst he gets his keys out of his jacket pocket, lets himself inside and takes off his shoes before walking into the kitchen to check on me. He expects his cup of tea to be waiting for him by the time he comes back from washing his hands in the cloakroom; a routine he follows religiously. I breathe slowly, in through my nose for three and out through my mouth for five, so that when he reappears and I pass him his favourite blue mug with one small spoonful of sugar, *can't you ever fucking get it right*, the trembling in my hands has stopped enough for him not to notice it.

He glances at the letters I've left in a neat pile on the counter, all addressed to him, frowning at a couple without opening them. I wait until he's finished his drink, trying to judge what kind of a mood he's in before I ask him anything. His eyes flicker over the pristine granite surfaces, never quite meeting my own, and I steel myself, waiting to see if I've passed his inspection.

He goes upstairs, taking the letters with him. It's a few minutes' respite from the hours I must sit through until I can go to bed, hoping he'll stay in the sitting room watching TV. The alternative is that he follows me up and that's always so much worse. Those memories take longer to fade than the bruises. I stay quite still, listening to the sounds that tell me what he's doing as clearly as if I was standing in the room with him. The soft thud of his trousers dropping onto the floor, the squeak of our wardrobe door as he opens it to reach inside for a hanger on which to put his jacket. The bang as he slams it shut. The creak of the floorboard by the side of his bed as he sits down to read the post. I've learned to recognise them all over the years as sounds don't allow him to hide things in the same way as he does with words. Nothing can disguise the noise of a door being shut. Especially when your fingers are trapped in the frame.

I double check the kitchen table is laid properly; all the

condiments set out exactly how he likes them, including the tomato ketchup that he insists smothering over whatever I cook. I loathe the stuff; it's too sweet for my taste. And then I hear his footsteps as he walks across the landing and back down the stairs. My body tenses, an unconscious movement, one of the only things I have left to shield myself against whatever will come next.

'Your mum gone?' he asks. I nod. 'When's the meeting with the solicitor?'

'Tuesday.'

He runs his forefinger across the counter, inspecting it for dust.

'She's going to tell Jo?' he asks. I nod. 'If you get what it's worth, it'll be more than enough to finance the site development. Maybe even another one I'm looking at as well. What's for dinner?' he asks.

'Lasagne.' He stares at me and I add, 'The one from Delia that you like.' He looks at the table, checking to see if he can find anything missing. 'Do you want some salad?' I ask.

He shakes his head. 'What time did your mum leave?'

'After lunch.'

'What have you done since she left?'

'Put some washing on. Cleaned the kitchen.'

He runs his finger under the tap and wipes it on a tea towel. 'I've spent the best part of a day of what's supposed to be my weekend in the office with fucking morons, trying to sort out something they should have dealt with yesterday. That's what happens if I take a day off.' I swallow and don't speak, letting my thoughts run through my head like water, small streams that flow in endless circles, never joining together with others to make a coherent conversation. 'Anyone call?' he asks casually.

I shake my head. 'No.' He picks up my phone off the side of the counter and keys in the digits of my pin, scrolling through my recent call history. He'll only find his number. I don't look at him as I put on the oven gloves to take the dinner out of the oven.

'You're sure?' he asks, I know he's watching me; I can feel my skin burn and have to hope that the blast of heat as I open the oven door will hide the flush that spreads across my face. I focus on not dropping the heavy dish as I put it down on the chopping board.

'Yes,' I say. 'Quite sure. No one's called; I've been on my own since Mum left.'

He doesn't reply, disappearing out of the room as I carefully cut him a portion of the steaming food, trying to keep the segment intact as I take it out of the china container, wiping the side of his plate to clean up the small trail of sauce that's dripped over the edge. I carry both plates onto the table and sit down, the familiar noise of our home phone in the study bleeping as he presses 1471 to listen to the last number that was dialled. I know he'll be checking the call history by scrolling through the numbers on the screen but I'm not stupid enough to use it. I only made that mistake once. He comes back into the kitchen and his mobile buzzes. He takes it out of his pocket and glances at the message before he sits down, smiling. I contract the muscles around my mouth so I look like I'm smiling too. He squeezes out a large globule of tomato ketchup and spreads it across the top of his lasagne. I don't let him see me wince, the sickly sweet smell making me nauseous.

'Do you want a glass of wine?' he asks. I try not to let the surprise show on my face. I can't remember the last time we had a drink together. Years ago we used to sit on the sofa, my legs across his lap, a couple of glasses of Shiraz on the table in front of us, him telling me his plans for the business whilst I resisted the urge to reach out and touch his face, needing to feel his skin with my fingers to believe he was actually sitting beside me.

'Sure,' I say. 'I think there's white or red in the rack. Which do you fancy?'

'Red,' he replies. I get up and bring back a bottle of Montepulciano and the corkscrew. He waves me away as I attempt to open it.

'I'll do it.' I put a couple of wine glasses on the table as he pours a small amount into the bottom of each glass. 'To us,' he says as he raises his towards mine. They clink as they meet and I wonder if he can hear my brain frantically flicking through various possibilities as to what could have happened to have put him in this mood.

'To us,' I say, as he picks up his fork.

'I think I've sorted the planning permission for that new plot,' he says. 'Haven't got it in writing yet but I'm pretty sure the Council are going to support it.' I nod, and he frowns, mid-mouthful.

'What have you put in this?' he asks.

I pause. 'Nothing . . . just the usual. Mince, onion, tomatoes . . . why?'

'What cheese sauce did you use? Was it out of a jar?' I shake my head. 'It tastes vile. How hard can it be to make a decent sauce?' I don't answer and keep very still, staring at the loose threads on the edge of the tablecloth. He lowers his cutlery onto his plate. 'I can't eat this. Clearly. I'll have to get myself something else that's actually edible.'

'Do you want me to . . .?' I go to get up but he grabs my hand.

'Sit down.' I sit. I've learned by now there is nothing I can do to stop him once he's started. I focus on trying not to let the terror that's twisting my insides show on my face. He looks at me, staring into my eyes, searching for the fear that he swallows greedily, feeding what is an inexhaustible appetite.

'There's no point wasting it,' he says, picking up his plate and sliding the contents onto mine. 'You can have it.'

'I don't . . .'

He stares at me. 'You will eat it. And you will finish every mouthful.' He picks up his glass as he pushes back his chair and stands up, hesitating for a fraction of a second before he takes mine as well and pours the remaining red liquid from both down the sink, the droplets splashing up the sides of the white porcelain like blood.

He leans against the sink at one end of the kitchen, his arms folded, waiting for me to finish what's on my plate. His body is so rigid I can almost see the anger flowing just below the surface of his skin, about to break through at any moment. I close my eyes as I swallow each mouthful, trying not to breathe through my nose so I don't taste the ketchup that snakes in crimson trails through each forkful. My stomach protests and for a moment I think I might be sick, but I keep eating until there's nothing left, and he uncrosses his arms, the muscle in his jaw flickering. I put my cutlery on the plate and carry it across the room to stack it in the dishwasher but my fork slides off, clattering against the tiles. I wince as I pick it up and get a glass out of the cupboard to gulp some water to get rid of the taste of ketchup.

'You missed a bit,' he says, bending down. He wipes the tile with his finger and steps towards me, holding it out, a couple of pieces of mince half-buried in a globule of cheese sauce. I open my mouth obediently, swallowing the tiny mouthful, my eyes bright, ignoring the greasy smear on the floor.

'Look what you made me do,' he says, putting his arms round my waist. 'I don't like getting cross. I look forward to eating something nice when I get in. I was hoping we could make a bit more of an effort now it's just the two of us here. And if the meeting with the solicitor goes well, it'll mean you won't have to work anymore. I can take care of both of us. I do love you, you know.' I feel his body tense, waiting for me to respond. He nuzzles his head into the back of my neck as I rinse out the glass, placing it carefully upside down on the draining board, wondering what Adam might be doing at this moment and whether the pain in my stomach is as a result of what I've eaten, or because I miss my son. I force myself to relax into Rob's arms, hoping my softness is infectious, that I can use it to mould him into how he used to be.

'I love you too,' I say, no longer sure if I'm lying to him or to myself. I still catch the occasional glimpse of the man I married, fleeting moments that I cling on to, folding them away in my head like tissue paper, fragile layers that tear into tiny pieces when I try to remember them. I promised I'd never leave him. Until death do us part. That was the deal.

You don't know I'm watching you. Or perhaps you do and you're just pretending not to notice. Or maybe, to you, I'm simply invisible. One of those people whose name you ask and they reply, but, in the same breath, tell you that you've already met. And you nod vigorously, unsure who is most embarrassed, pretending that of course you remember, and at the same time running through the occasion mentioned over and over again in your head. You wonder if I've dyed my hair, or had it cut, as you can't picture me ever being there at all. You can't remember us ever having had a conversation and want to ask me what it was about; whether we were both part of a larger group and I contributed the odd snippet from the sidelines, in which case you could perhaps understand why my presence is now a blank, or whether we talked for a while, one-on-one. And if it was the latter, you want to know what I said, but even if I repeated it, I suspect the words would slide out as a murky shade of beige, so unremarkable and inoffensive that they'd cancel themselves out, swallowed up by something far more colourful that attracted your attention. I can already tell you're the kind of person who is always looking to find the next new and exciting thing and I've decided that's going to be me.

SUNDAY

Jo

I ring the bell for the second time but when there's still no answer I flick through the keys on my keyring, trying to find the one Dad had given me. My mother said she'd be home by now. I find it and open the door, breathing in the unmistakably familiar smell that tells me I'm home, a heady mix of leather and polish and old books. I clear my throat to break the silence that greets me, half expecting to hear the familiar sound of clinking china from Dad making tea – always on a tray with cups and saucers; never a mug.

I peer into the sitting room, hovering in the entrance, refusing to cross the threshold. His hospital bed has gone, four indentations in the thick green carpet the only evidence it was ever there at all. I turn away, not wanting to remember.

As I walk down the hall, there's a rustling noise. I stop and listen, but the house is silent apart from the sound of my breathing, emptier than ever. The dark furniture and thick wooden doors trap the heat that settles in an invisible haze, pressing against me from all sides. The thermometer in the car had said it was twenty-eight degrees today but it feels hotter in here. Despite the years of being away, the sense of claustrophobia never changes whenever I return; I regress to being a teenager the minute I walk inside this house. If it wasn't for the thought of my mother's reaction at not finding me here as we'd agreed, I'd walk straight back out of the front door and wouldn't look back.

I swallow, forcing myself to breathe slowly as I lift my hair off the back of my neck, wiping the sheen of sweat off my skin, wondering if I should open a window. As I put my hand on the bannister at the bottom of the stairs I hear the noise again. Like scratching. It's louder this time; coming from behind the closed door of Dad's study.

I try to put any thoughts of rats out of my head as I walk towards the door, hesitating before I turn the old metal knob. It creaks ominously as it swings open and I wish I'd brought Buddy with me. That dog wouldn't hurt a fly, but he runs after anything that moves. I don't even have anything to throw in case something scuttles out in front of my feet. I peer into the gloom, feeling for the switch on the wall. The heavy velvet curtains covering the windows are still drawn, making it difficult to see anything. As my fingers find what they're looking for and the room lights up, a figure standing by the desk turns slowly towards me. I recoil, banging my elbow against the door frame.

'Jesus, Caroline,' I say. 'Mum said you weren't coming until twelve. You scared me.' My voice comes out high-pitched and I feel as if I'm thirteen again, standing in the same room, defending my behaviour, my heart thumping at a ridiculous pace.

'Rob's meeting got cancelled so he didn't need me to give him a lift. His car's in the garage, the brake lights aren't working. Typical that it goes wrong in the first week after he bought it brand new.' I tell myself I'm being paranoid at the emphasis she puts on 'new', not wanting to start an argument.

'I'm surprised you can see what you're doing,' I say. 'Why haven't you put the light on?'

She shrugs. 'I didn't need to.' She doesn't seem to have cleared anything away. Books and newspapers are stacked in unstable piles on every surface. 'There's so much to do, isn't there?' she says, looking at her handbag that's lying on the floor beside her, something blue poking out of the top.

'You didn't park on the drive?' I say, pulling back the curtains, wincing as the sunlight streams into the airless room.

'I hate reversing out. It's easier to leave it on the road.' We're back to the conversations I remember of our childhood. Clipped back-and-forth exchanges, like a game of tennis, each more aggressive than the last. I can tell she hasn't forgiven me after our last argument and realise with a jolt that Dad had still been alive then. It already feels like a lifetime ago. Losing my father has nudged my world off its axis, spinning it in a direction I could never have foreseen. His death should have brought us closer but it's had the opposite effect; created barriers that neither of us know how to cross. I've buried my memories of his last few days somewhere so deep I don't have to think about them, let alone share them with my sister.

'Sorry,' I say. 'I'm not having a go at you; you just startled me. I didn't realise anyone else was here. I've brought some dustbin liners,' I add, reaching into my bag and holding them out as a peace offering. 'Help yourself.'

I glance at my father's desk, the dark wooden piece of

furniture covered in a pile of envelopes, many of them un-opened. I think of the one I'd stuffed in the pocket of my jacket when it had arrived last Thursday. I'd briefly scanned the contents, knowing deep down what the letter inside was going to say. Seeing the words in black and white had still come as a shock and I hadn't wanted Paul to read it, telling myself I'd wait for a better time to show him, but I'm begin-ning to wonder whether I should show him at all.

'There are probably a lot of things that can go to charity,' I suggest.

She wrinkles her nose. 'Possibly. But I think we'll have to chuck most of it. No one wants this kind of stuff anymore.' I feel myself bristle, but don't reply. They're only things, I tell myself. Just things. The memories will still be there. A few good ones amongst the multitude I'd rather not remember. I notice the packet of playing cards on the shelf that he'd taught Grace to play Patience with and pick them up, putting them in my pocket, not able to bear the thought of them being thrown away.

'Does Mum want us to make a start without her?' I ask. 'Or should we wait?' I notice Caroline's hair is different. Normally she has it tied off her face in a ponytail, but today she's wearing it loose and it suits her. The temperature in here clearly doesn't bother her in the same way as it does me; she's still as elegant as ever. She sees me staring and tucks one of the auburn strands behind her ear, self-consciously.

We both look up as we hear the front door opening.

'Jo?' I'd recognise my mother's voice anywhere; her tone slices through my skin like a scalpel, dissecting the flesh be-neath, exposing my vulnerabilities.

'I'm in the study, Mum. With Caroline.'

She walks in and I'm struck all over again by the resemblance to my sister. It's not just the colour of their hair that everyone comments on, it's the way they both hold themselves, almost as if they glide across the floor, unaffected by the laws of gravity that govern the rest of us.

'Sorry I'm a bit late.' She goes to kiss Caroline first, their faces never quite touching. 'I won't keep you long. I just wanted to let you both know I'm seeing the solicitor on Tuesday. You don't have to come.' She fixes her eyes on me whilst she's speaking and I glance across at Caroline whose expression doesn't alter.

'Course we'll be there,' Caroline says before I've had a chance to think of a response.

'Why do we need . . .?' I stumble.

'Your father's will,' my mother replies icily. 'It's only a formality, but his solicitor insists we go.'

'I'll be there,' I say hastily, knowing it's the last thing I want to do. My mother stares at me and I flinch under her gaze, shrivelling even more than I am already in this heat. It's as if she can see exactly what I'm thinking and for a moment I think she knows. I step backwards, putting my hand on his desk to steady myself.

'Are you all right?' Caroline asks.

'Fine.' I wipe my sticky palms against my trousers.

'I'll open a window,' my mother says. 'It is a bit stuffy in here. We shut everything to stop your father's papers being disturbed.' She unfastens the latch, pushing hard on the glass to get it to budge; the wooden frame has warped slightly. I lean against the sill, not wanting to sit in Dad's empty chair that she's moved to stand beside as if he's still here, joining in the conversation, waiting to divulge my secret. I close my eyes and take deep breaths, repeating the same words in my head that I've said over and over again in the past weeks. *I'm sorry. I'm so sorry.*

'Before we see the solicitor, I want to let you know that I've made a decision to sell the business.' My mother's words cut through the fog of heat as if someone has dropped an ice cube down my back. I glance at Caroline but the expression on her face tells me this isn't a shock. She already knows.

'What? Why?'

'I'll own the majority of the shares once your father's will is settled and I think it's the best thing to do to ensure our financial security.'

I clear my throat.

'Shouldn't we at least discuss it? Dad wouldn't have wanted this.' My mother gives me a look that makes me wish I hadn't spoken.

'It's not your place to tell me what your father would have wanted, Joanna. I was married to him for over forty years. For some reason you seem to think you knew him better than I did when you've only worked with him for the last three. I'm doing what I think is best for all of us.' Her response is like a slap in the face and I dig my nails into my palm, holding back the words I'm tempted to let tumble out of my mouth, aware there will be no way to put them back. Caroline stays silent, avoiding my gaze.

'Did you know about this?' I ask. She glances at my mother before shaking her head. She's lying. 'And you agree with Mum's decision, I presume?'

My mother raises her hand, an attempt to stop me talking. 'Joanna, it isn't up to –'

Caroline interrupts before she can finish her sentence. 'Dad's gone, Jo. And we need to do what's best for all of us. We're the ones who are still here.'

She stares at me and for a moment I imagine I see a plea for help in her eyes, the same look she used to give me years ago when she was in trouble and wanted me to cover for her, but then she blinks and it's gone.

'Caroline's right.' My mother breaks the fragile connection, siding with my sister as usual.

'Why doesn't that surprise me?' I retort, watching my mother's face harden. I have a sudden overwhelming desire for my dad to be here, to feel that I have someone on my side. And then the guilt descends again, a sledge hammer this time, crushing me so hard that I want to curl up on the floor.

'I – I just need a moment.' I walk out of the room, down the corridor into the cloakroom, where I sit down on top of the closed toilet seat. One of my father's coats is hanging up on the back of the door, an empty shell on a hanger, his familiar earthy smell the only part of him that still remains. I take a deep breath. He's gone and I'm not in a position to question my mother's decision after what I've done. I try to swallow the lump in my throat and splash some water on my face, ignoring the face of the fourteen-year-old girl who stares back at me in the mirror. I rub my hand over the sleeve of my father's jacket, wishing he was still inside it as I unlock the door.

The whispering stops as my footsteps echo on the wooden floorboards in the hall. I walk back into the study and notice

33

Caroline looking at my father's desk. The bottom drawer isn't shut properly; I can see the row upon row of blue cardboard files hanging suspended from metal rails.

'It's your choice,' I hear myself say. 'Do whatever you think is best.' My mother smiles at me, her red lipstick parting to reveal her immaculate white veneers and I know she'd have done it anyway, with or without my approval.

'I'm so glad that's sorted.' She glances at Caroline who smiles and I get the familiar feeling that they've had a whole conversation which I haven't been part of.

I can't see any tables in the shade that aren't already occupied. We should have reserved one outside but I hadn't realised the pub would be so busy this early. Paul keeps checking his mobile as the girls walk over to the swings and the benches at the bottom of the garden.

'You expecting a call?' I ask, when his eyes slide away from me for what feels like the fiftieth time.

'Potential new client,' he replies.

'Can you get some drinks and order food whilst I find us somewhere to sit?' I ask, irritated at having to fight for his attention. He was the same when I got home from visiting Dad when he'd first been ill; his phone constantly in his hand or next to him on the arm of the sofa, never out of reach. 'The girls will have burgers and I'll just have a salad. No dressing.' I'm the one who wants him to focus more on getting new business, I tell myself as he walks inside towards the bar. I can't complain if he's doing what I ask.

I spot a free table on the edge of the patio where I can keep an eye on the girls and struggle to open the large cream parasol that's frayed along the edges, the rusty mechanism catching on the pole as I try to push it upwards. I can feel the sun burning the back of my neck before I finally get it to move; the shade expanding and blocking out the heat just as my frustration reaches a peak. A wasp buzzes around my head and I wave it away as I see Anna walking towards me.

'Not easy to open, are they?' she asks, leaning over to give me a hand.

'No,' I reply, 'and I don't want to sit out here without one. The girls haven't got any suncream on. Are you here for lunch? Do you want to join us?'

She shakes her head. 'Thanks, but we've just eaten. The girls spotted Livvi and Grace on the swings so I said they could have five minutes together.'

'Andy not with you?'

'He's gone to see his sister.' She sits down opposite me, winding her long blonde hair back off her face into a messy bun. I wish I could do that with mine but it's too thick and frizzy and I'm conscious it's making me overheat, hanging over the back of my neck like a blanket.

'Thanks so much again for having the girls for me on Friday,' I say.

She smiles. 'It really wasn't a problem. You know they're welcome anytime.'

'Well, I owe you; I know we were home late. I thought we'd be back by seven.'

Anna's forehead creases. 'I could have sworn I saw your lights go on earlier than that. I thought you needed a bit of time to . . . sort yourselves out.'

'No. I came straight over to get the girls after the taxi

dropped us off.' I frown as I try to think back. 'Maybe I forgot to switch them off in the kitchen.'

'They were on upstairs. Grace pointed it out,' she says. 'She noticed when they were eating tea.'

'One of the girls must have left them on,' I say, flapping at the wasp that has returned for a second attempt at landing. Anna looks across the grass to where Livvi is pushing Jess on the swings.

'How are the girls coping?' she asks.

I swallow. 'Kids are resilient, aren't they?' I reply, trying not to think about how upset Grace has been.

'It's early days,' Anna says. 'At least now the funeral's over.'

I nod, knowing she's trying to be helpful, those milestones in the grieving process you're supposed to reach and clamber over, a sense of achievement waiting on the other side, the road a little easier to navigate. She has no idea it's not like that for me; I feel as if I am slowly suffocating; each breath slightly harder to take than the last.

'Paul seems to be making an effort to help with the school runs,' she says.

'Most of the time he does,' I reply. 'But he's been a bit distant recently. Work's been tricky.'

Grace walks up the lawn and sits down beside me. 'Can I get a drink, Mum?'

'Dad's just getting them. He'll be out any minute.'

'We should go,' Anna says. 'Let me know when things have settled down a bit, it would be great if you can both come over.'

I nod. 'I'll check dates with Paul and text you.' I watch as she walks back into the pub before turning around to look at

36

Livvi on the swing, her body silhouetted against the sun as she flies up in the air, again and again, shrieking with laughter.

'Are Grandma or Auntie Caroline coming for lunch?' Grace asks, fiddling with the strap on her sandal.

'Not today, sweetheart.' I keep telling myself that things will get easier, that I'll think about it less, but at the moment guilt fills my brain, pushing everything else into a tiny gap at the side, making my head hurt. There's a buzzing sound and Grace lets out a shriek as the wasp lands on her arm. I tell her to keep still as I lean over the table and flick it off. She rubs her skin, checking it hasn't stung her as we both look around, waiting for it to come back. I wonder how much longer Paul is going to be and squint through the open door of the pub, trying to spot him. I can see him talking to Anna at the bar, but it's another couple of minutes before he finally appears outside with a tray of drinks and picks up a large glass of lager.

'Remember you're driving,' I say. 'Grace, can you go and get your sister?'

She runs off down the garden, her shoe still undone.

'Don't lecture me, Jo,' he retorts. 'It's one glass. It's been a stressful day.' I can feel the distance between us grow a couple of inches wider as we sit in silence.

'Is something the matter?' I ask, eventually.

He rubs his forehead, avoiding eye contact. 'Just work. I've got a few issues with my biggest client.' He takes another mouthful of lager. 'How was your mum?'

'Same as always,' I say. 'She's had Dad's hospital bed taken away.' As I hear myself say the words, I realise that although I knew it would happen, the reality feels like someone has detached a part of my body. It takes a huge effort to blink back the tears that prick the back of my eyes.

I can't get the image of the floral pattern on Dad's pillowcase and duvet cover out of my head; my mother's crass attempt to brighten the room that towards the end had just served to highlight the greyness of his skin. I want to be able to talk to Paul about it, but I can't. He wouldn't understand. No one would. And although I keep thinking he's pulling away from me, perhaps I am the one who is actually retreating. Shutting myself off so he can't see what I'm trying to hide.

'Caroline was there as well,' I add quickly, needing to change the subject. 'We discussed the business. Mum wants to sell it.'

He looks at me. 'Are you OK with that?'

'I don't have a choice. When Mum inherits Dad's shares, she'll be able to do what she wants. It's not what Dad would have wanted, but you know my mother.'

He smiles, briefly. 'Yes. I do.' The wasp returns, circling round his head. 'Bloody things. They're everywhere at the moment,' he says, attempting to swat it away. I grab his hand mid-air, waiting until the insect lands on the table, then pick up my glass and bring it down hard, squashing it underneath, its body making an unpleasant crunching noise as the buzzing noise stops. He raises his eyebrows.

'That was a bit brutal.'

'It should have learned the first time,' I say, pushing it off the table onto the patio where it lands on the ground in a curled-up ball. 'Are you around on Tuesday to get the girls from school?' I ask, changing the subject. 'I've got to go to the solicitor's with my mother.'

'Sure,' he says, pulling out his phone and putting it down on the table. 'Do you know how much you get if the business is sold?'

'I've no idea,' I reply, 'but I own ten per cent of the company so it should be enough to keep us going until I find another job.'

'You'll find something else.'

'That's not the point. We moved back here because Dad asked me to help save the business, not get rid of it.' Paul stares at me, his eyes asking the questions that we've been over so many times before. 'He'd just been diagnosed, Paul. He was desperate. What did you want me to say?'

'There are other accountants, Jo. He could have found someone else.'

'He could. But I'm the only one who knew how much the estate agency meant to him. And you weren't exactly overwhelmed with work. You agreed that you could carry on web designing from anywhere; we didn't have to be in Bristol.' I stop myself before I say anything else, feeling the need to defend a decision which we made jointly, but which recently Paul has twisted into sounding as if it had been all mine.

Paul hesitates, whatever he was about to say interrupted by the waiter arriving with the food. I remind myself that my salad has at least a thousand less calories than the burgers and chips that now look so much more appealing. He stands up, as if relieved to be able to get away, the tension between us easing as he walks off, as though someone had lifted up a blanket.

*

39

I carry my jacket upstairs with me and put it away in my wardrobe as I tuck the girls into bed later that evening. I'm going to have to talk to Paul at some point about the contents of the letter that rustles in the pocket, but I need to find the right time.

'Paul?' I say, as he goes upstairs to kiss Livvi and Grace goodnight. 'When we got back from the funeral and I went over to Anna's to pick up the girls, were the lights on when you came in?'

He frowns. 'I can't remember. Why?'

'Anna said they were.'

He shrugs. 'Perhaps you left them on?'

I hesitate, convinced I hadn't. 'Maybe.' I listen to his footsteps as he goes first into Livvi's bedroom, and then into Grace's. She's been finding it difficult to sleep since Dad died. She confides in Paul more than she does in me; he seems to be able to reassure her when I can't find the right words.

Livvi's more easily distracted. I think she's too young to understand the finality of death. She's drawn pictures for Dad and pinned them up on our noticeboard; blue skies with pink flowers and big yellow suns whose rays stretch right across the page. 'So he can see them.' I'd watched as Grace had stared at her, torn between wanting to impart her superior knowledge that Dad couldn't see anything anymore and wanting to cling to the hope afforded by childhood that perhaps he still could. Finally, Grace had seen me looking at her and had stayed silent, averting her gaze when our eyes met.

I sit on the sofa, waiting for Paul, but he doesn't come back downstairs. I wonder if I'm being paranoid, but in the last few months it feels as if he's been avoiding me at every possible opportunity. I pour myself another glass of wine and flick across the TV channels, unable to concentrate. Buddy jumps up beside me, pushing his nose into my hand, knowing something's wrong and I can't give him the reassurance he's looking for.

I put my empty glass in the dishwasher and scrape the remains of my barely touched dinner off my plate. Since Paul and I have been together, I've eaten three meals a day, determined to set a good example for the girls, but in the last couple of weeks I feel as if I've regressed back to the teenager I once was; restricting the calories I put into my body in an effort to try to keep control over the way my life is slipping through my fingers. The empty, gnawing feeling I'm left with isn't strong enough to distract me from the guilt that sits at the bottom of my stomach. I don't think Paul has noticed. He hasn't seemed to notice much about what I do recently.

As I walk up the stairs onto the landing, something glints on the wooden floorboards and I bend down to see what it is. Something metal is stuck in the small gap between them. I pick it out with my nail and put it on the palm of my hand. A gold earring in the shape of a flower. The butterfly is missing. I have no idea how it got there and as, instinctively, I reach my hand up to my ears, I'm not sure what I think I'm going to find. Mine aren't pierced and never have been. One of Grace's friends must have dropped it. I make a mental note to ask her whether any of them has mentioned losing one. The post digs into my skin when I close my fingers around it, sharper than I expected, leaving a small red dot of blood on my palm when I tip it onto my dressing table, a reminder of its presence.

MONDAY

Caroline

Rob has left early this morning to play a game of squash before he goes to work. He says it helps to keep him fit but I met Tim, the other property developer he's playing against, at the firm's Christmas party last year and can't imagine he'll make Rob run around much. Especially in this heat. Even at this time in the morning it feels too warm to do anything more energetic than walk. It should be an easy win, which is why he's agreed to play; keeping fit is just an excuse. Apart from tennis elbow and an allergy to pet hair, my husband is pretty healthy for forty-nine.

When Dad was dying, I'd wondered what would happen if Rob collapsed from a heart attack or got run over crossing the road. I'd imagined how his body would look, stiff and cold, the creases on his forehead frozen permanently into his skin. And then I'd felt guilty for thinking something so awful. As he always tells me, I wouldn't be able to cope on my own. And he's right; I wouldn't – the house, the bills and the bank accounts are all in his name and up until recently I've had Adam. I would never abandon my son, and he knows it, holding the prospect of never seeing him again over me as a permanent threat. His words used to ring constantly in my ears, like an announcement proclaimed by church bells, a truth so solid it could never be broken. But their permanence has dissolved since Adam left to go travelling and I'm not sure what I can hear instead.

I make myself a cup of tea and open the bin to dispose of the used teabag, frowning as I catch a glimpse of something familiar poking out from amongst the discarded orange peel and remains of last night's dinner. I pull at it, and the T-shirt I'd been wearing yesterday reveals itself, the soft fabric covered in pieces of food. I take it out slowly, trying to keep the rubbish that's been shoved on top of it from falling all over the floor. I hold it over the sink, scraping off the worst of the mess. At first, I think there's a chance of getting the stains out if I leave it to soak for a few hours, but as I turn it over to check the damage, I realise that's impossible as there's a large hole ripped in the back. I run my fingers over the unsoiled edge of the material. He knows how much I loved it. Adam had bought it for me before he'd left. One of the only new items of clothing in my wardrobe this year. There's a tightness at the back of my throat when I think about him and I have to swallow to stop it closing up, to prevent my body from physically shutting down, unable to function without him here.

My mobile buzzes on the counter and I pick it up.

'Everything OK?'

I blink away the tears that blur my vision as I reply with a lie, trying to work out when the small things I'd agreed to at the beginning of our relationship – the *maybe it's not a good idea to eat chocolate if you're trying to lose weight* had tipped over into this. Or whether it had been a gradual descent into a nightmare, the boundaries blurred over time, and it's been so long that I can't remember how to wake up. I remind myself he hasn't always been like this. That if I could cut him open, I might still be able to find what had used to make me burn with desire, his need to stare at me almost unbearable, my skin on fire.

I push the T-shirt back into the bin, wincing as I dig around in the surrounding waste to scatter some of it over the top of the material to make it look as if I haven't touched it. I wash my hands twice, scrubbing them with soap to get rid of the greasy residue, and then wipe round the sink to get rid of the blobs of food that are stuck to the edge. Even after I've cleaned everything, I can still smell something other than the orange blossom fragrance of the washing-up liquid on my fingers. Something faintly rancid.

I look at my mobile that's lying on the counter. I need to remember to take it with me; he's got an app on his phone that tells him where I am and I know he checks it, even when I'm at work. I wish I didn't have to go – I don't want to have to face Jo; I don't like having to hide things from her, despite the fact that I've done it for so long it has become ingrained, as much a part of me as the freckles I can see on my skin when I look in the mirror. Sometimes I'm not even sure what the truth is anymore. I worry that she can see through me, reading my thoughts I'd assumed were invisible, ones I hadn't buried deep enough in the dark.

I pull on my shoes as the post comes through the letter-box. Picking up the assortment of paper off the floor, I sort through it, discarding the junk mail, putting all the letters onto the counter for Rob to open when he gets home. The postcard is at the bottom of the pile. The photo on the front shows a stretch of turquoise ocean lapping at the edge of powder-white sand, a few beach huts scattered at one end in front of dense green foliage. I read it and smile in relief, the hard ball that's been sitting in my stomach since my son left, dissolving slightly. He'd made it.

Dear Mum & Dad,
Namaste! Experienced epic diving at Pulukan. Lodgings are nice. Plan on investigating surfing on Nusa – heard it's mental?!
Love, Adam

I shut my eyes and run my fingers over the letters he's written in black biro, feeling the tiny indents in the surface of the card. He'd created those. I'm touching where his hands were a few days earlier. I hold it against my face but there's no trace of his smell. I'm overwhelmed by a physical ache to be able to hold him, wishing he was here, but then think about Rob and I'm glad he's not. He's safe. No longer feeling an obligation to protect me. I get out his sweatshirt that's hanging up amongst my clothes in my wardrobe underneath under one of my shirts so Rob won't find it, burying my head in the material, breathing in his scent until it becomes so familiar, I can't smell it anymore.

I walk into the room next to ours that used to be his bedroom. It's been stripped bare apart from his bed, his old chest of drawers replaced by one from IKEA and the walls re-painted. The dark patches left by now-discarded posters of unfamiliar bands are no longer visible. Rob has tried to erase him from our lives completely and the void in my heart is like a black hole that pulls in every single particle of joy from the rest of my body.

I can see our entire lawn from the window in this room, all the way across to my greenhouse that sits at the bottom of the garden on one side of the fence, next-doors bi-folds on the other, their umbrella plant pushed up against the pane of glass. Dad's got one of them in his study. Except he hasn't, as he's not here anymore. He hasn't *got* anything. He *had* the same plant. I hate having to consign him grammatically to the past – it makes him feel even further away. I can see the tips of the leaves are all turning brown. It's inside, dying, when only a few feet away from it stands the place I use for the sole purpose of generating life. I wish I could open their doors and bring it over here, but I know that's impossible. Just as it's impossible for me to tell Jo why I need her to sell the business. I'd been tempted to blurt it out after she told me Dad had died, but hadn't been able to get the image of her holding his hand out of my head, her fingers pressing into his paper thin skin as if it was her property, something she'd take away with her, leaving nothing for anyone else.

I take one last look at the postcard and then slide it as far as I can underneath the mattress on what is now our spare bed. We never have any guests to stay and I know Rob won't look in here. He hates this room; it reminds him of the person he regarded as competition for my affection for the entire eighteen years he lived with us. My fingers encounter the edge of another familiar object which I touch briefly, letting it know I haven't forgotten about it, not allowing myself to get it out, before I slip Adam's postcard on top of it.

*

As I get into the car, I notice the deep azure sky hasn't changed colour since the day of Dad's funeral, as if it's in shock, refusing to move on, like us. The houses along our road are set back from the road, their sizeable front gardens all similar; the bright green striped lawns interspersed with beige gravel driveways and brick paths. Most have solar lights outside, illuminating the house names that can be difficult to see at night, camouflaged by the bushes and tall fences that form a boundary with the pavement. We don't have a light; Rob says they're an attraction to burglars, but I think it's because he knows there is less chance of anyone witnessing what he does in the dark.

I drive the short distance into town and park next to the office, taking the opportunity to nip into the sale that's on this week in the small toy shop a few doors down before I head into work. My phone buzzes in my pocket. I look at the message.

Where are you?

I type a quick reply.

Getting Livvi a birthday present.

It buzzes again.

You should have told me you were going shopping.

I don't reply, holding my phone in one hand as I walk past the shelves stacked high with different-sized boxes, their transparent plastic windows giving a sneak preview of the toys inside. I head past the dolls and remote-control cars round to where they keep the Sylvanian Family sets. I glance at the various shops, houses and vehicles, all accompanied by miniature animals, overwhelmed by the variety of options. I pick up a castle with a slide. Would she like that? I'm not very good at choosing things for other people. A quick glance at the price tag tells me it's within Rob's budget. I take it to the till where the owner wraps it in shiny paper, saving me the job, and puts it in a bag. I give her my card to pay when Katherine, Rob's secretary, walks into the shop.

'Caroline!' She smiles as she spots me standing at the till. 'Bought anything nice?'

'Just a gift for my niece. Her birthday's coming up soon.' I tell her as my phone buzzes again.

'I'm looking for presents too. I always leave it to the last minute.' She laughs and I mumble sympathetically in response. 'We'll have to have a proper catch-up next week.'

I stare at her blankly.

'You are still coming?' she says.

'Am I?' I say, not meaning to sound so surprised.

'Rob said you could both make it. It's only a few drinks and nibbles. Nothing formal. Simon wanted to do something to celebrate the planning permission coming through. Just pop in when you fancy.'

My mobile buzzes again and I take it out of my pocket and glance at the screen. Two messages.

Why didn't you tell me?

Why the fuck aren't you answering my texts?

'That'll be lovely,' I say, my face flushed. 'Thank you. When was it again?' My phone starts to ring and Katherine stares at me. 'Sorry,' I say, 'I . . . I need to get this.' I take the call, pressing the phone into my ear so she can't hear what he says.

'Why aren't you answering me?'

'I've just bumped into Katherine. She was telling me about the get-together Simon's organised.'

'You should be at work,' he says, hanging up.

'Yes, see you later,' I say into the silence on the other end of the phone. I put my mobile into my bag and turn towards Katherine. 'He's really looking forward to it,' I say.

She smiles. 'Great. Next Wednesday. Anytime from seven?'

I half walk, half jog the short distance into work, the present heavy in the bottom of the gift bag the sales assistant has given me, checking my messages before I walk inside, but my phone screen is blank. He'll be able to see where I am, but that doesn't ease the dread that swills around in the pit of my stomach, rising in waves whenever I think about it. Jo looks up briefly as I walk past her office and I hesitate, wondering whether to go in.

'I'm finishing the month-end accounts,' she says, staring back at her PC screen, making the decision for me. I hover in the doorway.

'I thought we could talk about what Mum said yesterday.'

The crease between her eyebrows deepens. 'I don't think there's anything to discuss. You made it clear you want to sell Dad's business. Where you work.'

'Jo, I –'

She cuts me off. 'It's fine, Caroline.' She wrinkles her nose in the way she used to do when she was younger, a way of denying she was upset when I'd irritated her. She thinks I'm siding with our mother but she doesn't understand I don't have a choice. 'I really need to finish these,' she continues, her tone of voice making it clear that there's no point in trying to have a conversation with her at the moment.

When I get home, he steps out from behind the kitchen door and I almost drop Livvi's present in shock.

'Got you.' He smiles.

I hesitate, my heart thumping from the rush of adrenaline before I smile back, putting the bag down on the counter. 'Did you win your match?'

He nods. 'Thrashed him. I wanted to surprise you.' He's speaking louder than usual, buoyed up by excitement. There was a time he'd have lifted me off my feet to hug me, but he hasn't done that for years. I stay a few feet away, just out of his reach, as he glances at the bag. 'What have you bought?' he asks.

'A Sylvanian family set. For Livvi's birthday,' I say.

'Have you got the receipt?' he asks. I fish around in my purse, relieved I remembered to keep it, and he examines it as he gulps down a large glass of water.

'Thirty quid? For some bits of plastic?'

I nod.

He screws up the piece of paper and throws it in the bin. 'Lucky she's my favourite niece, isn't it?'

I don't reply. He's stating the truth. He gets on so much

better with Livvi than with Grace. Perhaps it's because he's had the opportunity to spend more time with her than with Grace whilst she was younger. He says it's because Grace takes after her mother and Jo has never liked him.

'Make sure you answer your phone straight away next time,' he adds. 'I need to be able to get hold of you.'

He walks up to me and I freeze as he puts his hands on my shoulders, sliding them up slowly so they're pressing uncomfortably round my neck. I remind myself I used to crave this physical contact and try not to think about how much things have changed. He stares directly into my eyes before he leans forward and kisses me, his tongue insistent between my lips. I stand quite still, forcing myself not to pull away, his beard abrasive against my skin. He smiles as he peels himself off and lowers his hands. 'I worry if I don't know where you are,' he says, 'in case something bad happens to you.'

I talked to you a lot this week. You don't realise it yet but we're really getting to know one another. Almost all our conversations are inside my head, but that doesn't matter for now. Do you ever do that? I doubt it. I think you're the kind of person who lives firmly in the real world. We talk about lots of things, you and I. I make you laugh, which I think is important. You told me about that time when you fell off your bike when you were little and scraped your finger which is how you ended up with that scar. You said your brother had pushed you, a lie to get your mother's attention, a secret you hadn't shared with anyone else. I don't hold it against you. I don't think you noticed that I pick the skin at the side of my nails when I'm nervous. I watched your face carefully when we were chatting and you didn't make any of those sideways glances that people do when they try to pretend they haven't seen it when, really, they have. Sometimes I smile at you, and when you smile back it's like we're sharing a private joke, but then I remember what I'm thinking about never actually happened, so that can't be the case at all. In my head you're like a piece of Plasticine that I can mould into the person I want you to be, but it's not as easy to do that in real life. I'll just have to find a way to make it happen.

TUESDAY

Jo

'Come on, Grace. Get your shoes on. We need to leave.'
She's sitting on the bottom of the stairs, fiddling with her
laces. She stares at me and, for a moment, I think she's going
to say something, but then she turns away and picks up her
school rucksack. She's been so quiet since Dad died. Even
before that, now I think back. I'm going to have to ask Paul
to try to talk to her, as all my attempts to find the right words
have failed. She refuses to discuss how she's feeling and I
don't want to force her, in case it drives her further away.

Livvi's already waiting. I check I've turned off all the lights
and that Buddy's shut in the utility room before ushering the
girls out of the front door. Livvi walks over to the car and
I point my keys towards it, unlocking the boot so she can
put her bag inside. I look behind me to see that Grace has
stopped. She's standing motionless halfway down the drive,
staring back at the house.

'Grace?' I shout. 'Come on. We're going to be late.' I
can hear the buzz of the traffic at the end of the road telling
me the school-run rush hour has started and twist my wedding ring round on my finger, impatient for her to move.

53

She turns towards me in slow motion, her face drained of colour. 'What is it?' I ask. 'Are you OK?' She hesitates, then suddenly runs towards the car, her shoes barely touching the gravel. 'Slow down!' I shout. 'You'll trip over.' She holds onto my wrist when she reaches me, her grip so hard it's uncomfortable.

'There was someone at the window,' she whispers and I can hear the fear in her voice.

'Maybe it was Daddy,' Livvi says.

'He's already left,' I say. 'He had a meeting early this morning. Stay there.' I unpeel Grace's hand and walk back up the drive, the noise of the dry gravel crunching under my feet. Pressing my face against the pane of glass I look inside. The hall is empty and the kitchen door is pulled shut, just as we left it.

'There's no one here, Grace. You can come and see if you want.' She shakes her head. I'm beginning to wonder if Dad's death has affected her more deeply than either Paul or I have realised. I turn away from the window, the blurred circle of condensation from my breath in the centre of the pane of glass already starting to fade as I walk back to the car. Grace climbs into the back seat and I shut the door, looking back at the house, holding my hand up to my forehead as I squint against the sun. I pause, unsure for a moment if I imagine the shadow that flickers across the hall before telling myself I'm being paranoid. I reverse down the drive, forcing myself to concentrate on where I'm going.

Grace stares out of the window and doesn't say a word for the entire journey. As I pull up at the school gates, she hesitates, not opening her door.

'You're seeing Auntie Caroline today, aren't you?' she asks.

'Yes. And Grandma.' I glance at the clock. Still enough time to get to the solicitor's.

'Are they coming back to our house after your meeting?'

'I doubt it. And if they do, you'll be at school.' I twist round in my seat to look at her, but her expression is unreadable. 'Grace, is this about the argument I had with Auntie Caroline? Neither of us meant to upset you. Sisters argue sometimes. You know you and Livvi can –'

'I'll see you later.' She cuts me off and turns away, pulling on the door handle, the noise of traffic and schoolchildren drowning out the end of my sentence. I want to tell her to wait, to come back inside so we can talk about whatever it is that's bothering her but she slides out of the car closely followed by Livvi and I'm left swallowing a sense of failure that tastes like ashes in my mouth.

The solicitor's office isn't what I'd imagined. I'd pictured an antique desk, cracked leather sofas and floor-to-ceiling bookcases but, instead, I walk into a modern building, am handed a security pass at a sleek reception desk before being ushered into a glass-walled office with a large table surrounded by Aeron chairs which my mother and sister are already sitting in.

I text Paul to let him know I've arrived, but he doesn't answer. I hope his meeting goes well; he could do with taking on more clients if I end up having to look for a new job. I'd hoped he'd expand his web design consultancy after we relocated back here – use some of Dad's contacts to generate more business, but he'd refused my suggestions of help, insisting on finding his own leads, finding it all more difficult than he'd expected.

Caroline stares at her phone, avoiding my gaze and I shuffle uncomfortably on my seat, torn between my previous commitment to be here and my desire to walk out. The look on my sister's face as she'd shrieked at me across Dad's bed replays on a continuous loop in my head. She'd accused me of wanting him all to myself. She hadn't understood. And I hadn't been able to explain. Dad had squeezed my hand and I'd looked up to see Grace standing in the doorway, frozen, watching us tear into one another, our words more corrosive than acid. My mother had appeared behind her, demanding that we stop or get out. She'd stared at me whilst she'd said it, never once looking in Caroline's direction.

The solicitor in charge of executing my Dad's will walks into the room and introduces herself. I freeze, feeling a thrumming in my chest. She glances at me before inviting us to help ourselves to the refreshments on the table and I pour myself a large cup of black coffee, my hands shaking, leaving the white linen napkin with the pastries on it untouched. Caroline takes a cinnamon roll, licking the sticky icing sugar off the tips of her fingers. She picks up the plate and holds it out to me; a test of my willpower which I pass, shaking my head. My trousers dig into my stomach and I sit up a bit straighter as the solicitor shuffles a set of papers. My mother takes a blue folder out of her bag and puts it on the table in front of her.

'I've brought my own copy.' My mother speaks first, an attempt to exert her authority, tapping the folder with her immaculately manicured nails.

I stare at it, flinching at the sound of her voice, the blue card looking familiar. I realise where I've seen it before; in Caroline's bag at Dad's house. The coffee I'm drinking suddenly tastes bitter in my mouth. That's what she was doing when I found her in his study. Looking through Dad's desk. I blink back tears. I'd let myself believe over the last couple of years that we'd forged a tentative connection; restarting a relationship that was perhaps still salvageable after so much time apart. I should have known that we are condemned to play the roles handed out to us in childhood, two puppets dancing around each other whilst my mother pulls the strings.

I let the solicitor's words wash over me, focusing on breathing slowly until I'm confident the tears welling up in my eyes won't spill down my cheeks. Through the window in the building opposite, I can see a woman sitting with her back to me, staring at the computer screen on her desk. She's completely unaware of my existence. Has Caroline been doing the same thing to me since I came back and I've just never noticed? Ignoring me while I thought we were making repairs?

My mother tenses beside me.

'But that's just not possible.' Her tone makes me shiver. It's the one I used to hear a lot when I was younger, the one that warns me her anger is about to spill over into something more unpleasant. I look at my sister, who stares at me, blankly. What have I missed?

'It is, Mrs Wright. As you can see, the document in your folder is dated the tenth of November 2010, but this one was signed and lodged with us on the ninth of May 2018.'

The ninth of May. Less than two weeks before he died. I

cross my legs under the table as the solicitor hands out three stapled documents, one for each of us, hesitating before she offers me mine. Caroline examines what she's been given, picking up the one from my mother's folder and comparing them. She frowns as she reads down the page.

'You got what you wanted, then,' my sister says. 'How long did it take you to get him to agree to it?'

'Agree to what?' I don't understand what she's talking about.

'That's why you insisted on spending so much time with him, isn't it? I knew there must have been a reason. All those days you just wanted to sit with him by yourself.' Her voice is bitter, I know she thinks I've planned this and I can feel the goodwill that I've tried so hard to build up over the last couple of years draining away, like water through my fingers, spilling onto the document, the words floating in front of me, impossible to read. My mother stares at me, picking up her diary and flicking through it. I turn to the solicitor who is sitting at the other end of the table.

'I'm sorry, I don't understand?' I say.

'Did you not hear what I said, Mrs Lawrence?' she replies.

I shake my head, confused. My mother lets out a small snort beside me, her way of letting me know that I'm the last one to catch on, as usual.

'Both documents are copies of your father's will,' the solicitor says. 'However, the most recently dated one clearly states that it revokes the one made several years earlier, so that is the official document we all need to look at. It declares that your father left Joanna his shares in T. C. J. Wrights.' She looks at me. 'That means that, combined with your existing shareholding, you now own seventy per cent of the company, which gives you effective control of the business.'

I swallow in the silence that follows. 'Did he say why?' My words come out as barely more than a whisper. The solicitor shakes her head, but I don't need her to tell me. I already know.

'You were with him on the ninth of May,' my mother says to me, 'I've got it written here.' She points at an entry in her diary. 'I was at the dentist. Caroline took me as I had to get root canal treatment and I wasn't sure how I'd feel driving home after the anaesthetic.' She stares at me, not vocalising the question I know she wants to ask. I can't bring myself to meet her gaze.

'Mrs Wright,' the solicitor interjects, 'your husband's most recent will is legal.'

'How do you know?' my mother snaps.

'Because I drafted it and it was witnessed by one of my colleagues. Your husband specifically asked us to come round for that purpose.'

'You were in my house?' My mother narrows her eyes.

The solicitor nods. 'Only because your husband asked me to be there.'

'But . . .' my mother trails off as she sees my face, putting her diary down on the table. 'You knew?' she says, looking at me.

My voice trembles. 'Dad just asked me to let her in. I thought it was something about the business. I had no idea he was going to make another will.'

Caroline and my mother exchange glances.

'I can assure you, Mrs Wright, that your daughter is telling the truth,' the solicitor says. 'My colleague and I spoke to your husband alone and he asked for this matter to remain confidential until after his death.'

'We'll contest it, of course.' My mother looks at Caroline who picks up her copy of the will as my mother's voice cuts across the room. 'He clearly had no idea what he was signing.' She turns away from the solicitor and addresses me directly. 'You always were able to twist him round your little finger.' Shooting me a look of pure hatred, she picks up her handbag and walks out of the office, closely followed by my sister. I'm left with the solicitor, an uncomfortable silence expanding to fill the gap left by their presence.

I leave the office early so I can go home and talk to Paul before I have to collect the girls. I haven't seen Caroline since she left the solicitor's; no doubt she's spent the afternoon with my mother discussing things without me. The feeling of being left out bothers me more than it used to. I should have expected her to let me down again; it's what she's always done, her behaviour hard-wired since we were young; a tried and tested way of maintaining her position as my mother's golden child. I'd become accustomed to it years ago, but for some reason I'd thought it would be different this time. I thought the business meant something to her, too.

I let myself in through the front door and shout Paul's name but there's no answer and Buddy doesn't come racing out of the kitchen as he normally does. I walk to the end of the kitchen, opening the patio doors to let in some air, closing my eyes briefly as the afternoon sun hits my face. I hear voices as I go to step back inside, and peer down towards the bottom of the garden. Paul's office door is open and I hear a woman's voice. For a moment I think Caroline has come over and something in my chest lifts at the possibility of reconciliation despite myself. Then Anna steps out onto the lawn, the sun behind her, laughing. Paul follows, their silhouettes against the sun so close they appear as one. For a second, I think I see his hand on her waist but then their outline separates in half and I force myself to take a couple of deep breaths. Anna is one of my best friends. I've known her since we moved back here. I trust her. She is not my sister.

I stand rooted to the spot in the doorway as she looks up, sees me, and waves. I fix a smile onto my face and wave back, swallowing a flash of resentment at her apparent familiarity with my dog as she walks over, Buddy following at her feet.

'Hi, Jo. I just popped over to quiz Paul about websites. Andy's thinking of getting his updated. I didn't realise you were coming back early.'

I pat Buddy who is now trying to jump up to get my attention. 'Can I get you a drink?' I ask.

'Oh yes, please. Something cold would be great.' She walks inside with me and sits down on one of the chairs at our kitchen table. I'm tempted to pour us both a glass of wine but it's only three-thirty and I still have to pick the girls up. I get out two large tumblers, filling them up instead with sparkling water. The ice cubes crack as I add the liquid, a sharp noise that cuts across the silence. I gulp several large mouthfuls, waiting for the coolness to spread through my body.

'Work not busy?' she asks.

'I just wanted to collect the girls from school today,' I reply. 'I'm a bit worried about Grace.'

Anna stares at her glass. 'She and your dad were very close, Jo. Give her some time.'

'I know, I know,' I say. 'But she won't talk to me. She insists on having Buddy sleep in her room. And Paul has been working so bloody hard I haven't had a chance to speak to him properly about it.'

Anna glances out of the patio doors towards his office. 'Well, I'm always here if you need to chat.'

I smile. 'I know, and I'm grateful.' I daren't tell her there are some things that I can't talk about. Things that I should have told Paul and haven't as I'm scared what he'll say. 'I wish he was around more,' I say. 'The girls need him. Especially Grace.'

'The girls? Or you?' Anna reaches over and squeezes my hand.

'All of us.' I almost give in to the temptation to tell her about the earring I found, wanting to see her reaction, but I stop myself.

She looks at me. 'You need a break.'

I clear my throat, not wanting her to hear the tremble in my voice. 'Paul says that's impossible. His business hasn't had a great year.'

'I'm more than happy to have the girls if you want to get away, or just have some time on your own at home, even if it's for a weekend. I can get them for you this afternoon, if you'd like.'

'Thanks, but I want to chat to Grace.'

'No worries.' She leans forward to give me a hug. 'I often pop over to see if I can give them a lift before I go and collect Jess and Maddie. Saves both of us doing it.' I don't tell her that Paul hasn't told me this, pushing away the niggling doubt that crawls around in my head, wondering if visiting Paul's office is something she does regularly and how much time she spends with my husband, telling myself in the same breath that I'm being as ridiculous as Grace was this morning – imagining things that are not there.

Two glasses of wine on an empty stomach make my brain fuzzy but I pour another in an attempt to dull the memories of my meeting at the solicitor's. Buddy sits beside me on the sofa, his tail thumping against my stomach, my feet on Paul's lap whilst he reads through the copy of the will that I've got out to show him.

'Did you have any idea your dad was going to do this?' he asks. I shake my head, watching him as he reads carefully through the pages. He's not usually this interested in anything administrative. I'm the one who deals with all of that.

'I had no idea he'd even changed his will until today.'

'Bloody hell,' he says, looking up when he gets to the end. The wine has loosened the control I'm fighting to keep over my emotions and, for a moment, I'm tempted to blurt out what I want to tell him into the silence. To share the burden of guilt. But then he starts talking again and the opportunity passes. 'What did your mum say?'

'What do you think?' I reply tightly. 'She accused me of orchestrating the whole thing.'

'And Caroline?'

'The same. She thinks I asked Dad to do it. You should have seen the way she looked at me.' The recollection is still painfully raw, like a graze inside my chest. He puts down the copy of the will and stares at me. 'You know this means that you'll get most of the proceeds if you sell the business?'

'I'm not going to sell it. It's not what Dad would have wanted.'

He hesitates for a moment, as if he's deciding what to say next. 'Maybe it's something you should consider.'

'Why?'

'The money would come in handy, for a start.' A feeling of unease rises in my stomach.

'Are you worried about our finances?' I ask.

He looks back at the will lying on the table, avoiding my gaze. 'My main client cancelled their contract today,' he replies.

'Oh shit, Paul. Why?'

He shrugs. 'These things happen. Said they wanted to use another designer who charged a lower rate. I did tell them they wouldn't get the same level of ongoing support but they decided to move anyway.'

'Did anything come of your meeting this morning?' I ask. For a moment he looks blank before shaking his head. 'You'll get another client,' I say. 'It's not a reason to sell Dad's business.'

'I'm not telling you what to do, Jo. I just think that you've been trying to build bridges with your sister and this is going to cause all kinds of problems. It's not like you're going to be able to carry on working together in the same office.'

'I'll find someone to replace her.' He raises an eyebrow and I know I'm being petty. I'm still hurt by the fact that Caroline thinks I planned this. That she's not given me the benefit of the doubt. A memory that I've buried for years rises in my head and I block it out.

'What if it had been the other way around?' he says. 'What if your dad had left it all to her, how would you feel?' I don't answer. 'I hope he had a good reason for doing this,' he adds. I want to tell him he did, that leaving me the business doesn't make up for it, but the words stick in my throat. Paul pushes my feet off his lap. 'I'm going to bed.' He looks irritated, as if I've done something to annoy him. 'Are you taking the girls to school in the morning?'

'Yes,' I reply. 'I'll drop them on my way into the office. Are you collecting them?'

He picks my empty glass up off the table. 'I always do, don't I?' He carries it over to the dishwasher, puts it on top of the counter and walks out of the room, leaving me wondering whether to tell him that I know he's lying to me.

WEDNESDAY

Caroline

I come downstairs at six-thirty, the heat outside pressing heavily against the kitchen windows. It's still over twenty degrees, even this late in the day. Rob's leaning against the counter, trying to get one cuff-link through his shirt, his jacket flung over the back of a chair. He's been in such a foul mood since he heard what happened at the solicitor's yesterday that I'm not sure whether he still wants us to go to the function Simon has organised.

My mother had expected him to be able to perform a miracle, repeating over and over again that there must be something he could do until, finally, he'd walked out of the room, pretending he needed to make a phone call, his jaw so tense I could see the outline of muscle under his skin.

His irritation at not being able to fasten his shirt spills over into the room as he curses loudly, and I stand quite still, waiting for his anger to dissipate. He holds out his wrist, expecting me to do it. I step forward tentatively, eyeing him like a wounded animal, one who will snap at any moment. He hands me the cuff-link and I push the gold bar easily through the gap in the material, folding it down at the back.

'Is that what you're wearing?' he asks, looking at me.

'I – I was going to,' I reply.

'It's a bit tight.'

I don't say anything as he turns away from me to pick up his jacket, the scent of the aftershave he's slathered himself with clogging my nostrils, making me cough. I walk back upstairs and pick out a navy dress from my wardrobe, holding it up to the light to check it hasn't got any marks on it.

'Wear that pink one you've got. That looks OK.' His voice sounds muted through the floorboards but I can feel him staring up in my direction as I hang the dress I've got out back onto the metal rail and flick through the other items of clothing to find the one I know he's referring to. Unzipping what I've got on, I take it off and step into the pink material before I shut the wardrobe door, catching a glimpse of myself in the mirror. The colour clashes with my red hair. I hate it.

'Hurry up. We need to go,' he shouts as I walk downstairs. His lips twitch as he looks at me, crushing the last fragment of affection I had for him this evening. 'You're not going to be able to walk in those shoes. Wear something flat. I've got a pair out for you. Come on, we're due there at seven.'

I grab a cardigan for later as he opens the front door. The only lights in our road come from other people's windows and I stumble in the dimness on the uneven pavement as we walk towards Simon's house.

'I bet you're glad I told you to wear flats now, aren't you?' he says, a couple of strides ahead of me. I don't answer, hurrying to keep up. I think about what Adam might be doing tonight. I know Bali is eight hours ahead of us so he's already in a new day. Separated from me by time and space. The further away the better. I hope he had a fun evening. I want him to enjoy every minute.

Simon's house is similar to ours. They all are in this road. This village. And the next. My husband would describe them as detached, character properties with good-sized gardens in a highly desirable area. All with three or four bedrooms, built in the same period, red brick and leaded windows. The kind of place my father had aspired to upgrade to from where he was brought up; rows of flat-fronted identical terrace houses squashed together on either side of a narrow street, where you stepped out of the front door directly onto the pavement. I wonder if he'd realised the problems found inside are all still the same. The buildings around here are just bigger and more spread out, allowing people more privacy to hide their secrets. No one to overhear what's happening on the other side of a thin partition wall.

Some of our neighbours have extended, building garden rooms at the back, additional space to spread themselves out into whilst complaining about the cost but Rob has kept ours the same size as when we bought it. I know all the prices they've sold for. He makes a point of tracking them, looking through the property details on various websites to see if there's anything we should copy.

We walk up the drive, the glow from inside the house spilling out from behind the blinds at the windows, lighting up the gravel. The guests are gathered around the large granite island in the kitchen where Simon is pouring drinks. I smile as he hands me a glass of Prosecco.

'Cheers!' He raises his glass towards mine and I can tell he's looking at my dress. I shuffle uncomfortably, feeling a hand on my shoulder.

'All right?' My husband is standing behind me, staring at Simon, who points at a bottle of beer, raising his eyebrows in a question before opening it and passing it across. Rob's hand drops from my shoulder down to my waist, his fingers pressing firmly into my side. I go to step away but he digs them in further, smiling as he looks at me. He doesn't need to say anything. I get the message, staying exactly where I am.

By a quarter to midnight I'm desperate for the toilet. Rob's the focus of attention amongst the group, I can see the woman standing next to him listening intently to what he's saying, just like I used to, but tonight my cheeks ache from holding a smile. He revels in the attention; when he's being charming, he attracts others with a force as powerful as gravity. I know. Once it was me.

Simon tops up my glass and I'm conscious I've barely eaten anything; Rob has moved me from one conversation to another. I wonder whether anyone else feels that people are speaking a different language at these occasions. I don't know how they manage to think up things to say, how they throw words around like balls, backwards and forwards to one another, with no hesitation. I can't relax and join in. Unless I drink too much. And Rob hates it when I do that.

A teenage girl whose parents are here is waitressing. I can see her at the other end of the kitchen. She'd come around with a plate of beetroot and smoked salmon blinis earlier, but my husband had dropped his as he'd taken one, marking her white shirt. He'd been a bit too eager to clean up the mess with a napkin, letting go of my waist for the first time in hours, and she hasn't been back since.

'I'm just going to the ladies,' I say, but he doesn't hear me, too busy discussing house prices with a man I've never met as I walk into the hallway to the cloakroom. I open the door to the smell of air freshener, the artificial fragrance bearing no resemblance to damask rose which is written in gold lettering on the label. I shove the bolt across the door, relishing the moment of privacy and sink down onto the oak seat, my bladder emptying in relief. Simon's wife must have lit a candle in here as well. Another fragrance to add to the floral mix. A wave of nausea sweeps over me. I've had a lot of Prosecco. I stare at my flat shoes, trying to focus, but can't quite manage it, unable to keep my gaze still for long enough.

I rip off a few pieces of toilet roll, stuffing them into a thick ball as I wipe myself before pulling up my knickers. I flush the chain, wash my hands, then stick one hand under the tap and use it as a cup to scoop water into my mouth, swallowing until my stomach feels bloated, not allowing myself to breathe until my lungs feel as if they're going to burst, a way of punishing myself for having drunk too much, for letting my guard down. I splash my face, glance at the damp hand towel draped over a hook on the wall and decide to ignore it, pulling off another long piece of loo roll to dry my hands and mouth, staring at myself in the mirror.

My reflection gazes back and smiles, her eyes wide. She doesn't look like me. The wrinkles either side of my eyes and across my forehead are a sign of how much time has passed since I last saw the girl I remember from twenty years ago. The one who'd danced on the table when a band had played in the local pub. The one who'd ridden on the back of a motorbike with no crash-helmet, her face pressed against the leather jacket in front of her. But the physical changes are nothing compared to the ones inside. The ones no one else can see. I close my eyes, gripping the edge of the sink, blocking out the memories. It terrifies me how easily I can travel through time, all those days, hours and minutes compressed into a single second, the vividness of the emotions I felt long ago strengthened a million times until I think they'll crush me with their force.

There's a gentle tap on the door. I need to hurry up. I flick my hair behind my shoulders and take a deep breath as I slide back the lock. Katherine is standing in the hall.

'Everything OK?' she asks.

'Yes, fine,' I reply. 'Sorry, were you waiting?'

'I wasn't sure if anyone was in there. The door sticks sometimes.' She looks at me. Perhaps it's obvious I've drunk too much. 'You've got such lovely hair, you know,' she says.

'Thanks.' I tuck it behind my ear self-consciously. 'It could do with a wash.'

'Rubbish. It looks nice down; you should wear it like that more often. I always see you with it up. Such an unusual colour.' She hesitates. 'You've had a few people admiring it this evening. Rob should watch out.' She laughs as I run my hand over my head, her words making my cheeks colour. 'He's in the kitchen,' she continues. 'He's got everyone in hysterics telling them stories about nightmare builders.'

I smile as she walks into the toilet and shuts the door.

I don't want to have to go back to join him and am tempted

to go and sit on the bottom of the stairs for a few minutes but as I turn around, I see him standing in the doorway of the kitchen. He's staring at me and I know he's overheard the entire conversation. He holds out his hand.

'Time to go, I think,' he says.

I glance at the clock in the hallway, trying to ignore the growing feeling of tension in my stomach, like someone pulling an elastic band, wondering how far it'll stretch before it snaps.

'I'm happy to stay a bit longer if you want,' I say.

'We need to get back,' he replies. 'I've got to get up early tomorrow. And I don't think you need any more *admiring glances*.'

'Katherine was only joking. Shouldn't we wait to thank Simon for having us?' I'm trying to play for time and he knows it. Until recently, Adam would have been there whenever we got home, his presence the one constraint on Rob's behaviour. But he's not there any longer, and my husband knows it; I can see it in his eyes.

'No need. I already told him we're leaving.' He opens the front door. 'Now.' He practically drags me outside, the night air cool against my face.

'Can I have my cardigan?' I ask. He's still holding it.

'You don't need it. It's not far.' I look at him, but say nothing. I know when he's in this kind of mood there's no point. I walk quickly, glad that I did wear flat shoes in the end, my body beginning to shiver, unaccustomed to the colder night air, any feeling of inebriation eradicated. Our house isn't far; about three hundred metres, a four-minute walk away, two hundred and forty seconds. I count each one in my head, feeling the goosebumps rise up on my arms as I wrap them around myself in front of me.

'You're going to have to contest it,' he says. 'If you and your mother both say he wasn't of sound mind, then they'll have to reconsider.' It takes me a moment to adjust to the shift in the conversation. I realise he's been thinking about this all day, and it's the best solution he can come up with. I don't contradict him, not now, not tonight. I'll come off worse if I do, but I know what he's suggesting is a waste of time. Dad's will had been signed and witnessed by two solicitors. They'll both confirm he had been perfectly capable of making a rational decision.

'And if that doesn't work, we're going to have to find a way to approach Jo.' His words send quivers of panic down my spine. I don't want him anywhere near my sister.

He opens the front door and follows me upstairs. I clean my teeth as fast as possible, expecting him to appear behind me at any moment. He removed the bolt from the bathroom door a while ago, a way of ensuring I'm accessible at all times. I fight to get my pyjamas on, catching my toe in the hem, the cotton threads breaking before I curl up beneath the duvet. I wait for him to turn towards me, but he doesn't – he stays on his side, nowhere near touching distance. My limbs relax as he begins to snore; I'd prepared myself for something so much worse. He can't bear to hear me receive compliments from anyone else. I stay awake as long as I can, but as the warmth spreads through me, I drift off, surrendering to sleep.

In the morning, the first thing I notice is that he's no longer lying next to me, the bed on his side empty apart from something on top of the duvet, something metallic that flashes in the sunshine edging through the gap in the curtains. As I sit up to see what it is, I notice my pillow is covered in red streaks. I bend down to examine them more closely, unable to see anything clearly without my contact lenses in. They're not marks at all. My heart races as I pick up a thick strand of hair between my fingers, running my other hand through what's left on my head. A tear escapes down my cheek as I realise what the object is on the duvet. My kitchen scissors.

I never fitted in at the last place I worked. I stayed less than a week. Left on the Thursday and never went back. They didn't ask why. It had been like being back at school all over again. I knew they didn't like me but it's what they didn't say that I heard the most. The way they cut me out of their conversations, keeping the topic on something I couldn't get involved in, any attempt to change it met with a return to the original, a never-ending loop from which I couldn't escape. And when I did manage to speak, the loaded pause afterwards, long enough to make me question what I'd said, running over my words again and again in my head to make sure they made sense, long enough to plant the suggestion of doubt in everyone else's mind too. The way they stood in a group, everyone huddled together, leaving a space that was too small for me to fit in, forcing me to take a step backwards, the odd one out in an otherwise perfect circle. The way they looked at me; their lips raised in a smile, always a smile, but no effort to disguise the crease between their eyebrows, one that deepened as I spoke, as if my words were a jigsaw puzzle with missing pieces that they couldn't be expected to find. I couldn't confront them. There was nothing solid for me to grab hold of. Only the way they made me feel; as invisible and as all-encompassing as air. You'll never make me feel like that. When we're together, I know you'll listen to every word I say.

THURSDAY

Jo

I wake up at four and lie there for an hour, unable to go back to sleep, too preoccupied by the thoughts running around inside my head. Glancing across at Paul, I check he's still dead to the world before sliding out of bed, silently pulling on my leggings and a T-shirt. I creep into Grace's room to get Buddy, changing my mind when I see she's got her arms wrapped tightly around him. I've grown used to the sight of him curled up on her bed at night, barely able to distinguish between his soft brown fur and her hair, the pale blonde colour she'd had as a baby long since disappeared. He looks up at me, his tail thumps weakly a couple of times but he doesn't move, and I let myself out of the house, alone.

The air feels warm as I set off at a slow jog down the drive, as if it has retained some of the heat from the previous day, and as I pass the lavender bushes, I'm aware of their faint scent in my nostrils. Dad would have said it was perfect gardening weather; the time of year you have to be most vigilant. Everything is fighting to grow and you have to be ruthless in choosing what survives. Why me? I ask him silently. I only came back because you said you

76

needed me to help you. Had you planned this from the start?

I run to clear my head. I used to do it every day after I'd first met Paul, logging my time and speed in a diary in order to calculate how many calories I'd burned off. There weren't apps that did it for you back then. I'd written the figures in a notebook I'd kept by my bed, a way of playing mind games with myself, seeing if I could stick to a strict daily calorie allowance but knowing I had the extra ones from my exercise as a backup in case I slipped up. Or if Paul chose what to cook or if he bought dessert. There were only so many times I could insist on a smaller portion or throw half of mine away without causing offence. If I exceeded my permitted total, I punished myself by lowering the number of calories I was allowed the following day. Compared to what I'd put myself through as a teenager; four years of binging and purging and laxatives, this was relatively measured behaviour. I hadn't told him what I was doing, what I'd done for so many years that it had become an ingrained habit, part of who I was, not even something that I noticed anymore; a life governed by measuring and weighing and counting.

I'd turned over one morning beside him in bed after forgetting to set my alarm, choosing to thread my legs in between his rather than force them into a pair of trainers. In the months that followed I'd written in my food diary less and less frequently, the calculations in my head becoming fewer and fewer, until eventually I'd stopped doing them at all. I'd put the diary away in the bottom of a drawer, releasing it like an anchor that fell away through a bottomless ocean but the urge to punish my body has stayed with me, like having a tap dripping constantly in the background. I can block it out most of the time, but I'm never able to turn it off completely and in the past few months the sound has got louder again. Last night I'd picked up a crisp out of the bowl on the table, my first conscious thought being the thirteen calories it contained, rather than the salt and vinegar flavour, as I'd put it in my mouth.

I run down the road, along the footpath behind the small row of shops, through the woods, pounding the ground with my feet, trying to rid myself of the tight ball that burns in my chest, accelerating my pace, pushing myself to the brink of exhaustion. I'm out of practice. I stop by a tree, my throat raw, my breath coming in gasps, kicking the trunk until my toes hurt and the fronts of my trainers are covered in bark. I refuse to let myself cry, swallowing the metallic taste in my mouth. I glance at my watch. Six o'clock. I'm sweating like it's the middle of the day. I need to get back to get ready for work and take the girls to school. The thought of facing Caroline in the office makes it more difficult to breathe as I set off again, but I don't have a choice.

I'm back at the house before six-thirty. Paul doesn't say anything, standing at the sink cleaning his teeth as I turn on the shower.

'I needed to clear my head,' I say, pulling a towel round me. He nods, not asking why. 'Is Grace awake?'

'I haven't seen her yet. I thought I'd leave her to have a lie in after last night.' We'd both fallen silent when she'd appeared downstairs long after we'd put her to bed, the click of the old-fashioned latch on the kitchen door interrupting our conversation. She'd stood in the doorway in her pyjamas, staring at us with a blank expression. Paul had reached for her hand to take her back to her room, leading her back upstairs as something cold had buried itself in my chest.

'Can you try and talk to her later?' I ask him. 'She's been making excuses to try and get out of going to school this week. She might listen to you.' He nods, drying off his newly shaved face with a towel before patting it with aftershave, examining himself in the mirror.

Paul goes straight outside to his office when we get downstairs and I sit on my own at the kitchen table, not wanting any breakfast, the cup of tea he's made me turning colder the longer I stare at it. My lips feel greasy after taking the first sip – he's added too much milk. Livvi walks into the kitchen, her red hair unbrushed, the similarity to my sister and mother difficult to ignore.

'Where's Daddy?' she asks.

'He's gone out to his office, sweetheart. I'm taking you to school.'

She yawns. 'Can I have Nutella on my toast?'

'Sure,' I say, getting it out of the cupboard. 'Is your sister awake?'

'I don't know,' she says. I slide a piece of bread into the toaster. 'She was in the night, though.'

I frown. 'Did you hear her come downstairs?' I'd checked on Livvi after Paul had taken Grace back to bed and had thought she'd been asleep.

'No. But she woke me up,' Livvi says.

'She came into your bedroom?'

'No, I heard her talking.'

The weight that I'd felt pressing on my chest earlier returns. 'Could you hear what she said?' I ask.

Livvi hesitates whilst she dips her finger into the jar of Nutella. 'Nope. I can't remember.' The toast pops up, making me jump. I put it on a plate and take it over to the table.

'Maybe she was talking in her sleep?' I say, watching Livvi's face.

She spreads on a thick layer of the chocolate spread. 'Maybe. Jess says she does that. But if she's asleep, then how does she know?' I put the lid on the jar to stop her taking any more out. Perhaps I should speak to the doctor. If Grace isn't sleeping it might explain why she looks exhausted. I need to remember to phone the surgery when they open as it's impossible to get an appointment without a few days' notice. I pour a glass of orange juice and put it beside Livvi's plate.

'She wasn't happy with that man, though,' she says, staring at me as she licks the dark stripes off her fingers.

I freeze. 'What man?'

'The one in her room. She told him to get off her chair.' I suppress the shiver that runs down my spine, my face hidden behind the fridge door as I put the carton of juice back.

'You heard her say that?' I keep my voice deliberately light.

'Yes, that's what woke me up. She shouted. And Buddy barked. Didn't you hear him?'

I try to think. I can't remember hearing anything, but our room is at the other end of the long corridor. She'd been fast asleep when I'd gone in at five-thirty. I'm about to go and wake her when the door creaks and Buddy walks into the kitchen, tail wagging, followed by Grace who looks as if she hasn't slept at all, her blue eyes a steel-grey colour. She yawns as she sits down.

'Did you sleep OK, sweetheart?' I ask, already knowing

the answer. She nods, slowly. 'You don't remember coming down here last night?'

She frowns at me. 'No. I didn't come down. Can I have some toast?' she asks. I look at her as I put another slice in the toaster. Maybe she really doesn't remember. I hope Paul manages to talk to her this afternoon. I tip my cup of tea down the sink; my stomach turning at the sight of the thin skin that's formed on top of the cold liquid.

The alarm system beeps as I unlock the door to our office building and enter the keypad code to make it stop. I'm the first one here, arriving before Alice, our secretary, which is unusual. I wonder if Caroline is going to come in at all. She can't avoid me indefinitely. I look across reception to Dad's office; his door locked, his brass nameplate still attached to the outside: Thomas J. Wright in large black letters. Dad had insisted on having it but Caroline and I don't have one, preferring the anonymity. We need to sort out his things, but neither of us has been able to face touching them since he died.

I put down my bag, open Alice's drawer to get the key for his door and force myself to go into the stationery cupboard, every step hampered by the fact that my legs feel heavy, almost as if I'm carrying him with me. I don't want to do it but it might be easier when there's no one here to watch, no witnesses to the destruction of a place he'd considered sacred, lovingly tended for over forty years. I pull out a bundle of flat-packed boxes that we use for filing, snipping off the plastic straps that hold them together, folding the cardboard along the scored lines and tucking the edges into the slots to make them up. I tell myself I can manage to fill at least two, that it can be a gradual process, as if this will somehow lessen the pain. I carry them into Dad's room, emptying his shelf of A4 files, keeping a record on a separate piece of paper of what I'm putting into each box in case we ever need it again. I wonder if the process will be cathartic, whether I'll be able to remove the guilt that is sitting in my chest and pack it away too, or whether I'll be forced to carry it around with me forever, a burden so much heavier than my father, even before he was ill.

The sudden burst of traffic noise interrupts the silence.

'Caroline?' I shout. There's no reply but I hear a door slam. I leave the second box half packed and walk into reception where my mother is standing, a smile painted onto her face in familiar red lipstick.

'Hello, Joanna.'

'Mum.' I edge around her to get back to my office, into familiar territory, unwilling to have this confrontation in the open. 'I wasn't expecting you.'

'I thought I'd pop in. I was hoping to catch up with Caroline, actually, but I can see she's not here.' I watch her face as she speaks, unsure if she's lying. The truth isn't something that is solid and fixed for my mother. She has a way of stretching and twisting it to make her own version which doesn't always resemble the original.

'No, she's not in yet.' My mother hovers in the doorway, and I don't offer her a seat. She'll take one if she wants one, but I'm not going to encourage her to stay. She glances across reception through Dad's door, noting the filing box I've left on his desk.

'Packing up his things already?' she asks. I look down at some correspondence, pretending to read it, hoping she doesn't notice the flush that rises on my cheeks.

'Yes. Let me know if there's anything you want to keep, otherwise I was just going to put it all into storage. We'll keep his paperwork here, all the rest I'll take home. Unless you want it?'

My mother doesn't answer, and I wonder if she's even heard what I said. She taps her nails on my door handle, not moving.

'I wanted to ask if you'd thought any more about what we discussed at the solicitor's?' she asks. I stare at her. So, this is the real reason she's come.

'We didn't discuss anything, Mum. You walked out of the meeting before we'd had a chance to do that.'

'It came as a shock,' she says. 'I'm sure you can understand. After forty years of marriage, it's not easy to hear that your husband has kept things from you.' She presses her lips together and for a moment I think I see a crack in her veneer, but then it's gone. My guilt is making me imagine things; she wants me to feel sorry for her.

'I don't know what I'm going to do with the business yet,' I tell her. 'I'm thinking about it. But I don't want to sell it.'

My mother walks across reception into Dad's office, picks up the silver photo frame off his desk and brings it back into my room, putting it down in front of me.

'Look. We're all there. Our family. Your father, me, you and Caroline. We need to stick together. *That's* what he would have wanted.' I look at her, and something inside me breaks.

'How would you know what he wanted, Mum? You weren't interested in the business. That photo doesn't show the reality of our family. We haven't been close for years. Perhaps if there'd been a picture of you and Caroline together . . .'

'How dare you.' She cuts me off and stares at me, her eyes searching inside my head for what I'm trying to hide; something so black and ugly that I'm surprised she can't spot it. I glare back, trying to disguise the fact that my hands are trembling. 'You were the one who decided to leave us, Joanna. You disappeared for years with barely a visit and only the odd phone call until –'

We're interrupted by the sound of the office door opening and I look up as Caroline walks in. She's had her hair cut. I've never seen it short before but it suits her. My mother reaches into her pocket for a tissue, pretending I've upset her but I ignore it. I've seen her do this before. She's a better actress than either me or my sister. Caroline puts her arm round my mother's shoulders as she dabs her eyes. The familiar feeling of being the odd one out again reignites a fire that's been smouldering for years and I slam my hand down on the desk.

'I'm not the one here who's done anything wrong,' I shout. 'I haven't taken the morning off work to go to the bloody hairdresser's. I'm not the one who went through Dad's things in his study.' Caroline flushes. 'I saw that folder Mum had at the solicitor's,' I continue, looking at my sister. 'You took it, didn't you?'

There's an uncomfortable silence.

'I'm starting to think it would be better if we kept our distance for a while,' I say. 'You know your niece doesn't even want to see you at the moment?' My sister's eyes widen. 'Grace keeps asking if you're coming over. She's scared you'll start shouting again.' Caroline stares at me, her fingers reaching to tuck her newly cut hair behind her ear, the same motion over and over, as if she can't get it to stay where she wants. 'I thought we were making progress,' I say. 'I thought we were starting to – oh, forget it.' I pick up my bag and walk out of the office, not wanting to go back until I'm absolutely sure my mother has gone.

I pull into our drive after leaving work and take a couple of deep breaths before getting out of the car. I check my phone but there are no messages from my mother. Caroline had left a note in the office to let me know she was going out on viewings this afternoon so I hadn't had to face her but we can't continue to run the business like this. Alice had left her packed lunch in a carrier bag under her desk yesterday, untouched, disappearing outside to get something to eat just to keep out of our way.

I pick up one of the filing boxes full of Dad's belongings off the back seat and walk into the house. For a split second, I think the hall smells different and try to work out what it reminds me of; as if someone has put out a new diffuser, but I know that's impossible. Paul wouldn't know what a diffuser is. By the time I've put the box down, whatever was there has gone, and I can only detect the faint scent of school shoes, washing powder and Buddy's fur.

The girls are out in the garden bouncing on the trampoline, and I wave at them, kicking off my shoes that stick to my feet. I give Paul a kiss on the cheek as I sit down at the garden table, wondering if I imagine his slight flinch as my lips touch his skin.

'Did Livvi remember to bring her recorder home?' I ask.

'I'm not sure. Why?'

'She's got a concert next week and is supposed to practise. The teacher said she'd remind them all when she sent them home.'

'Livvi didn't say anything to me about it,' he replies, staring at his laptop.

'I'm surprised you can read what's on that screen,' I say. 'It's so bright out here.'

He pushes the lid shut as I peer over his shoulder. I wonder how long the girls will be occupied on the trampoline, whether now is a good time to tell him what happened today with my mother, but before I can decide, he leans forward and takes my hand, squeezing it between his own.

'They've had a ball since they got back this afternoon,' he says, looking over at Livvi whose shrieks of laughter echo across the garden. 'Have you thought any more about –'

'Did you spray something in the hall?' I cut him off, deliberately changing the subject; I can't deal with that conversation on top of everything else.

'What?' Paul squints at me, the expression on my face hidden in the shade.

'The house smelt funny when I came in,' I say. 'I wondered if you or the girls had sprayed air-freshener or something?' He shakes his head and stands up, his earlier question apparently forgotten, but I see the vein on his forehead pulsating beneath his skin as he walks away stiffly towards the trampoline. He looks scared. And I have no idea why.

FRIDAY

Caroline

As Rob leaves for work, he tells me he'll meet me at the office at twelve-thirty to pick me up. A surprise to make up for last night. My heart sinks but I smile as he kisses me goodbye and I lie in bed for a few minutes after hearing the front door shut, feeling my heartbeat slow down, readjusting into a normal rhythm.

I catch a glimpse of myself in the full-length mirrored wardrobe doors in our bedroom as I put my clothes on. The semi-circular red mark just above my left breast has faded to a silvery white; from the colour of blood to the colour of bone. Less obvious unless you're looking for it, but a scar I can never get rid of. It will always be a part of me now, just like the other imperfections that originate from his handiwork, ways of permanently engraving himself into me. It feels smoother than the rest of my skin when I touch it, and it isn't until I look closely that I can see the narrow strips of unmarked skin that run between each blemish, as if my body has tried to knit itself back together, tiny streams of normality that flow between the horror. I hate the fact each mark is shiny, that they catch the light when I put on my bra, emphasising their presence. I open my mouth and look in the mirror. I wonder if mine would leave a similar imprint. I tell myself it could have been worse; it could have been a full circle but I'd got away from him before he'd managed to close his mouth.

Before I get dressed, I walk into Adam's old room, remembering a time when Rob had wanted our son, when he was still part of me, something he could claim responsibility for, before he turned into a living, breathing individual. I slide my hand under the mattress, feeling for the postcard I put there a few days ago. My fingers find the edge and I pull it out, leaving the other object where it is. I can't deal with that yet, I'm not ready. Adam has to come first. Until I'm sure he's safe and settled, I can't risk getting it out.

I read his message again, even though I've memorised it off by heart, staring at the colour of the ocean in the photograph. A proper turquoise-blue. I press it against my face, trying to persuade myself that I can still feel the imprint of his hands on the paper. I haven't mentioned his name for days and I say it out loud now, over and over, fracturing the silence in the room; a small cry of resistance to let him know he's not forgotten. After a while the syllables lose their meaning and I force myself to stop. I know it won't bring him back but as I slide the card under the mattress, I remind myself that I wouldn't want it to.

I check my reflection once more before I leave for work. My short hair still takes me by surprise. I'd cut it at home myself to try and neaten up some of the mess before I'd gone to see the hairdresser, my tears mingling with the chopped strands and smears of toothpaste in the bathroom sink until it had all been a horrible wet mess that I'd had to dig out of the plughole and wrap in some toilet roll before throwing it in the bin. I'd driven to a salon where they wouldn't recognise me and where I'll never go back, sitting outside before they opened yesterday morning to get the first emergency appointment.

The stylist had frowned as she'd stood behind me, running her fingers through the uneven lengths as if they were a puzzle she could fit back together. I'd watched her eyes narrow in the mirror as I'd told her my story about letting a friend who was training to be a hairdresser have a go at doing it. The lies had slid off my tongue like so many others had before and she'd seen them for what they were, but had said nothing. I'd understood. It's easier to swallow a mouthful of deceit than taste something unpalatable. She'd shaped it into a short bob with lots of layers to try to disguise the bits he'd cut off down to the scalp and had told me it would keep its shape as it grew out if I wanted to have it longer again. But I'm not sure I do. It gives him less to get hold of like this.

Jo has already arrived when I get to work, her office door firmly shut. She's always busy at this time of the month finishing the accounts, but I wonder if she's using it as an excuse not to talk to me. I debate whether to knock, but I don't know what to say to her. She won't believe me if I tell her I'm doing this for her own good, but if I don't do what Rob has asked, there will be consequences for all of us, her included.

I think of Grace and feel my cheeks burn. I hadn't meant to upset her. I should apologise, but I don't know if Jo will give me the chance. I'd been losing Dad and the desperation

I'd felt to be there for him in his last few days had hit me just at the wrong moment; my grief mingling with childhood jealousy. I'd worked with him since I'd left school but he and I had never got much beyond polite conversation; it had been like standing ankle deep in the shallow end of a swimming pool whilst having to watch Jo diving underwater. We'd hardly seen her for years until Dad's diagnosis and yet, within weeks of moving back, she'd seemed closer to him than I'd ever been. She'd slotted back into our lives like the final piece of a jigsaw puzzle and I'd resented her for it, just like I'd resented how much time he'd spent with her when we were younger.

I hadn't realised until a few months after she'd come back that he'd gone to see her in Bristol, had begged her to move a hundred miles across the country, saying he needed her financial expertise. She'd managed to turn a loss-making business into something highly profitable in less than two years; moving all the books and records into an online accounting system, redesigning the firm's online presence, cutting our costs and making a sales assistant redundant whose lunches alone had cost the firm more than he'd ever brought in. I thought she'd done it because she wanted to prove to my mother as well as Dad that she was capable of it, but now I wonder whether it had been her plan to take over the business all along.

Rob appears in reception at twelve twenty-five.

'Ready to go?' he asks. I nod. He glances at Jo's door. 'Is she in?'

'Yes, but she's with a client.' He walks over to Dad's office, the desk where he used to sit clearly visible through the open door.

I hurry after him. 'You shouldn't go in there. Jo won't like it.'

'She's busy,' he retorts, glancing around the room. 'Where are all his things?'

I frown, confused. 'Jo's sorting them out. Why?'

He doesn't answer my question. 'What's she done with them?'

'We're filing some stuff here, but she's taken the rest home.'

'Filing it where?'

'In the storage cupboard. What's this about, Rob?'

'Show me.' I stare at him, not moving, and he prods my shoulder. 'I said, show me.' I hesitate as I walk out of Dad's office into reception, thankful our secretary, Alice, isn't at her desk, opening the door into the small filing room.

'In here,' I say, looking at the dozens of boxes stacked on the shelves. The most recent ones containing Dad's paperwork are on the floor waiting to be filed. Rob crouches down and takes off their lids, flicking through the various documents.

'What are you —?' He puts his fingers to his lips and continues looking through the contents, searching for something. The conversation in Jo's office stops. I shove the lids back on the boxes and step out into reception as she opens her door.

'Jo. How are you?' he asks.

'Good, thanks.' At least they are being cordial.

'The girls?'

'They're fine.' She shuts the door of my father's old office, cutting off his view.

'It's Livvi's birthday soon, isn't it?' he asks. 'We need to drop her present over. Been a while since I've seen her.'

Jo nods but doesn't suggest any dates, and I wonder if she's noticed he hasn't mentioned Grace. She looks at me. 'Going out for lunch?'

I nod. 'Won't be long.'

Rob smiles at her as we walk out, but she doesn't smile back.

'Where are we going?' I ask.

'I told you, it's a surprise.' I don't tell him that, based on previous experience, his words do nothing to reassure me. I open the passenger door to see a bunch of chrysanthemums wrapped in cellophane lying on the seat. The sticker shows they've been reduced in price, the red label still stuck on the side, and I notice their narrow orange petals are beginning to curl at the edges. He watches as I pick them up. I try to smile but my lips stick to my teeth and I push my face into the flowers as I lean down to smell them, their musty fragrance filling my nostrils.

'Thank you. They're lovely.' I lift them up and put them carefully onto the back seat. 'So they don't get squashed,' I add.

'They aren't for you,' he says.

I bite my lip, feeling like an idiot. 'Oh. I didn't – why were you looking through Dad's things?'

He doesn't answer, putting his hand on my knee before he starts the engine and pulls away out of the car park, humming as he taps his fingers on the steering wheel. At the moment he's like a child on a day out – full of excitement; but I know only too well how quickly that can change. Every decision I make; what I do, what I say, is based on my prediction of his most likely reaction after an analysis of all the probabilities. Over the years I've got better at it. Faster. More accurate. But he savours his capriciousness and when I get it wrong, I know only too well what can happen.

I look at the road, the tarmac ahead shimmering in a heat haze. Rob stops at a set of traffic lights and a couple of shoppers walk across in front of us, lowering their sunglasses against the brightness. I wonder what Adam is looking at, unable to imagine him on the other side of the world. It doesn't seem two minutes since he was sitting in this car, travelling in silence when Rob had been driving, animated conversations cut short by our arrival at home when it had been just the two of us.

I think about turning on the radio but change my mind; Rob usually scoffs at my music preferences and switches stations anyway, so I concentrate instead on working out where we're going, my stomach tightening as I recognise the familiar route.

He pulls up beside the pavement and turns off the engine, leaning towards me and sliding his arm gently round my waist. For a moment I lean my head against his shoulder, breathing in the smell of his suit, surrendering to the unfamiliar feeling of comfort, wishing I could bottle this version of him and take it home.

I hesitate as he pulls a key out of his jacket pocket and hands it to me. My stomach falls, my last hope of this being some kind of hastily organised gathering obliterated.

'There's something I need you to get for me. For us.'

I look at him blankly. 'I don't understand.'

'Your mother told me your dad might have written another will. One that he signed more recently than the one you saw at the solicitor's. I need you to see if you can find it.'

'One more recent than a couple of weeks before he died? The solicitor would have told us.'

'Not if she hadn't drafted it. Your mother said he might have left it in his office. If Jo's been clearing out his things, she might have taken it home with her. I need you to check.'

'But I don't –'

He cuts across me. 'Just go inside and tell me if you can see any boxes that she's taken home from the office.'

'But Paul will be –'

'Paul will be out walking their dog. It's something he does every lunchtime and he'll be gone for at least half an hour.' I don't dare ask him how he knows this.

'What if someone –'

'You've got an excuse to be there. You can say you came around with the spare key Jo gave you to leave her some flowers after your argument yesterday.' He covers my hand with his own. 'So, you'll do it?' he asks. I look at him and nod, slowly. I don't have a choice.

'Keep your mobile on,' he says.

I nod. I get out of the car and walk up to the house, pausing for a few seconds after I open the door to listen, but there's only silence. The coat rack hanging on the wall is overloaded; school blazers piled on top of one another. It's too hot to wear anything other than short sleeves at the moment. I run my hand over one of the jackets that has fallen on the floor and pick it up, struggling to get the small thread loop at the base of the collar over one of the pegs.

I take my shoes off before I walk across the hall into the kitchen and put the flowers down on the island, knowing Jo won't ever believe I bought them if she comes back. We both hate chrysanthemums. I open a cupboard, glancing at the white china plates and bowls that are stacked in piles, and then look inside the dishwasher that's still full of clean crockery waiting to be emptied. I press the button on the front of the machine so the red light disappears. Rob's insistence on not wasting money is so deeply ingrained it has become part of my character.

I glance at my watch. Twenty past one. I hesitate at one end of the kitchen before stepping off the travertine tiles that are cold under my feet and onto the wooden flooring. I look in the utility, in the hall, upstairs in the bedrooms and on the shelves in the family room, but can't see any cardboard boxes.

I walk back through the kitchen, pausing in front of a drawing of a large sun and pink flowers that's pinned to the noticeboard. I run my fingers over the rays that have been coloured in so thickly with yellow crayon that the wax has formed an embossed shiny layer on the surface of the paper and have a perverse desire to scratch through it with my nail, ruining its smoothness with a jagged pattern.

There's something about the way it feels that reminds me of my skin, and I glance at the knife rack on the counter, pulling out one of the wooden handles, staring at the cold metal blade as I hold it against my wrist. It's so tempting. One deep cut and I wouldn't be here anymore. I wouldn't have to do any of this. I'd slip away into oblivion as fast as the dark stain would spread across the pale tiles and into the lines of grout. It's not as if I haven't contemplated it before. It would take less than a second to slice through the centimetre of flesh before I hit my radial artery that I can feel pulsing below the surface.

Adam's face flashes before me and I force myself to put the knife back in the block, my hands trembling. I take a last look at the picture where Livvi has scrawled her name across the bottom, pick up the bunch of flowers and walk back into the hall to put on my shoes, being careful not to knock her coat off its hook.

I open the car door and slide in, throwing the flowers onto the back seat.

'I can't find them,' I tell him. He thumps the steering wheel in frustration.

'Are you a hundred per cent certain?'

'Yes. I looked everywhere I could think of.'

'They've got to be there somewhere. I'll have to look when I've got more time.'

'What if she comes home when you're there? Or Paul walks in? Aren't you worried they'll find you?'

'No,' he says, smiling. 'I've got the perfect place to hide.'

I decided not to tell you about the visits to the counsellor. I don't want you tilting your head slightly to one side when you look at me, smiling with that 'I understand what you're going through' expression, a mask to cover up your panic because you have no idea what to say. By simply uttering the words I'll have changed myself from being just another person, to being another person with issues. Someone not to avoid, because you don't avoid people like me anymore; it's important to be inclusive, but someone to be wary of, to watch a bit more carefully than you do others, to keep an eye on what I'm doing, to excuse any odd behaviour as part of my problem when you don't even know what my problem was in the first place. It all happened so long ago that I don't think it's important and I've changed. The panic attacks have stopped and I'm calmer with you around. I don't want to be different. I want to blend in. I want to be one of those people who I see you look at, who laughs, who lives in the moment, every atom of their being immersed in what is going on. Not the person who is always thinking about what has gone before and what comes next. I know what comes next, anyway. I know we're going to be together. You just don't know it yet.

SATURDAY

Jo

When I come downstairs this morning, Paul's talking quietly on his phone, sitting at the kitchen table with his back to me, his knee jiggling in the way it does when I know he's stressed. He goes quiet as I open the door, his low murmurs switching to a series of monosyllabic replies that make it impossible for me to decipher the remainder of the conversation. I turn on the tap to fill the kettle, staring out of the window down our drive and across the road to the house opposite. I squint against the sun to see into Anna's kitchen window as her silhouette slides into view, her mobile tucked between her ear and her shoulder as she clears some plates off her draining board. She's smiling, her face reflecting a happiness I haven't felt for a long time and she doesn't look in my direction as I continue to watch her, only stopping when the water runs out of the spout of the kettle and over my wrist. I shake my hand, wiping my arm with the tea towel as Paul ends his conversation, finishing the call with a mumbled, '*You too.*' When I look again, I see Anna has put her phone down before disappearing from my view. I flick the switch down on the kettle.

'Who was that?' I ask.

He hesitates as I get a couple of mugs out of the cupboard. 'Your mum,' he replies.

'My mum?' I repeat. 'Why did she call you?'

He doesn't meet my gaze. 'She wants to know if she can meet up to talk things over.'

'With me?' The noise of the kettle reaches a crescendo as it hits boiling point.

'Yes.' I hand him his mug, unsure whether to believe him. I can't remember the last time my mother phoned him. She always calls me.

'Drink up,' he says quickly, 'and I'll tell the girls to get a move on. We want to be there before ten to avoid the crowds.' I nod, watching as he slides his phone into the pocket of his shorts, experiencing a flutter of annoyance that I can't see the number of the incoming caller.

The track to the National Trust property is bone dry, clouds of dust rise up like smoke in front of the windscreen, the parched earth letting out sharp sighs at being disturbed by the line of vehicles driving into the car park. Livvi jumps out as soon as we pull into a space, keen to get going. Grace shuffles across the back seat reluctantly, waiting until I open her door before she slides out. I run my finger over the hot paint-work, examining the shiny trail that's hidden underneath the dirt.

'Ready?' I say. She nods.

'You OK?' Paul asks her. 'You were a bit quiet in the car.'

'I'm fine,' she replies, hurrying ahead to catch up with her sister. We are swept along in a tide of buggies through the stone-walled entrance and funnelled past the reception counter where the girls are handed stickers to put on their T-shirts, emerging into the gardens with the other visitors like a breaking wave. Grace crumples hers up and puts it in her pocket, Livvi presses hers onto her chest, the three years between them sometimes seeming like so much more. It had been the same with Caroline and I; the four years between us hadn't been so noticeable when I'd been six or seven, but by the time she turned fifteen it felt like she'd chosen to step into a different universe, leaving me behind, one filled with boys and fashion and things I had no interest in.

Several paths criss-cross over the grass, bordered by lime trees, all leading down towards the large house. Being out of the direct sunlight is a relief and I'm almost tempted to get out the rug and not go any further, stopping here to eat our hastily concocted picnic.

A couple of families hover behind us as we walk, impatient to overtake, the rubber wheels of their prams echoing on the rough tarmac. I step off the path onto the grass to let them go by and Paul stares as they walk past, his eyes drawn to one of the small figures lying beneath the hood. I know what he's thinking. Guilt prods me in the chest with sharp fingers, reminding me of the letter in my jacket pocket. I need to talk to him. But not here, not in front of the girls.

I shout at Livvi, who is running ahead, to slow down, telling Paul that I don't want to lose sight of her, an excuse to cover the real reason I want the girls with me, their presence diluting the tension that hangs in the air between us.

I reach for Livvi's hand as she circles back and head inside the Edwardian building, relieved to be somewhere cool, the smell of furniture wax and dried flowers a welcome change from the sickly sweet heat. The rooms are huge, all high ceilings and ornate decoration. Livvi pulls on my arm, pointing at a black-and-white photograph of a woman with two children. Paul and Grace are on the other side of the room, admiring a small piano.

'So, they didn't actually go into school?' Livvi repeats, the concept clearly bewildering.

'No. They were taught here, in the house.'

'Did they not own a car?'

I blink, trying to assimilate my scant historical knowledge, watching Paul glance at his phone screen whilst Grace reaches up to touch a giant gold clock on the mantelpiece.

'It wasn't really about that,' I say. Paul runs his hand through his hair before texting something and putting his phone back in his pocket.

'They should have shared lifts,' she says. 'Like we do with Anna.'

'What?' I'm not concentrating on what she's saying, too busy watching Paul.

'Like sometimes Anna collects us if Dad's busy. Like she did last week. And sometimes we bring Jess and Maddie home.' The noise of Paul's ringtone cuts through the low murmurs of conversation in the room and he pulls it out of his pocket, embarrassed, fighting to mute the sound. He glances at me and I look away, wishing he'd just turn the bloody thing off.

Livvi takes her time examining the various objects in the room and I don't hurry her, reluctant to follow Paul who disappears with Grace down a corridor into another part of the house. Livvi crouches down in front of a glass cabinet, looking at the china ornaments and a man walks over and stands next to her, pointing at one of the ballet dancers.

'She looks a bit like you.' He's wearing a distinctive Balmain T-shirt and a watch with a heavy metal strap that is stretched tightly round his thick forearm, digging into his suntanned skin. Livvi turns towards him and smiles.

'I don't have pointe shoes yet.'

'Don't you? I bet you're good enough.' He's about my age but I can't see anyone else with him. I wonder if his family are in a different room.

'Miss Alex says I have to be eleven.'

He nods, glancing at her and then back at the figure in the cabinet. 'Not long to wait, then?'

She grins. 'I'm only seven but I'm almost eight. Miss Alex says sometimes you get them early if you're really good.'

He smiles at me, and I smile back, wanting to be polite. There's something about him that seems familiar even though I'm sure we've never met before. It makes me feel uncomfortable and I move a bit closer to Livvi, putting my arm round her shoulders.

'We'd better go and find Grace and Daddy, sweetheart.' I look up as Paul walks back into the room, almost tripping over on a rug as he marches across the floor.

'Come on,' he says. 'Grace and I are waiting.'

I raise my eyebrows. 'Calm down, we're not in a rush. Livvi's just looking at the china figures.'

'They're so pretty, Daddy, aren't they?'

He reaches for her hand and I notice he's trembling.

'They are. But it's time to move on now.'

The man standing next to Livvi looks at her. 'She's beautiful but she's very fragile, isn't she? That's why they've put her behind the glass. So she doesn't get broken.'

'Let's go, Livs.' Paul frowns as he takes her hand, pulling it with more force than is necessary as we walk out of the room. I linger in the vast hallway, admiring a tapestry but Paul strides ahead, straight out of the front door. I have to hurry to catch up with him.

'You don't need to go so fast,' I say as he looks back towards the house.

'I want to get outside. Have some lunch. Grace is hungry and I'm desperate for the Gents. Do you want to take the girls and go and set up the picnic over there?' He points at the expanse of lawn which is dotted with oversized deckchairs.

'Sure,' I reply. He hands me the rucksack and I watch as he disappears behind the Edwardian building, heading towards the toilets at the entrance. I walk over the lawn with the girls, looking for a space under one of the overhanging trees around the edge. Livvi points at the ice-cream van that's positioned on the other side of the grass.

'Can we get one?' she asks.

'You'll have to ask Dad,' I tell her, glancing over at the van, realising that Paul needn't have gone all the way back to the entrance. There's a block of Portaloos less than a hundred yards away.

We roll out of the car when we get home, the girls half-asleep, a combination of the drive and the late afternoon heat. Livvi's fingers are sticky with ice cream and the back of Grace's legs are pink from the sun. As I go to shut the car door, I notice something on the floor under the passenger seat and reach down to pick it up. A small, white portable mobile phone charger. I frown. It's not mine. I try to remember who else has been in the car recently. I don't think Paul owns anything like that. I turn it over in my hand and put it in my pocket to remind myself to ask Paul about it later, unease fluttering in the bottom of my stomach.

Paul and the girls throw open the back door to sit outside whilst I pour myself a glass of elderflower cordial and walk upstairs, picking up a jumble of clothes off Livvi's bedroom floor, sniffing them to work out which ones to dump in the washing basket, folding the rest into a pile on her dressing table. Her bed is untouched from where she got out of it this morning; the shape of her head still imprinted in the pillow. I plump it up and straighten out her pink duvet, tucking her teddy inside so its face peers out over the top of the cover. Clearing up after them usually irritates me, but today I want to do it. Anything to help keep my mind off the conversation I need to have with Paul.

Grace's room is tidier, she's always been the neat one. Her bed is made, her curtains drawn, fastened nicely with their matching star tiebacks, her reading books stacked in a pile on her bedside table. I sit down on her bed and lean back on her pillow, smiling as I look up at the ceiling to where she's stuck luminous glow-in-the-dark stars above her bed. I'm still worried about her. I couldn't get an appointment with the doctor until next week and I know she's still not sleeping properly.

I'm so tempted to shut my eyes and doze, but I can't. As I get up, I feel something hard under my head. I reach my hand under the pillow and pull out Grace's iPad. I frown. It's not in its usual cover, which annoys me as she knows that's where she's supposed to keep it. We'd bought her a thick rubber one at an extortionate cost as it had been the only one to guarantee the screen wouldn't smash even if it was dropped from a height of five feet, and had agreed all devices would be kept downstairs to charge at night. I go down to the kitchen and see it sitting by the plugged-in charger. I'd presumed the iPad was inside it, but clearly Grace had taken it out, leaving the cover downstairs and taking the iPad with her into her bedroom. No wonder she's so tired if she's been playing with it rather than sleeping at night. I shove it back roughly into its case. What on earth has she been doing on it? I type in her password. At least she hasn't changed that.

Has she been talking to someone online? She's had lectures at school about the importance of keeping her personal information private. How the nice twelve-year-old boy from a school down the road who asks to meet her might not actually be who he says he is. I take a couple of deep breaths, trying to slow my rising heart rate as I shake the thoughts of grooming and paedophiles out of my head.

I check her Internet browser history. A few searches for books on Amazon, pages on how to train your dog to do circus tricks and various music videos on YouTube. Nothing that raises cause for concern. Nothing in her emails, received or sent. I glance through her messages. Full of emojis and gifs, words abbreviated to numbers in an almost indecipherable language; but only conversations with Maddie and a few other girls in her class, and all before nine o'clock.

I scroll down a bit further and a couple of initials catch my eye. GT. I click on the bold letters and flick through multiple messages, long swathes of white writing in blue boxes, dating all the way back to a month ago. And not a single reply to any of them. I put my hand over my mouth to hold in the sob that rises up in my throat. All this time. I wish she'd told me. She's been writing him texts and hasn't said a word to me about it. I see the words of her first message without even meaning to read it.

I miss you. I had history today and we're learning about World War II but it was more fun when you told me about it. I'm sorry about Mum and Auntie Caroline arguing. I really hope it wasn't my fault.

GT. Grandpa Thomas. My eyes blur as I shut down the browser screens, take the iPad out of its case, carry it upstairs and slide it back under her pillow before going to sit on the closed toilet lid in the bathroom, burying my face in a handful of loo roll until Buddy comes in and pushes his nose into my legs. I kneel down on floor beside him, wiping away the tears that run down my face as he whines at my distress.

I try phoning my mother, but it goes straight to voicemail. I don't bother leaving a message, she'll see the missed call. As I open up the dishwasher to unload it, I curse as I realise everything is still dirty. I thought I'd put it on this morning before we left. It's been playing up this week – the other day I'd come home to find it had switched itself off before the cycle had finished. I need to get someone out to look at it but I'm waiting to see if it breaks completely as we could really do without spending the money at the moment.

Paul walks into the kitchen and I get out the mobile phone charger from my pocket, putting it on the counter.

'This was in your car,' I say.

He frowns, picking it up and turning it over in his hand. 'It's not mine,' he replies after a pause.

'Well, it's not mine either,' I retort. 'It was under the passenger seat.'

He shrugs and turns away, reaching for a glass in the cupboard. 'Maybe it belongs to one of Grace's friends?' he asks, turning on the tap and taking a sip of water. His face is flushed. After twelve years together I can tell when he's lying to me. An image of the earring I found on the landing pops into my head. Grace had confirmed that neither Maddie nor Katie had pierced ears.

'Most of them don't own a phone,' I say flatly. 'Let alone a charger. Are you sure you don't know anything about it?'

He shakes his head as Buddy dashes into the kitchen, one side of his coat much darker than the other, the smell of fox poo pungent on his fur.

'Jesus, Buddy. What have you been rolling in?' Paul tries to grab his collar as a combination of the stench in this heat and the fact that I barely touched any of the picnic at lunch overwhelms me and I dash out of the kitchen into the cloakroom, vomiting up the glass of elderflower I've just drunk, the sweet taste now acrid in my mouth. I pull off some toilet roll to wipe my mouth and splash my face with cold water, taking deep breaths.

Being sick terrifies me; the way my stomach feels so gloriously empty afterwards is a sensation that I used to crave above all others and one that I know I could slip back into coveting with so little effort. It's waiting for me, if I let it, reaching out to remind me it's still here even after all these years. I hold my wrists under the tap, the water refreshingly cool against my skin as I catch a glance of myself in the mirror, tracing my wet fingers across my cheekbones, one of the places I used to scrutinize to work out if I was putting on weight.

'I've hosed him off outside with some shampoo,' Paul says as I walk back into the kitchen. The look on his face reminds me of what I just saw when I stared in the mirror. The dishonesty of someone who's hiding something. I can hear the girls shouting outside in the garden and hope they stay out there whilst I say what I need to. I can't put it off any longer.

'Paul, there's something I need to –' He walks over to me and tucks a piece of my hair behind my ear.

'You should have told me before,' he says. 'I wish you had.' I frown, wondering if he's found the letter, a flush of embarrassment rising on my cheeks.

'I thought you'd –' I start to say before he wraps me in a hug that cuts me off, mid-sentence.

'You know how much I wanted this. I thought you'd been avoiding the topic as you weren't keen, but I'm over the moon.' He grins at me, and I'm speechless. 'We can keep it quiet for now if you don't want to say anything to the girls yet,' he continues.

Behind him, through the window, I see Anna walking up our drive. She waves but her eyes don't meet mine – she's staring directly at the back of Paul's head and I frown, the mobile charger on the counter catching my eye, taunting me with its presence, unanswered questions rising up in my head.

'Aren't you pleased?' He stares into my eyes and for the first time in weeks I feel I have his full attention. I think of the letter in my jacket pocket upstairs and swallow, wondering if I can pretend that it never arrived.

'It's early days,' I hear myself say, feeling something disintegrate between us as I commit to the lie, 'only a few weeks, so let's not say anything to anyone for now.' He hugs me again as Anna taps on the window and I smile, making sure she can see Paul embrace me as I point towards the back door to let her inside.

SUNDAY

Caroline

My mother wipes her face with her napkin, but I can see she's missed a bit, a small spot of gravy is still visible on her chin and I know Rob has noticed it too. He's on his best behaviour this afternoon, holding out the dish of roast potatoes so Mum can help herself, but she shakes her head and he has to swap it quickly for the one filled with broccoli, his lips pinched whilst she takes her time picking out a couple of limp stems. He clears his throat at regular intervals, a way of relieving his irritation, unused to having to hide his impatience in his own home.

I wonder how long he'll be able to keep up this pretence. He's managed it for a couple of months now, ever since Dad had taken a turn for the worse; starting his final journey down a road that had got gradually steeper until it had become a descent from which we knew he'd never return. My husband had begun popping over to their house more often, offering to send over a builder from one of his sites to fix a leak in their bathroom, coiling himself around my mother like a snake, an inch at a time, so slowly she didn't even realise it was happening.

Despite all that effort, despite all those hours of conversations where I know he's had to swallow his frustration until it's almost choked him, he's still having to sit at a table with my mother, pretending to be interested in how long this heatwave is expected to last. His knife shakes with the effort of maintaining his self-control as he digs it into a piece of lamb, conscious that what he really wants is moving ever further away. I can feel his desperation oozing from every pore.

Jo hadn't liked him when I'd first brought him home. I remember the way she'd moved when he'd sat down on the sofa, uncurling her skinny legs beneath her, all bones and angles, standing up awkwardly, like a baby giraffe, before walking out of the room. I'd warned him she was a difficult teenager, but I could see by his face he hadn't expected her to ignore him. And there'd been something else in his eyes too – a look of piqued interest at not being able to capture her attention. I'd slammed the door after her, a small part of me in awe that she seemed to care so little about his impression of her. Even though we lived in the same house, I'd been the one to inherit my mother's traits, her teachings so deep-rooted I wouldn't have been able to erase them, even if I'd wanted to.

'Did you speak to the solicitor, Cynthia?' Rob asks. My mother nods, her mouth still full. I grip my hands together under the table. 'Did she say there was a way we could challenge the will?'

My mother swallows as she looks at him. 'Apparently, that's not going to be possible.' She seems almost embarrassed to admit it, as if it's her fault.

Rob turns his head to look at me, his knuckles white as he grips his cutlery. 'Can you open a window, Caroline. It's rather hot in here.'

I push my chair away from the table and it squeaks in protest. Rob frowns and shuts his eyes briefly, forcing himself not to say anything. I press the small button on the window handle to turn it, pushing the casement outwards. There's no rush of cool air to ease the temperature. If anything, it's hotter outside than it is in here. I take a deep breath, trying to get rid of the greasy smell of roast lamb. Something else Rob insisted on having despite me suggesting a salad might be more suitable.

I press my back against the sill, watching my mother look at Rob. It's the same way she used to look at Dad. As if he can provide her with the answers she's searching for. She doesn't see the flaws that he hides so well, she never looks below the surface where the shadows lurk, those horrors reserved just for me.

I'd tried to tell her once, a few years ago, before Dad had got ill. Rob had been out for the afternoon and she'd come around to see Adam, not realising he wasn't home. She'd chatted whilst I'd made her a cup of tea, but I hadn't heard anything she'd said, my head too full of everything else I had to remember. What we were having for dinner, whether I'd cleaned the bedroom thoroughly and how I could tell without going to the doctor if a rib was really broken or just cracked. She'd stared at me, holding out her cup, surprised that I'd forgotten to put in her sweeteners. I hadn't been able to hide the tear that had slid down my cheek as I'd reached for the tub in the cupboard, clicking to release a couple of tiny tablets that disappeared into the hot liquid. She'd put her arm around my shoulders but I'd flinched, and she'd pulled back, misunderstanding, fiddling with the strap of her handbag that lay on the counter. I'd tried to catch her eye again as she'd carefully pulled out a single pristine tissue, still folded, from a cellophane packet and had handed it to me, staring at something over my shoulder, chattering incessantly, terrified of what would materialise if she left any opportunity for me to speak. Her fluttery hand movements betrayed her desperation to maintain the status quo, physically waving away any possibility of me saying anything that might change that. Once I'd wiped my eyes, screwing her tissue up into a small ball to throw in the bin along with the courage I'd gathered together, she'd paused, mid-sentence, before attempting to impart her knowledge based on experience.

'All marriages go through bad patches, Caroline.' I hadn't answered. I didn't have the words to bridge the gap between what her idea of a bad patch was and the reality of what I faced on a daily basis. 'Your dad and I . . . we had . . .' I'd put my arm on her shoulder, the physical contact making her go stiff, her body unconsciously repelling my attempt at reassurance.

'You don't need to explain,' I'd said, feeling her rigidity soften, as though I'd removed an obstacle she'd thought she'd have to face. I'd smiled, knowing the opportunity to say something had passed, wondering if it had ever been there at all. She'd chosen to look the other way, not because she didn't care, but because she couldn't bear to think about what had happened to her in the past. She'd presumed Paul was having an affair, her assumption based on her own life, the only time I'd ever seen her cry. She'd stayed with Dad after he'd confessed, the alternative too impossible to face, and they'd moved on, the incident shrinking to a tiny square in the patchwork quilt of their marriage. And I hadn't told a soul about the day before my eighth birthday when I'd found her in the garden, eyes red and puffy, pretending she'd had an allergic reaction to picking tomatoes, an early lesson in how perfection is only an illusion that hides something much darker beneath its surface. I might even have believed her if I hadn't heard her creeping across the landing into the spare room each night for months afterwards, the slight creases in the usually immaculate duvet cover each morning the only sign she'd ever been there.

'Aren't you going to sit down?' Rob raises his eyebrows and I detach myself from the windowsill to walk back to the table.

'Sorry, I was just getting some air.'

He sighs as he leans down to switch on the fan next to the table, the sharp blades whirring into action, the hot air in the room now moving around in warm gusts, more uncomfortable than before. The buzzing in my head gets louder and I'm not sure whether it's the fan, or me, or both.

'Should we speak to Jo?' my mother asks, looking at him.

'I'm not sure what we can say,' he says slowly.

'Well, if you had a word with her, you could make her see that selling would be the best thing for all of us. Her included.' She smiles as if this is an obvious solution.

He nods slowly. 'What do you think, Caroline?' He turns towards me, and I have to wipe my palms on my skirt to get rid of the perspiration, worried my fork will slip through my fingers.

'We could,' I say. 'Maybe we should ask her if we can look through the boxes she took home from the office to see if we can find the other will.'

'What other will?' Rob's voice is quiet and I can see my mother frown, straining to hear what he's saying, not wanting to have to ask him to repeat it.

'The one that you said –'

He reaches over the table and covers my hand with his own, squeezing it so hard that I kick out under the table, catching his shin. He's been lying to me. He never believed there was another will at all. He's had me searching for something he knows doesn't exist. He loosens his grip and looks at me, watching as this realisation sinks in. I swallow the words I was about to say, half wishing they'd already escaped.

I dig my fork into a piece of lamb, slicing it into ever smaller pieces to try and get rid of the fat and gristle attached to one side but it's threaded through the meat like veins; impossible to cut out. I put it into my mouth and chew, watching Rob who is watching me, trying to work out what he's so desperate to find in my father's belongings and wondering if in fact I already know.

You can tell a lot about someone from their habits. I've been trying to work out what yours are but they're not easy to see. We all have them – little things that give away something about ourselves without us meaning to, like a trail of breadcrumbs that you can follow back to find out what makes someone tick. You like things to be arranged in a specific order on your desk. I've seen you adjust your keyboard, making sure it aligns with the bottom of your PC, your notepad neatly beside it. It's important to care about the little details. Mine is making bets with myself. If I reach a particular point on the pavement before a car passes me, I'll have a great day. Harmless. Until I start making the point further and further away and have to run faster to reach it. So fast that I think my heart might burst out of my chest. Or until my brain bets me to do something without me wanting it to. The other day it gave me ten seconds to get outside the front door or I'd die. I was in the bathroom at the time and had to run all the way down the stairs to get out, slipping on the last step, stumbling to get over the threshold, arguing with myself before I'd even got there that getting one foot outside meant I'd done it. Nine point eight seconds. A success until I realised I couldn't be sure exactly when I'd started timing, curling myself into a ball, overwhelmed by the desire to scrape out the inside of my head to stop myself thinking at all. It's like I'm trying to sabotage my own life. And if I can do that to mine, I wonder what I could do to yours.

MONDAY

Jo

The sun is already filtering through the curtains when I open my eyes, creating shadows that dance across our duvet cover in a rhythm that matches the flutters in my stomach at the thought of having to get up for work. I realise Paul's not beside me. The sheet is cold when I reach across and run my hand over the permanent indent his body has formed in the mattress, the edges of the shape once as familiar as my own, now undefined. I look at his pillow, still creased from where his head has been and shiver, turning over to press the button on my alarm clock. The digits light up; six-ten. I can't hear him walking around or the low hum from our bathroom fan that starts up when anyone switches on the light.

He'd slid into bed late last night in the darkness and had put his arms around me, burying his face in the back of my neck. I hadn't turned around but he'd threaded his fingers through my own, linking us together, an attempt to restore a bond I wasn't sure still existed. I'd almost told him then, my face hidden, tempted to say I'd made a terrible mistake, that I'd done another pregnancy test and it had come out negative and then I'd remembered the way Anna had looked at the phone charger on our counter when she'd come into the kitchen; I'd been convinced I'd seen a flicker of recognition in her eyes, and I'd stayed silent instead, squeezing my guilt into a small hole in my chest where it had pressed tightly against my lungs. Anna had denied it was hers, but I'd caught the glance Paul had given her when I'd asked the question, and had felt like I'd done at school when I'd walked into a classroom at break time and everyone had stopped talking.

I get out of bed and pull on my dressing gown, walking past our empty bathroom and down the stairs, treading carefully so as not to wake the girls.

Paul is sitting at the kitchen table staring into space.

'Can't sleep?' I ask. He shrugs. I run through conversation topics in my head, like flicking through the pages of a book, trying to find one that isn't controversial. I'm conscious the silence between us is stretched tight with expectation, like an over-inflated balloon, ready to burst at any second. Putting my arm round his shoulders, I kiss the top of his head, but he feels different; the Paul I knew a few months ago would have responded, pulling me in for a kiss, but today he feels rigid, his hands remain firmly by his side and I recoil, feeling like I'm touching a stranger.

'Grace was up in the night,' I say. 'She had a nightmare. She thought someone was in her room.'

The colour drains from his face as he looks at me.

'It wasn't a big deal,' I reassure him. 'She was fine once I'd calmed her down.'

'Why would she think that?' he asks.

I shrug. 'She's finding Dad's death really difficult to deal with.'

He hesitates and reaches for my hand. 'I don't want you to worry,' he says.

'About what?'

'About – about the baby,' he says.

I pull away, desperate for him to retract the word he's said out loud. A lie that can't possibly develop into flesh and blood and one that I can't take back. I lean over the edge and dry retch, my body's attempt to cover up for me. He doesn't know it's because I haven't eaten. I should tell him the truth, but the look of concern on his face makes me put it off for a bit longer.

'Where's the charger?' I say, noticing the empty gap on the counter where it had been last night.

'I binned it,' he replies. 'It's useless without a lead. Can I get you a cup of . . .?'

'I'm fine. Honestly. We need to get the girls up for school,' I say, turning to go upstairs.

'I do love you, Jo,' he says, the words cutting across the silence in the kitchen but instead of bringing us together they push me further away and I leave the room without replying. I don't deserve his affection when I haven't told him the truth. But I'm convinced he's hiding something from me too.

I push open Grace's bedroom door a fraction and peer in. Buddy's sprawled out along her whole length, snuggling up to her like a hot-water bottle. I lean over her, a lump in my throat when I see how peaceful she looks when she's asleep, overwhelmed by a feeling of nostalgia, a sense that time is slipping away without me noticing. I creep out again, deciding to give her ten more minutes.

I walk back into my room where Livvi has already tucked herself under my duvet, her copy of *Rooftoppers* spread open in front of her as she tells me about Sophie and Charles in the bell tower of Notre Dame. I snuggle up to her, breathing in the smell of shampoo on her hair. She looks up at me, her brown eyes wide.

'Are you taking us to school?'

'Yes. I'll drop you on my way to the office.'

'And Dad will collect us?' she asks.

'Yes,' I reply. 'Same as usual.' I wonder if her need for reassurance is part of the grieving process too.

'Not Anna?'

I frown at her, my brain fumbling to fit together the pieces of conversation.

'No,' I say. 'Dad will.'

'He didn't last week,' she says. 'Not on Wednesday, Thursday or Friday. I told you, Mummy. And I don't mind going home with Jess because they have DVD screens in the back of the seats in their car, but sometimes her mum drives really fast and I feel a bit sick.' Paul hadn't told me Anna had collected the girls at all, let alone three days in a row. I try to think back to what he'd said when I'd come home from work. Had he actually lied, or just omitted to tell me? And if he's got fewer clients and less work on, why did he ask Anna to collect them at all?

'I'm going to take Grace to Paris,' Livvi continues.

'Are you?' I say. 'That would be lovely, wouldn't it?' My voice sounds unfamiliar, hoarse. I can't let her see me cry. I throw back the duvet as I clear my throat. 'Come on, you need to get ready for school.'

'The man in her room won't be able to follow us there,' she says, 'and Grace won't be sad anymore.'

'There wasn't anyone in Grace's room, sweetheart.'

'But I heard –'

'Grace was talking in her sleep because she had a bad dream. She's still very sad that Grandpa died. There wasn't actually anyone there.' I smile, an effort to convince myself as much as her.

Livvi's eyes narrow and I can see she doesn't believe me. She shuts her book, clasping it tightly as she squirms away from me, across to Paul's side of the bed where she buries her head in the pillow. I flinch, shutting my eyes to block out the memory that rises up in my head before I can stop it. She murmurs something I can't make out before sliding off and walking to the door, her ankles visible beneath her Disney pyjama bottoms, the Cinderella design so faded I can barely see it. She's grown. It's not until she's left the room that I realise what she's said. Two words of mumbled defiance that on top of her other revelation make my stomach contract into a hard knot. 'There was.'

As I walk into work after I've dropped the girls at school, I find Caroline already in my office, standing by my desk. I put my handbag down on the floor, unsure what to say to her.

'Have you got a minute?' she asks.

'I'm a bit busy.' My voice comes out harsher than I expected; an unconscious attempt to keep her at arm's length now she's shown that she doesn't trust me.

I dig my nails into my palm, trying to block out the memory of the girls waiting in the car before we'd left for school whilst I'd sifted through our kitchen bin, perspiration running in a stream down my chest, no sign of what I was searching for beneath the discarded yoghurt pots and plastic packaging. I'd resorted to taking everything out, one item at a time, putting it all into a new bag, desperate to believe that I hadn't looked properly. But I'd just ended up with another bag full of rubbish and no phone charger. I'd felt something break in my head, a small crack at first but as the realisation that Paul had lied to me sunk in, it had widened, spreading through my body like fine lines across a piece of china, fracturing my life into tiny pieces.

Caroline bites her lip, reminding me of how she used to look whenever Dad had told her off. 'We really need to talk.'

'What about?' I switch my computer on, as she pulls out a chair, the machine humming quietly into life.

'I'm sorry if I upset Grace. I didn't mean for her to see us arguing.' Her apology takes me off guard. I know I should accept it, but I don't want to open the door to let her back in, to pretend that everything is normal. She's ripped away a plaster that had been covering up a wound that had been slowly healing after so many years apart and I'm not sure I can face going through that pain again. I want her to leave my office so I can try to focus on work. Anything to keep my mind off Paul.

'It's fine,' I say. 'I'd better get on.'

She doesn't move. 'We need to discuss what you're going to do with the business,' she adds.

'I haven't decided,' I tell her.

'You won't even talk about it?' she asks. I knew she had an ulterior motive for apologising. When I was a teenager, she'd smuggled me packets of cigarettes that I'd used to hide in my bedroom, not old enough to buy them myself, waiting for me to smoke the first one out of the window before asking me to cover for her by telling Mum she was with her friends instead of out in some bar, knowing that by that point I didn't have a choice.

'What do you want me to say, Caroline? I don't want to sell. It's not what Dad would have wanted.'

She leans forward towards me, folding her hands together on the desk. 'But what do *you* want?' she asks.

The question takes me by surprise and I have to swallow before I answer. 'It doesn't matter what I want. Dad would never have sold it.'

'You don't have to defend him now he's gone,' she says quietly. 'He's not your responsibility.'

'What are you talking about?' I snap.

'You idolised him, Jo. You always have. When we were growing up, Mum and I were the enemy and you and Dad were always right.'

I frown, crossing my ankles under the desk, pressing them together. 'That's not true. Have you any idea what it was like growing up with you? The golden child? Mum's favourite the whole time?'

'That's not how it was.'

'That's how it felt.' I shuffle in my seat, exasperated by the way she can make me feel fourteen again, being lectured by my older sister who always seemed to take Mum's side.

She hesitates. 'I've apologised for upsetting Grace. You yelled at me, too. Can you not just consider for a moment that Mum and I might have good reasons for wanting to sell?'

'I'm sure you do. You want to get your hands on the money and use it to add an extension or something onto your already perfect house.' I raise my voice, furious that she thinks she can justify selling something that I've spent the last three years restructuring into a highly profitable business. Something that Dad had poured his life into. 'And I'd like to remind you that with Dad's shares I own seventy per cent of it,' I add. 'Which means I get seventy per cent of whatever it's sold for. You get ten. Surely that makes it hardly worth selling, from your point of view.'

'Fifty thousand.'

'What?'

'That's what I'd get out of it,' she says quietly. 'Ten per cent of the business. It's worth at least half a million. Mum showed me the figures from when it was last valued.'

I had no idea it was worth that much. I had no idea it had even been valued. My head begins to throb. Had Dad organised that, or had my mother done it without telling me?

'And there's every possibility Mum will have to sell the house if she can't get rid of the business. You know Dad didn't have a pension. He invested everything in the company.' I stare at her, trying to work out if she's lying. I can't believe Mum wouldn't have told me if she needed to sell the house.

'Mum knows where I am if she wants to talk to me.' I pick up my bag, needing to get outside, somewhere where I can get space to think.

'Jo?' she calls after me. I freeze, tempted to ignore her, reminding myself that whatever I say now will have reverberations for the future.

'Mum wants us to go and see her.'

I turn around. 'I'm busy.'

'How about Friday?' she continues. 'We could go over in the afternoon. There's nothing in your diary; I've checked. Just you, me and her. A chance for us all to talk.'

I hesitate. 'I'll think about it.'

'You can't see it, can you?' she says quietly, and I'm surprised to see her eyes fill with tears. 'Even when it's staring you in the face.' She blinks, furiously, and I sense she's waiting for me to say something, throwing me a rope that she's waiting to see if I'll grab hold of; a way into her life. But I don't reply and she pulls it away, clearing her throat. 'Don't you think Mum's been through enough? She doesn't understand why Dad would have done this in the first place. Neither do I. It feels so . . . vindictive.'

She looks at me, waiting for an explanation but I can't tell her the truth. She doesn't know I'd happily hand over every last share in the company if we could go back a month and swap places. She should be grateful; Dad's instructions hadn't been a punishment – he had spared her.

'Is that what you were trying to find in his study? A reason?' I leave the question hanging in the air as I lean against the door frame for support, my legs trembling.

She hesitates. 'I needed to know what his will said,' she says, a flush spreading across her cheeks.

I shake my head. 'You're unbelievable,' I say. 'Couldn't you have waited to hear it from the solicitor rather than sneaking round behind my back?'

'You're the one who has been sneaking around,' she replies. 'You've spent the last three years trying to impress Dad.

I've worked with him for seven times longer than that and he never listened to me the way he did to you. You asked him to leave you the business, didn't you?'

I sit back down on my chair, putting my head in my hands as it starts to spin with the unfairness of her accusations. I know she thinks I'm being a hypochondriac, something I used in order to listen to her whispering to Mum when I first stopped eating. Words as light as feathers that she didn't think I could hear, sounds that had stuck in my throat, choking me when I'd tried to swallow them. I remember her sitting next to me on the bed when I was ill, the tiny amount of heat my emaciated body had generated not sufficient to keep out the cold. She'd been fascinated and repelled by me at the same time; craving the attention I was getting yet unable to look at what I'd become. She'd wrapped the duvet around me, tucking in the edges; a gesture that I was pathetically grateful for, a kindness she rarely demonstrated unless my mother was watching.

I close my eyes, trying to block out the images of beds and duvets that rise up in my head, the same ones that return over and over again in my nightmares. I can hear Caroline saying my name but I'm already back in the sitting room at my parents' house and all I can see is the thin cotton of the pillowcase between my fingers, soft and shiny from having been washed so many times, the floral pattern faded. I can smell my mother's Summer Fresh fabric conditioner, the scent not strong enough to mask the horrible sweetness coming from the bed, an odour of acetone that stays with me long after I leave the room. I shut my eyes as I don't want to see but it doesn't help; I can't block out what is in front of me. The small bulge in the centre of the pillow barely noticeable, considering what's beneath it.

I had tried not to look as his hands had lifted themselves off the duvet, pale sticks of bone struggling to reach for mine, unable to stop himself despite all his previous assurances. It hadn't lasted long, the frantic struggling, but he'd said he wouldn't fight at all and I'd wanted to let go, the pillow only held in place by the promise I'd made, the look in his eyes as I'd agreed to do it, the one thing I still recognised in his ravaged body. The silence that followed had been so huge and black and dark that I'd prayed for it to swallow me up, to take me wherever I'd sent him. I'd retreated away from the bed, at first backwards, one step at a time, then had turned and run out of the room, trying to escape the horror of what I'd done.

There's an explosion so loud that I recoil, covering my ears in fright as I'm shocked back to the present. Caroline rushes out into reception. The large mirror on the wall of Dad's old office has cracked horizontally in half, the bottom piece smashing on the floor, leaving shards of glass sparkling on the green carpet, like tiny knives. Beautiful yet deadly.

TUESDAY
Caroline

I hear voices outside on our driveway after he shuts the front door, and have to hold onto the windowsill as I draw back our bedroom curtains a fraction, enough to look outside without him being able to see me. I breathe slowly, ensuring the material doesn't flutter when I exhale. He's talking to someone, their familiar red jacket causing my stomach to turn over. Not today, I think. Please not today. I promise to be a better wife this evening if it comes tomorrow instead, attempting to bargain with an entity that I'm not convinced exists. It's never helped me before, despite my frantic pleas, and on one occasion, screams so loud that even one of my neighbours had asked if everything was all right the following day.

I watch as the postman walks away, wheeling his trolley back to the pavement as my husband examines the pile of letters in his hand. He flicks through them, like a pack of cards, lifting up the front one and placing it behind the others as if he's shuffling them in slow motion. I can't see exactly what he's holding from where I'm standing as I haven't got my contact lenses in. I think he's about to get into his car when suddenly he turns around and looks straight up at the window I'm looking out of.

I don't make any sudden movement. My face is hidden behind the curtain and the gap that I'd made when I'd opened it is so small, I'm sure he can't see me. Can he? I can feel my heart hammering as acid rises in my throat. I listen, attempting to ignore the blood rushing in my ears, trying to work out what he's doing. Everything goes quiet until I hear his key turn in the lock and I run, silently, to the bed, sliding under the covers, hiding my face in the duvet as if I'm half-asleep. It sounds like he's moving around the hall and then I can hear him as he starts to walk up the stairs. Oh God, he hasn't even stopped to take his shoes off. Across the landing. Should I lie on my left side, or right? What looks most natural? Which side do I normally face when I sleep? Away from him. I turn over, grabbing one hand with the other for comfort.

He walks into the bedroom up to the side of the bed and I keep my eyes shut.

'You didn't tell me he was writing to us?' he says loudly.

I open my eyes slowly, pretending he's woken me up, trying to keep my expression neutral.

'What?' I mumble.

'You didn't tell me he was writing to us. Has he sent anything else?'

'I don't know what –'

'Don't act dumb.' He frowns and throws a postcard down in front of me as I push myself up onto the pillows, rubbing my eyes. I don't reach for it. I know that's what he wants me to do. As much as I'm desperate to see the words, I put my hands back under the duvet where he can't see them, clasping them together. He stares at me, waiting to see what I do next.

'Is it from Adam?' I ask.

'Why don't you have a look?' he says, sitting down on the side of the bed and I glance at him, trying to see if he's holding anything else. I think his hands are empty but it's hard to tell without my lenses in. 'Go on,' he says, 'look at it.'

I slide my hands out slowly from under the covers and reach for the postcard that's lying like a splash of colour on the expanse of white material. Holding it close to my face I can see it's a picture of a temple in the middle of a lake, surrounded by orange and pink flowering bushes. I'm reminded of the picture I saw on Jo's noticeboard on Friday. I can feel him watching me.

'Have you read it?' I ask.

'What do you think?' he replies.

I turn it over slowly, desperate not to reveal any sign of my eagerness in my tone or the way I move. I scan the page.

Dear Mum & Dad,
Massive, incredible sea shores, yachts of unbelievable –

He pulls it out of my hand.

'Has he written to you before?' he asks.

'No,' I lie. 'This is the first time I've heard from him.'

'He hasn't called you?'

'You know he hasn't. You look at my phone.' He relaxes slightly as I swallow to keep down the acid rising up in my throat. Then he reaches inside his suit jacket and brings out a lighter. I recognise it as the one we keep in the drawer in the hall. He watches my face as he flicks the spark wheel so the flame appears and holds it in front of my face. I stare at him, committing the words I saw on the postcard to memory, keeping my face neutral.

He moves the lighter to the edge of the card and the orange light travels up the side, the picture of the temple crumpling and twisting into blackness before it disappears. I stay completely still. As the heat reaches his skin, he drops what's left of the card onto the bed, the flame continuing to burn, and I throw back the duvet on top of it. There's a pungent smell of burning feathers. I don't say anything else as he flicks the wheel on the lighter a couple more times, not taking his eyes off me. Then he stands up, sticks it in his pocket and walks to the bedroom door. I suppress the shudder that crawls across my back.

'You tell me if he sends anything else.'

I nod.

I listen to the car as it leaves the drive, waiting a few minutes before getting up and checking through the curtains that he really has gone. Then I go downstairs, find a piece of paper and write down what was on the postcard. As much as I'd seen. I stare at it, and take it upstairs with me, lifting up the mattress in Adam's old room, putting the piece of paper on top of the things that are already there. Everything in one place. I run my fingers along the edge of the object under the postcard. It's still there, waiting for me. I need it to stay where it is for just a little bit longer.

He comes back from work early and I can hear him opening drawers and then slamming them shut. A couple of expletives.

He'd only come into the kitchen briefly before disappearing into the study and shutting the door. The dinner I've cooked is going to get cold and he hates that.

I think about Jo at home with Grace and Livvi; how the girl who once refused to eat is currently having dinner with her family and I am here, in a house that chills me to the bone despite the heat. I saw how she'd looked at me when I'd made that comment about Mum having to sell the house. A flicker of guilt that I hope has fractured her resolve, a small chink that I can force open into a large fissure.

My heart races as I watch the digits on the oven clock. Two minutes pass. I look out of the window to the faint outline of my greenhouse at the bottom of the garden, wishing I was inside it and not in this room. Three. I close my eyes, remembering the smell of the earth, feeling my heartbeat slow down. Four. I think about what's in there and remind myself things could be so much worse. Five. I hesitate, then walk over to the study door and knock, gently.

'Your tea's ready. I just wanted to let you know.' There's no reply and I'm about to walk away but then he answers.

'I'll be out in a minute.'

'I can bring it in there, if you want?' I can hear his laptop beep as it starts up.

'Fine.'

I take the plate of sausages, mashed potato and peas and put it onto a tray with his cutlery, a glass of squash and a bottle of tomato ketchup. Walking up to the study door, I try to hold the tray steady in one hand whilst I turn the handle, ignoring the sound of blood rushing in my ears. He's sitting with his laptop open in front of him, staring at the screen. I put the tray down beside him on the desk and turn to walk away when he grabs my hand. His eyes narrow and he looks at me accusingly.

'Are you absolutely sure you couldn't see where Jo put those boxes?'

'Yes. I checked everywhere.' I don't understand why he's still asking; we both know Dad hadn't made another will. 'Why do you need them? What are you looking for?' The questions slip out without me thinking about it and he stares at me, unused to any kind of interrogation. A jolt of adrenaline runs through me as I realise what I've done; a moment of terror at what the possible consequences will be, like spinning a coin and waiting to see which side it lands on as I glance down at where he's still holding my hand. To my surprise, he lets go. His laptop whirrs into life and he fixes his eyes on the screen as a multicoloured circle rotates in front of him. A small square containing fuzzy shapes appears and he clicks his mouse. I can hear voices, tinny to start with until he turns up the volume on the computer speaker, and listens, grinning. It's still difficult to hear anything clearly but I take a sharp breath as the shapes in the square suddenly sharpen and the familiar face of a girl and her mother fill the screen; Livvi's brown eyes staring directly at me.

I took something of yours yesterday. Not something you'll notice. You were fiddling with it as you were talking and put it down on the table before you walked away. I only picked it up to look at it; wanting to put my fingers where yours had been. I pressed the push button on the bottom of the biro and watched the thrust device drive the ink cartridge against the spring, the tiny silver metal spiral contracting tightly before the ball point emerged, the tension in the coil mirrored by a similar feeling in my stomach. The impact that one thing has on another is obvious through the transparency of the barrel. One tiny change can affect the outcome of everything else – The Butterfly Effect, I think they call it. The clicking noise was addictive, the sound transforming into words that arrived in my head out of nowhere – you are, you aren't, you are, you aren't – a kind of twisted onomatopoeia that took over my brain and I had to force myself to put the pen down, the desire to keep pressing it leaving me nauseous. I put it in my pocket. You won't miss it. You won't even remember you had it. It's amazing how quickly you forget one thing when it's replaced by another. A bit like relationships. If you're with the wrong person, sometimes you just need a little bit of help to see it, and then you can move on with someone more suitable. Someone like me.

WEDNESDAY

Jo

The letter in the pocket of my jacket rustles as I move the hanger along the rail of my wardrobe to reach a pair of trousers. I wonder if it's just me who hears the noise and glance round, looking at Paul, but he's still asleep, one hand stretched out over the duvet, his wedding ring visible; the metal band a symbol that's held us together for twelve years. I want to get rid of the sheet of paper, to throw away the whole envelope, but I'm too scared to take it out in case he opens his eyes and asks what I'm doing.

I slip on my trousers, the crepe fabric cool against my skin, noticing the gap between the waistband and my skin is wider than ever. I'll have to safety-pin it when I get downstairs or they'll gape. Three months ago, that would have made me happy, but now it just feels like the secrets I'm carrying around are eating me up from the inside, like Dad's cancer, punishing me for what I've done. I couldn't face dinner last night; Paul thinks it's because I've got morning sickness. He's expecting me to grow outwards, not inwards, and I'm going to have to tell him it's not going to happen. Not now, not ever.

I try to mute the voice inside my head that makes excuses for the lies I've told him as I go downstairs to make breakfast for the girls. I look at him lying in bed before I leave the bedroom, attempting to keep faith in the part of me that refuses to accept he would betray me, or the girls, a tiny life raft in an ocean of doubt. But we've been together for so many years that I know when he's hiding something and, as much as I try to persuade myself otherwise, a hard ball sits inside my chest, rolling from one side to the other, every movement telling me differently. I'd convinced myself when Dad was dying that he'd just been distracted as he'd had to look after the girls more, but since then things have got worse, not better.

I glance at the various photos in the frames hanging on the wall above the mantelpiece as I fish around for a safety pin in the drawer of our hall console, the early morning sun bleaching the colour out of the pictures, turning them a sepia colour, images captured in a different era. A montage of our family through the years. One of Grace and Livvi in their swimming costumes in the garden, screaming with laughter as they'd squirted each other with the hose. I can't remember the last time I saw Grace laugh like that – her eyes showing her utterly caught in the moment, the joy spilling out of her. Recently, every move she makes seems heavy, weighed down with an unhappiness that seems more than just part of the grieving process.

Another one from a couple of years ago with Anna and her family, all of us standing in front of a giant bell tent after we'd been camping for a long weekend. Livvi and Jess look so tiny. Andy is holding Maddie on his shoulders and Paul has one arm around Anna and the other around Grace. Everyone's smiling. I'm not in that one. I must have been taking the shot.

I push the safety-pin through the waistband of my trousers, the sharp point difficult to get through the thick layer of material until it suddenly finds a way out the other side and the sharp tip pricks my skin. I flinch, fastening it up, the small drop of blood sinking into the pale material, wondering if it's an omen of what is to come.

As I pull up outside the school gates, Grace leans down to grab her bag before she gets out and I notice she's bitten her nails down so far that the white tips are no longer visible. I'd hoped, since she hadn't woken up last night, that things might be getting better.

We'd been to the doctor's after school yesterday, the GP smiling as he'd ushered us into his office. Grace had responded to his questions by squirming in her seat, eyeing me nervously before finally mumbling a response. She didn't know I'd phoned him beforehand, my voice catching as I'd told him what I'd found on her iPad, reassuring me it was probably part of the grieving process. He'd advised us that if things didn't improve, we could discuss the possibility of her seeing someone. I'm not sure if it was the suggestion of professional intervention, or the kindness in his manner that had caused a tear to slide down my face. Grace had stared down at her hands when he'd pushed the box of tissues across his desk. I'd wondered if he thought I was making the whole thing up. Pretending Grace had an issue when in fact it was me who wasn't coping. He knew my medical history and what was written in the letter still stuffed in my jacket pocket.

Grace had looked out of the car window all the way home. She hadn't mentioned the messages she'd been writing to Thomas. Neither had I.

Anna pulls up behind me, Maddie in the seat beside her. She raises her hand and waves at me as she gets out of the car and walks over. I press the button to wind down my window, stopping after a few inches, just enough of a gap for her to speak through. I'm wary and our usually relaxed communication feels tight, like pulling on a sweater that's got too small.

'Everything OK?' she asks.

I nod. 'Fine. You?'

She smiles. 'Not bad. Jess has got a sore throat so I've kept her at home today.'

'Hope she feels better.' I look at Maddie. 'Grace has just gone in, if you want to catch her up?'

Maddie stares at the pavement, not moving and Anna flushes. I wish I could take back the comment, a motherly instinct to protect my daughter. She hasn't mentioned anything to me about them falling out, but Maddie's reluctance to see Grace is obvious.

'We're going in to see Maddie's teacher about the form trip next week.' Anna's reply is too quick. I smile to hide my confusion.

'Well, I'm sure you'll catch up with her in class. I'd better go, got to get to work.' Anna pulls a sympathetic face.

I put my window up, wanting to get away, and watch through the glass as Maddie bends down, scrabbling about by her feet for a few seconds before standing up and handing something to her mother. Anna wipes it on her sleeve, then reaches one hand up to her ear, holding the object in the other as she pushes it through the tiny hole before turning away and crossing the road.

I decide to go the back route to work, delaying the inevitable, hoping my sister will decide not to come in at all. I turn off the main road into town, almost subconsciously, driving for a mile or so, the summer foliage making the familiar lane appear narrower than usual, pulling into the small car park at the edge of the green that overlooks the playground where Mum used to take Caroline and me when we were little. It's changed from how I remember it – the metal climbing frame, witches' hat and spinning barrels have been replaced by a wooden fort, swings and a slide. A layer of black rubber now covers the grass surface that used to stain the knees of our jeans.

When I was eight, Caroline had dared me to climb up to the top of the climbing frame where she was already standing; her twelve-year-old legs able to scramble up that high so much more easily than mine. The wooden bench where my mother had sat watching us has long since disappeared, bare metal visible underneath the peeling red paint. I'd been desperate to get up to the same place as her, wanting to prove to my mother that I was as capable as my sister. That I could do something she'd be proud of.

I'd almost made it; feeling the final rung beneath my fingertips as I'd stood on one foot, stretching out so far, I'd thought I might snap. But then Caroline had clapped, her feet firmly wedged against the bars to keep her stable; and the sudden burst of applause had startled me. I remember my fingers brushing the metal as I'd desperately scrabbled to hold on, before I'd fallen, my sister's red hair tumbling across the grey steel as she'd leaned forward to see me hit the grass below.

Caroline had screamed. A proper scream, not just the girly shrieks I'd been used to hearing at home when she wanted attention. I'd been too winded to utter a sound. I don't know whether it had been the shock, but my mother had seemed to move in slow motion, getting up off the bench and walking towards the climbing frame as if she couldn't quite believe what had happened. Other adults had run over, their footsteps vibrating through the earth, violent explosions inside my concussed head. And I remember, as my mother had come towards me, it hadn't been me she'd been looking at. Her eyes had been fixed on my sister, still standing at the top of the bars, her red hair whipping round her face in the wind like flames.

The office is already busy when I walk in to start my day. Alice is on the phone in reception and Caroline is sitting at her desk talking to a client, her voice the one I recognise above the low humming of computers and the noise of the photocopier. I wonder if years of conditioning means I'm attuned to her distinctive tones, responding like one of Pavlov's dogs, my chest tightening in anticipation.

I open up Xero to finish off the accounts, pausing after a few minutes, aware I'm waiting for something before realising with a crushing sense of disappointment that I won't ever hear Dad's footsteps again on his regular morning visit to my office. He'd always appeared with an excuse to go through the budget or to look at the latest cash flow forecast, but our interactions had ended up being so much more than that. Small spaces of time that had allowed us to get to know each other in a way I'd never have had the opportunity to do otherwise. As his illness had progressed, his visits had become more infrequent, interspersed with hospital visits and days at home, but losing him still has the ability to hit me when I least expect it. Especially as I know it's my fault.

I look up to see Caroline standing in my doorway, her client meeting finished.

'Morning.'

'Morning.' We're being cautiously polite, but I know it's only a matter of time before she brings up the subject of Dad's will again. Her words from Monday have stayed with me, her questions spinning around in my head.

'How's Grace?' she says.

'Fine.' I'm pleased she's asked, but I wait, convinced she's just delaying what she really wants to say. Getting to know my sister involves peeling away multiple layers, and I'm not sure I've ever really found her centre. She opens her mouth to say something else, but there's a tremendous crash that halts her words in their tracks. Caroline cowers instinctively, her body frozen in response to the sound of splintering glass that echoes around us followed by a horrible silence. Alice appears in the doorway, eyes wide, as I push my chair back and turn around.

The window in my office that faces out onto the pavement is smashed, an ugly hole in the centre of the pane surrounded by a myriad of cracks that spiral outwards, like a deranged spider's web. A piece of brick sits on the floor, a dark trail behind where it landed.

'Christ.' My voice quavers.

'Don't touch it.' Alice's voice echoes from the doorway. I walk over towards the window, standing on tiptoe to look out through the hole to the street outside, not sure what I'm expecting to see. People continue to walk past and there's no one standing looking back at me.

'It'll be kids messing around. I'll call the police.' Alice walks away and Caroline comes to stand next to me, staring at the brick as if it's still dangerous.

'Why would someone do that?' she asks. Her hands are trembling.

'God knows,' I say. 'Look, it's only a window. We can get it replaced.'

'But why us?' Her voice is shaky.

'I don't think it was personal.' Her eyes well up and I wonder if she's going to cry.

'It could have hurt you,' Caroline stutters.

I put my hands on her shoulders. 'But it didn't, did it? I'm absolutely fine.'

She steps away from me, rubbing the back of her neck.

'Can you ask Paul if he'll fix it until we can get a glazier out?'

I stare at her. I can see it's really bothered her, but I don't want to call Paul. Not until I've decided what I'm going to say to him about the charger.

'Wouldn't it be better to ask Rob?' I ask. 'He could send round a builder off one of his sites?'

Caroline shakes her head. 'He hates me disturbing him at work. Can you ask Paul? Please?'

'I'll try a glazier first. You go and find a dustpan and brush to clear up the glass.'

★

Paul arrives shortly after the police have left. I'd tried five glaziers but none could get here until tomorrow at the earliest. I watch as he struggles through reception with a couple of large pieces of plywood that he leans up against the wall before walking into my office.

'What did the police say?' he asks, breathless with the effort.

'They've taken the brick away and they're going to see if there's anything on CCTV, but it doesn't sound like they're holding out a lot of hope,' I reply flatly.

'That's no bloody good, is it?' he says angrily. 'What if this guy comes back, what if . . .?'

'Calm down, Paul. As they said, it's probably just kids, messing around.' He walks over to me and takes my face in his hands.

'I'm worried about you,' he says. 'What if it had hit you? What about the –'

I cut him off, pushing his hands away. 'But it didn't, did it?'

My sister emerges from her office and stands in the doorway, smiling at him. 'Thanks for doing this,' Caroline says to him. 'I would have asked Rob, but I know he's busy on site today.'

Paul and I exchange glances.

'I've cleared up the worst of it,' I say, staring at my carpet which is still covered in small pieces of glass.

'I'll put the panel over the hole and the glazier can deal with the rest,' Paul says. 'Have you got a hoover? I'll go over the floor when I'm done.'

I shake my head. 'The cleaning company does all of that.

143

I'll give them a call to let them know what to expect when they come in tonight.' I walk into reception where Paul has left his wallet and phone on Alice's desk. I can hear him shuffling around in my office. Alice is typing, absorbed with something on her screen, her headset on. I pick up Paul's mobile, turning my back to her, tapping the screen which lights up, a photo of both the girls at the beach in Devon last year. A lifetime ago.

Paul starts hammering, the sound reverberating in my head, my heart beat speeding up as I realise what I'm about to do. I type his passcode into his phone, half expecting to find that he's changed it, but he hasn't. It's still the four digits of his birthday, without the year. I take a deep breath, double checking that the hammering hasn't stopped as I scroll down his messages, stopping a few from the top. Anna's name is there. My heart thumps faster and I hesitate before I click on it to open the thread, asking myself whether I really want to do this.

The thread unravels as I press the screen. I scan down the texts, my mouth dry, forcing myself to read slowly, anxious to absorb the contents as the words blur in front of my eyes. They're not what I expected. There's nothing salacious here, no suggestion Paul is having an affair. Just offers and acceptances of school pick-ups. I click out of the thread and back to the main screen where there's a number in the list of messages that I don't recognise amongst all the familiar names, underneath which is written:

Tuesday 19th. 1 p.m.

144

Next Tuesday. I'm about to click on it to open up the thread when the hammering stops. I swipe the screen shut and slide his phone back upside down onto Alice's desk whilst she's busy searching through her filing cabinet. It's probably a meeting with a potential client. But why hasn't he mentioned it? I remind myself we haven't had the opportunity to talk much recently, perhaps he just hasn't had a chance. Or maybe he doesn't want to get my hopes up. I hear Paul's voice coming from my office and walk over; Caroline is talking to him whilst he holds the bottom of the piece of plywood, preparing to hammer in another set of nails.

As I watch him, the implications of what I've just done suddenly hit me. I don't know who to trust anymore. I can't even trust myself.

'You OK?' Caroline turns to look at me as I lean against the wall, trying to stop the buzzing noise in my brain that seems to be getting louder, like an advancing swarm of bees. 'Sit down for a minute, you look awful.' She pulls out a chair and I lower myself into it, her voice getting fainter, and I feel someone pushing my head down between my knees as the volume in the room slowly turns itself up again.

'Here.' Caroline hands me a glass of water. 'Have you eaten anything today?'

I don't answer. I know she recognises the all-too-familiar signs from when I was a teenager. Paul is kneeling on the floor beside me, his hand holding mine.

'You need to take more care of yourself,' he says.

'I'm fine,' I say weakly.

'You clearly aren't. You're doing too much. You –' His

voice is too loud and I see Caroline look at him, her forehead creasing at his reaction. I take a sip of water.

'Better?' he asks. I nod as I go to stand up but am over-whelmed by a wave of nausea and have to sit back down again.

'Oh my God,' I hear my sister say, 'are you pregnant?' I start to shake my head, but it's too late, she's looking at Paul who's already smiling at her.

'It's early days,' he says. 'And we haven't told anyone yet, including the girls, but I want you to keep an eye on her. She needs to take things more slowly.'

Caroline nods, but I notice her hesitate before she offers her congratulations, kneeling down to kiss me on the cheeks. She doesn't take her eyes off me as she gives Paul a hug and I can tell by the look on her face she doesn't believe the news he's just told her.

THURSDAY

Caroline

I dip the tip of my toe into the water. It's hot. So hot it actually feels cold for a couple of seconds before the heat burns through, making me wince. I never know how far I can raise the temperature before there's visible damage. I look down at the top of my foot which is now a bright pink colour, checking for any blisters. There are no tell-tale lumps in my skin. I hang my dressing gown over the hook on the door and take a deep breath. Putting one hand on the side of the bath, I lower one leg into the thick layer of bubbles so it disappears slowly, an inch at a time. I breathe in and out, little panting breaths, like they taught me to do when I gave birth to Adam to manage the pain. The steam coming off the water brushes against my face, making me blink. Then I put the other leg in. I've learned that if I do it one at a time there are fewer ripples which stops the heat from moving about. I slide the rest of my body into the bath until I'm sitting in the water which comes up high enough to cover my waist. My body is on fire but I welcome it. I need it to burn to feel clean again. Taking a deep breath, I submerge myself completely, feeling the bottom of the bath hard beneath my head. I keep quite still, listening to the roar in my ears, the flames now inside my chest as well as on my skin, consuming me from the inside as I count off the seconds, each one representing a year that I've been here.

I wonder what would happen if I stayed underwater. Could I hold my breath long enough to pass out? Would I float away in the water to another life? The fire in my chest builds, a furnace now, a pressure I can't resist; it pushes me to the surface and I break through with a gasp, filling my lungs with air. My skin has adjusted to the temperature. The human body can adapt to most things, given time, but it's turned a pink fleshy colour that reminds me of raw meat. The chrome tap at the side of the bath is covered in condensation. I turn it on again, very slightly, to keep the water topped up, watching the small rivers disappearing out of the holes in the overflow beside me, wishing I could go with them. I try to think about what it would be like without him; the thought of coping on my own still too frightening to contemplate. It's not until I notice the goosebumps on my arm that I realise the water dribbling out of the tap has gone cold, the hot water tank in the airing cupboard finally empty.

I stand up very slowly, holding onto the edge of the bath. I fell once, stumbling as I put one leg down onto the bathmat. Luckily, I hadn't hit my head when I landed; only bruised my shoulder, a mark he'd noticed a couple of days later, pressing his finger into it curiously as he watched the reaction on my face. I'd told him I'd caught it on a door, but it had taught me to be more careful.

I start to dry myself with the bathroom towel and then stop, dropping it on the floor as I go and get a fresh one out of the airing cupboard, not wanting the smell of his aftershave on my skin. I rub it gently over my body, looking down at the stretch marks on my stomach that appeared when I was carrying Adam. They run silvery white across my red skin like branches, the tips growing and spreading as he'd got bigger. I think of Jo's announcement yesterday and wonder if this will happen to her, too. I have a feeling it won't, years of practice with Rob have made me very good at spotting when someone is lying and her eyes hadn't reflected the words Paul had said. They'd seemed empty, not full of that secret delight I'd been expecting to see. She hadn't kept her pregnancy a secret when she'd found out she was carrying Grace or Livvi; she'd told Mum and I before she'd got to her twelve-week scan, her announcements cutting into me like a knife, the champagne my mother had forced me to swallow after Jo's phone calls tasting like cotton wool in my mouth. I don't understand why it would be different this time. And if she's not pregnant, I wonder why Paul thinks she is.

I open the bathroom cabinet and move Rob's asthma in-haler, a tube of 'Deep Heat' and a box of plasters to one side on the narrow shelf, making room for my bubble-bath that I pick up from where I left it next to the taps. I'd decanted it out of its original container into an old bottle of Calpol so it doesn't look out of place as I put it back in the cupboard, arranging the other things in front of it. He doesn't like me spending money on anything he considers unnecessary. I stare at myself in the mirrored doors. The colour of my face looks scarlet beneath my short hair – as if I've been lying in the sun all day without any cream on. But I know it won't last. In an hour or so it'll fade to its usual pale milky-white and by the time I get to work, Jo won't notice. I turn the extractor fan on as I leave the bathroom, shutting the door behind me so the steam doesn't make the bedroom walls damp.

Seeing Livvi on his screen like that had made me realise what he's capable of. My whole body had frozen in a state of disbelief at the video of her moving around, playing with her toys, oblivious to the fact that her every move was being recorded. He'd told me he'd put something in their house so he could record what they were saying and play it back later. Listen to their conversations in case Jo mentioned where she'd put the filing boxes with Dad's things. I wonder how many times he's been into their house, taking the set of spare keys Jo had given me in case of emergencies. He keeps them with him now; I've seen the keyring in the drawer of his bedside table. He claims the SD card had got hours of footage on it, enough to give him the information he's so desperate for. He hasn't explained what he's looking for and I haven't asked. He won't tell me anyway. But I have a horrible feeling it has something to do with what's hidden under our spare-room mattress.

I walk into our bedroom and open the window that looks out over the driveway to get rid of the familiar musty smell with the slight tang of ammonia that lingers on the sheets. One of the many ways he marks his territory. I strip the pillow cases and pull off the duvet cover, leaving the duvet itself in a pile on the floor at the bottom of the bed. It looks naked – the wrinkled grubby bundle no longer hidden beneath clean white cotton. I shut my eyes briefly, holding back the tears that threaten to fall, not wanting to be reminded of what happened last night. I rip the sheet off the bed, squashing it into a ball. I don't think about the way he did the same thing with my pyjama top whilst I'd still been half-asleep. I open the airing cupboard and get out a set of new linen, reassured by the smoothness of the ironed material under my fingers. I make the bed, adjusting the covers, so that by the time I'm finished everything looks tidy and pristine. I get dressed and do my make-up, glancing at my reflection in the mirror on the wardrobe door before I go downstairs, satisfied that anyone in the office who sees me will think exactly the same thing.

You offered to give me a lift to work yesterday. I mentioned the office was quite a walk from the station and you said you were passing, anyway, so could pick me up, starting tomorrow. I didn't even have to ask. I've seen your car in the office car park. It's a BMW. A black one, sporty. I looked through one of the back windows on my lunchbreak; it was difficult to see much as they're tinted, but I know you've got leather seats and satnav and an air-freshener shaped like a dog that hangs from the rear-view mirror. Dogs are my favourite animal so I think it's got to be fate. Some kind of sign. Not like horoscopes — they're a load of crap. It doesn't make any sense to me that six hundred million people all have similar character traits. I hope being in your car with you on our own will give us some time to really get to know each other properly. There are so many things I want to ask you, but I think I know your answers already. We have so much in common. You are the last thing I think of at night and the first thing my mind turns to when I wake up, but I never dream about you; I can't make you stay in my head when I'm asleep. My subconscious blanks you out, as if it needs a break. I wish I could keep you with me, that I could reach for your hand to hold in the dead of night. I don't think I'll have long to wait; once I'm in your car I can find out so much more about you. Little things that are so important. Like where you live.

FRIDAY

Jo

I'm lying on a towel in the garden, the afternoon sun heating my skin to the point where it's almost uncomfortable, a tingling on the cusp of pain that tells me it's time to move, but I can't be bothered. Paul's just cut the grass and the smell is intoxicating, a drug that encapsulates everything about summer, one that I can't get enough of. I sense someone walking towards me and open my eyes a crack, raising my hand up to my face to shield my eyes against the brightness as a familiar silhouette heads across the garden. Anna sits down beside me.

'Shouldn't you be at work?' she asks.

'Not today,' I tell her. 'I've got a day off.'

She rolls out another towel next to mine, laying it down so the edges touch. I don't understand why she can't put hers somewhere else – she's got an entire garden to choose from. I'm going to have to get up and I don't want to, as I know it'll sharpen the lovely blurred feeling I have at the moment. I try shuffling surreptitiously to one side but she keeps moving with me. I'm about to ask her what she's doing here when the ground moves beneath me, as if there's an animal trapped underneath my towel, trying to get out. I sit up with a jerk.

'What?' Anna rolls lazily onto her side and looks at me.

'I felt something move,' I say. 'Under my towel.'

I retreat, onto the grass, about to lift up the dark blue material to look underneath it.

Anna puts her hand on my arm. 'Are you sure you want to do that?' she asks. 'If you lift it up, you can't put it back.'

I frown at her and pick it up to see the undisturbed lawn below, the blades of grass flattened from the weight of my body, knotted together in intricate patterns that don't seem to start or finish in any particular place.

'There.' Anna points but I can't see anything, the sun is so bright. 'Can't you see it?' she asks. I want to go inside to sit in the shade but Anna has pulled herself up onto her hands and knees in the space where my towel used to be.

'You need to dig,' she says and I see my mother's teeth as she smiles at me, whiter than white, a flash of brightness that makes my head hurt. Anna puts her hand into the earth and I don't understand how she manages to get through the grass, but it's too late to ask. Now she's making a hole and I don't want her doing this to my garden and try to get her to stop but she won't listen. She grabs my arm, her fingers black with earth.

'Look,' she says, pulling me closer. 'There.' The dry soil is crumbling where she's dug into it, little rivers of dirt that run down a slope to the bottom, a landslide in miniature and my head sings like it did when I had gas and air giving birth to Grace. Suddenly I can see what she's looking at as it emerges from the earth, like a plant reaching for the sunlight.

First a nose, then a mouth and then the rest of my father's face. I scream and grab my towel, trying to cover it up, pressing down on whatever it is that Anna's uncovered but she's laughing as she knows it's impossible and I wake up with a jolt, slicing through the cord that links me to sleep with one swift motion.

I throw off the duvet, my chest covered in sweat, gasping to catch my breath as my brain catches up with reality. My fingers come away wet as I touch my face and I shiver in the dark, waiting for my breathing to return to normal, Paul's familiar shape a mound beside me that I can't bring myself to disturb to share my burden.

My nightmare lingers all morning, like a hangover, and I feel as if I'm trying to work through a dull fog in my head. Alice puts a call through to me just before lunch and as soon as she says the name my heart sinks.

'Mrs Lawrence?'

'Yes?'

'It's Mrs Kennedy from the school office. There's been an incident with Grace.'

'Is she OK?'

'Yes, she's fine. She's with the school nurse. Are you able to come and pick her up?'

'What's happened?'

'She fell over and says she feels a bit dizzy.'

'I'll be there as soon as I can.' I call Paul's mobile. He mumbles something unintelligible when he answers. 'It's me,' I say. 'Grace isn't well. We've got to pick her up. Are you busy?'

He clears his throat. 'Can you go? I've got some stuff to do for a client.'

'I thought you didn't have much work on at the moment?'

'Someone's contacted me today and I want to look keen.'

'Right,' I say stiffly. 'I'll need to drop her off with you as I've got to go to Mum's with Caroline. I don't really want to take Grace with me. She can sit on the sofa and watch TV, she won't disturb you.'

There's a silence on the other end of the phone.

'How long will you be?' he asks.

'At my Mum's? I don't know. A couple of hours maybe?'

'No, now. Getting Grace.'

I look at my watch. 'If I leave now, I should be home by one.'

There's another longer pause. 'OK. I'll see you then.'

I half run, half walk across the tarmac towards the door of the school office, catching a glimpse of a reflection I barely recognise in the glass window of the door as they buzz me inside. My hair lies in damp strands around my face, and I run my hand through it in an effort to look presentable. The school nurse ushers me into a small room where Grace is sitting on a bed, sipping a plastic cup of water. I give her a hug, feeling her body crumble beneath mine.

'You're all right now, Grace, aren't you?' the nurse says, looking at her before turning her attention to me. 'She had a bit of a falling out with a couple of other girls. There was a bit of pushing and shoving and Grace got knocked over. I've put a plaster and some antiseptic on her knee but she says she feels a bit dizzy. She didn't hit her head as far as we're aware, but perhaps to be on the safe side she'd be better off going home for the afternoon so you can keep an eye on her.'

'Pushing and shoving?' I say. 'You mean she was fighting?'

The nurse hesitates. 'I think it would be better for you to talk to the Head about it, Mrs Lawrence. But I can assure you that Grace has been checked over and she's fine.'

'Is the Head around now?' I ask.

'She's in a meeting at the moment. But she did say she'll call you later.'

I weigh up whether to demand a meeting now, look at Grace and decide against it.

'Have you got your bag and anything else you need?' Grace nods, her lip trembling. 'Let's go, then.'

I usher her out of the office and across the playground, glancing from left to right over the empty space, biting the skin at the side of my nail. It doesn't feel right to be trespassing in a place that should be filled with noise and laughter. The tarmac smells like it does when it's first been laid; a burning that sticks in the back of my throat. Cracks have appeared in the previously smooth surface, bisecting the yellow lines that mark out the netball court. Grace screws up her eyes against the sun as I open the passenger door, and I hurry around to my side, telling myself to stay calm.

'Fighting?' I say, as I start the engine, handing her my mobile. 'What has got into you? Can you call Dad, please? I said we'd let him know you're OK.'

She sits with the phone on her lap and dials the number, putting it on speaker. I can hear a rustling in the background and a noise I can't make out before the line cuts off. I frown, but before I have a chance to say anything he rings back and

Grace answers. His voice sounds strained as it echoes through the car speakers.

'Not sure what happened there.'

'It's just me, Dad,' Grace says. 'Mum wanted me to call to let you know I'm OK. We'll be home in about fifteen minutes.'

'OK. See you then.'

'Is someone with you?' I ask. There's a beat before he answers.

'No,' he says, 'I'm in my office. Just trying to get stuff done so I can look after Grace when you're back. I'll see you in a bit.' He hangs up and Grace glances at me as my shoulders stiffen.

'What happened at school?' I ask her.

She shrugs, staring straight ahead. 'It was nothing.'

'The nurse said you were fighting.' I try and concentrate on the road to avoid eye-contact, remembering how much I hated conversations like this with my mother, feeling as if I was backed into a corner.

'It wasn't a fight,' she says quietly. 'Maddie and I were just –'

I interrupt, not able to stop myself. 'You were fighting with Maddie?'

'If you're not going to let me explain, Mum, then there's no point in talking to you.' She turns her head away from me to look out of the window and I notice her fingers tighten their grip on my phone in her lap.

When we get back, she runs upstairs to her room and slams the door without stopping to take off her shoes. I can hear Buddy whining when I walk into the kitchen and open the back door to let him inside. He dashes past me and I hear him going up to Grace's room. I glance at my watch. I need to get to Mum's. I make up a glass of orange squash, grab a cereal bar from the snack cupboard and walk quickly up the stairs, knocking on Grace's door.

'What?' she asks. I grit my teeth as I put the drink and biscuit down on her dressing table. Buddy is lying next to her on the bed and I can tell she's been crying.

'If there's something you want to tell me, Grace, I'll listen,' I say. 'I'm worried about you.'

'I'm fine, Mum. It wasn't anything. Maddie and I just got into a stupid argument as she told Katie something she'd promised me she wouldn't.'

'Is it something I should know about?' I ask.

She shakes her head.

'Secrets always have a habit of coming out in the end,' I say. 'That's what Grandpa always used to say.' The words escape without me thinking and as soon as I've said them, I want to take them back. The feeling of guilt returns; like a buoy that's suddenly been released underwater, shooting up to the surface. I hear the back door open and shut downstairs. Paul must have come in from his office. Grace puts her hands over her face as Buddy tries to lick her fingers. I put my arm around her.

'Are you sleeping OK?'

She hesitates before nodding and I want to tell her that the dark shadows under her eyes tell a different story. 'I know how much you miss Grandpa,' I say carefully. 'We all do.' I'm conscious my words sound inadequate. Hollow. They're not what I want to say but I can't find the right ones. She shakes her head, not able to speak through the sobs. I sit with her until her body stops shaking.

'We can talk some more when I get back,' I say. 'But I've got to go and see Grandma now. Dad's here if you need him.'

'Why do you have to go?' she asks.

'I've got to sort out some things about Grandpa's will.'

'Is Grandma OK?' she asks.

'She's fine,' I say, tightly.

'Will she be coming over for Livvi's birthday?' she asks.

'I'm not sure yet. Probably.'

'What about Auntie Caroline and Uncle Rob?' she asks, sniffing.

'You're going to have to see them at some point, Grace. I know Auntie Caroline wants to apologise to you. She only said those things because she was very upset. Can you maybe try and forgive her for it?' I ask. 'We all make mistakes.'

She doesn't look at me as she answers. 'I'll try,' she says quietly. I give her a hug before I walk downstairs, wondering why I still feel like I've missed the point of what she was trying to tell me.

The journey to Mum's isn't far. Fifteen minutes at the most. The house is at the end of a short cul-de-sac, the entrance to the gravel drive partially obscured by thick laurel bushes. Large beech trees line the pavement on either side, dating back to when the houses had been built in the 1920s, planted to give an air of authenticity to the name of the road; Beech Avenue. They've grown over twenty metres tall since then and form a thick canopy that almost meets in the middle, tiny slivers of blue visible through the green as I drive beneath them. Caroline used to tell me to hold my breath until we got past them or it would be bad luck and I feel myself doing it now, the pressure a burning pain in my chest as I speed up to reach the open patch of sunlight, letting out my breath in a gasp as I pull onto the gravel.

I park on the drive in a way that doesn't leave any room for my sister to get her car in next to mine, experiencing a perverse sense of satisfaction that I've managed to get here ahead of her. My mother opens the front door before I reach it and I wonder if she's been watching out of the window, waiting for us to arrive. I remember her doing that when Caroline had been a teenager; sitting up in her dressing gown in the dark with the sitting-room curtains pulled back, refusing to go to bed until she'd got home. I don't remember her doing it for me. It was always Dad who'd stayed up on the rare occasion when I'd been well enough to go out.

'Joanna.' I walk into the hallway and my mother shuts the door behind me, glancing outside one last time for any sign of my sister. 'Come through. I've made us some lunch.'

'You didn't need to do that, Mum,' I reply.

'It's only something light. Caroline said you hadn't eaten.' Something slithers between her seemingly innocuous words, a reference to old habits and a hint to conversations that have taken place without me.

'You've spoken to her already?'

'Yes. She called me to say she might be running a bit late.' My mother pours out a perfectly chilled glass of Sauvignon and hands it to me. 'She works too hard.'

I swallow a large mouthful. 'Are you saying I don't?'

My mother sighs. 'It's not a competition. Help yourself to cheese and crackers and there's salad if you want it. Your favourite.' I sit down at the dining table, the room too warm despite the fact she's lowered the blinds in an attempt to block out the sun, something that just increases the sense of claustrophobia. I dig into the wilted leaves of lettuce, lifting them out onto my plate.

'I know how close you were to your father, Joanna,' she says, passing me a bottle of dressing which I take but don't open, her change of subject making me reach for my wine glass again. 'And I know how grateful he was to you for your help with the business when he needed it.'

'Help?' I say, struggling to keep my voice level. 'I uprooted my entire family and moved across the country, changed the girls' schools and Paul's job because Dad begged me to. Telling me he'd lose the business if I didn't. And now you want to sell it?'

She hesitates. 'The company is doing very well at the moment partly due to your efforts, but also due to the amount of business that your father generated through his personal contacts. With him no longer here, I know those contacts are going to go elsewhere. We need to sell it whilst we have the chance. Someone I know has made a decent offer –'

I interrupt her. 'You've told people it's for sale?'

'I didn't say that. The subject came up in conversation.'

I screw up my toes in my shoes under the table. 'You have absolutely no right to do that,' I tell her. 'I own the business. Dad left it to me.' My knife rattles against my plate.

'Joanna, you need to calm down.'

I stare at her. 'Dad trusted me with it, not you.'

My mother's face is pale. I want to stab my words into her, for them to pierce through her apparent lack of emotion, to spill out whatever's inside all over her perfectly set table.

'Despite what you might think, your father and I had a very close relationship,' she says quietly.

I finish the last mouthful of wine in my glass and pour myself another. 'Really?' I ask, my bitterness echoing more loudly than I expect. I think of all the times over the last few weeks she'd insisted on carrying out pointless tasks; changing the sheets in the spare bedroom that no one had slept in, clearing out cupboards to pack up unwanted items into boxes to take to the charity shop. Anything, it had seemed, to avoid spending time by the side of that bed.

She doesn't answer, but I can see from her pursed lips that she knows exactly what I'm accusing her of. She's giving me the chance to leave the conversation where it is, to move on like we normally do, burying any awkwardness so we can't see it, leaving it to grow like seeds and reappear later. But sometimes I don't know when to stop.

'If you were that close, why didn't you want to be with him at the end?' A tear slides down my face, more anger than grief. 'You left me with him.'

My mother doesn't move, focusing her gaze on the salad. Her apparent composure lights something inside me, a blast of heat that makes me blurt out what I want to say; desperate to provoke her into a response.

'He asked me to help him, when it should have been you.' Guilt seeps out through my pores and I wish she could see it; I want her to know what I've done so I don't have to hide it anymore.

She smiles sadly at me, her white veneers brighter than ever.

'Oh, Joanna. He might have asked you but we both know you aren't capable of finishing a job properly.'

I look at her in confusion, her words not making any sense. I wonder if she's actually understood what I'm trying to say.

'He begged me to help him,' I say. 'He said he didn't want to carry on anymore and so I did what he asked. Do you understand what I'm saying, Mum? I murdered him.'

She looks at me, her face expressionless.

'I went back into his room that morning after you ran out,' she says as if I haven't spoken. 'Your father was most definitely still alive, so I finished what you'd started. Just like I sorted out so many other messes you left me with when you were a teenager.'

I stare at her, as she spears a piece of lettuce with her fork. 'You didn't kill him, Joanna, so you can drop the self-pity. I did.'

SATURDAY

Caroline

I hear Rob's car pull into the driveway. He's back later than usual from work. He hasn't spoken to me today, coming home last night from work bringing with him an atmosphere so charged with frustration I'd almost been able to touch it, like static electricity on a balloon. I'd watched as he'd paced around the kitchen, keeping my distance by taking my time to lay the table; a grotesque dance that I choreographed in a similar way each night.

I hadn't thought it was possible to be so invisible, to be looked *through*, rather than *at*, as if my skin and internal organs were wholly transparent. Ever since I'd had Adam, he'd avoided looking at me directly, as if he couldn't quite fathom what I'd become. He'd watched me breastfeeding when we'd first got home from the hospital and had gone out shortly after, returning with dozens of cartons of formula milk. I'd known, without him saying, that he couldn't bear the bond he'd seen between us, as if love was a finite thing that had to be shared and he'd known he'd end up with less than he had before.

Before we'd had Adam, I'd recognised when he'd been

stressed before he'd even spoken by the way he came through the door. I'd been able to make him laugh as I'd wrapped my arms around him and he'd kissed my hair, feeling our closeness as a single heartbeat.

Last night he'd come downstairs and had poured himself a large whisky, dropping the ice cubes into the dark liquid with such force, it had splashed over the side of the glass onto the granite surface of the counter. I'd been careful not to look at him whilst he was doing it, not wanting to give him an excuse to find somewhere to direct his exasperation. Sometimes I delude myself into thinking my avoidance tactics work, that I've found a way to make myself invisible, a way of neutralising his potential attack. But I know that's not true. There isn't a strategy that works. His unpredictability makes him lethal.

I'd been late to meet him on our fourth date as my train had been delayed. He'd punched a wall in front of me and then had apologised, telling me he'd thought I'd decided not to come. I'd told him he didn't need to worry. That I wouldn't leave him. That it would be OK. And I was arrogant enough to believe it would. That I could fix him. As if he was a piece of machinery where a part was missing, and I just needed to find a spare which I could slot in and then he'd function in the same way as everyone else. I hadn't realised it was an impossible task. That a whole system of wiring and connections had somehow got tangled up and whether it had been his parents' divorce, or the fact that he hadn't fitted in at school, I hadn't been able to work out how to put him back together.

If I think about it when he's not here, I'm overwhelmed

with sadness for what we've lost. Part of me believes he can still change. And then he comes home, and I'm forced to recognise the gap between my expectations and reality; like a nightmare Groundhog Day that I repeat over and over again, hope running through my fingers like water, impossible to hold onto.

The car engine goes silent and I glance around the kitchen. I don't think I've left anything out of place. The card that had arrived in the post this morning has been put away upstairs with the one that's already under the mattress in the spare room. I'd hidden it in the kitchen drawer until he'd gone out so he hadn't seen it. I try not to let the warmth that floods through my stomach show on my face when I think about it. I'd read the words as if Adam had been standing beside me, picturing him lying on a sun-drenched beach, wondering what it would feel like to start a new life.

> Dear Mum & Dad,
> I think Seminyak's awesome. Lovely, magnificent ocean, seen twelve turtles incubating many eggs. Baby elephants randomly emerged at dusk yesterday.
> Love, Adam

Even if I had a passport, I couldn't have gone with him. I know my husband. He'd told me if I ever left, he wouldn't stop looking until he found me. And if he discovered me with Adam, I don't like to think about what he'd do. It would be worse for both of us than me being here, dying slowly.

I wait until I hear his key turn in the lock before I lift the clean cutlery basket out of the dishwasher where I'd left it earlier, taking it over to the kitchen drawer to unload it.

The constant need to get the timing exactly right on every single thing I do to ensure I look busy, but still available, is exhausting. Sometimes I feel as if I'm living the reality of a giant flowchart, with endless possibilities of yes and no options, varying my decisions again and again, wondering whether one day I'll be able to get it right.

I hear him walk towards the study, then stop and turn around, his footsteps getting louder as he comes back towards the kitchen. Oh God. The tiny bubble of hope that has risen in my chest bursts as I realise he's not going to switch on his computer. I should have known better. He never changes his routine. I feel a twinge in my bladder and wish I'd been to the toilet before he got back. He pushes open the door and I grab a handful of knives and forks, the metal still warm, fixing a smile onto my face.

'What's for dinner?' he asks.

'Fish and chips,' I reply. 'How was your day?' He doesn't answer as he walks over to me, staring at my face. 'What the hell have you got on?' he asks. I look down at my clothes, confused, and he puts his hand under my chin, pushing it upwards so I'm looking directly into his eyes. 'Not your outfit. This.' He presses his finger onto my lips and drags it across my face before pulling it away and holding it out for me to look at. 'What are you wearing that for?' I stare at the raspberry-pink colour on his skin and run my tongue over my lips in an effort to remove the rest.

'I – I put it on earlier,' I stutter.

'I can see that,' he says, almost wearily, like he's talking to a child. It's the same voice he used to use when Adam was still here, the one that told him to *Put your hands in your lap when you've finished eating.'* He'd demanded obedience at all times. I'm surprised Adam hadn't rebelled earlier.

'I remember you saying how much you liked the colour,' I say, deciding it's something he won't expect to hear. He doesn't realise how long I've had to watch and learn from him and that I can change too when he's least expecting it. And I'm getting better at it. Not much longer and I'll be almost perfect. His eyes flicker, a sign his brain is processing the implications of what I've just said and he's unsure how to deal with it.

'Wipe the rest of it off your cheek,' he says. 'It's smudged.'

We eat our fish and chips in silence, the acid of the vinegar stinging the graze on my lip where I'd rubbed the lipstick off. I'd forgotten I still had it on. I'd found it in my make-up bag earlier, the cellophane wrapping around the small tube still intact. I'd torn it off and opened it up, hearing that satisfying noise as I'd pulled the lid off, the same sound as when you press your lips together and pull them apart after you put it on. I hadn't heard it for years. The stick of colour had been smooth and untouched and had smelt faintly of vanilla. I hadn't been able to resist it, applying it to see what it looked like, pouting in front of the mirror like a teenager, imagining I was somewhere hot, sucking up the ice-cold liquid of a frozen margarita in the heat of the sun, leaving behind a raspberry-coloured mark on a white straw. It had been stupid. I never should have done it. I can't get carried away. It only leads to disappointment.

Last night I'd been in the kitchen when I'd heard him storm out of his study, slamming the door, his footsteps thudding all the way upstairs. I'd stood by the sink, washing up the saucepan, every one of my senses alert, trying to anticipate what he'd do next. I'd dried my hands on the tea towel and had walked into the hall, listening to the sound of the tap running upstairs, presuming he'd been running a bath.

I'd pressed down the handle of the door very slowly, careful not to make a sound. His laptop had been open on the desk; the screen blank. I had bent down in front of it and jiggled the mouse, but nothing had happened. I'd lifted up his headphones, still plugged into the laptop, and had put them over my ears, pressing the volume button on the keyboard, watching as a small line of white dots had appeared, but I hadn't been able to hear anything apart from a barely detectable low humming noise.

I'd felt a hand on my shoulder.

'What d'you think you're doing?'

I'd whirled around, the cable from the headphones tangling round my neck as he'd tried to pull them off. I'd backed away from him, dragging the laptop with me off the desk where it had landed with a crash on the floor. 'You fucking stupid idiot,' he'd shouted, picking up the machine and ripping out the headphone lead, leaving me to unwind it from round myself. He hadn't looked at me as he'd sat down in front of the screen, rebooting the computer, double clicking the mouse to enter his password.

I'd watched, praying it would start, anxiety scratching at the bottom of my stomach with sharp claws. I'd learned to fold up my fear and bury it inside me, but sometimes, like at that moment, I'd seen the look on his face and hadn't been able to stop it escaping. I'd had a sudden urge to empty my bladder, a feeling of lightness that I'd wished would envelop me so I'd disappear. The machine had whirred back into life. I'd let out a deep breath. I hadn't broken it. He'd snatched the headphones back, the look on his face letting me know I'd pay for it later. And I had. Another scar to add to his collection.

'All those conversations and they don't even mention the bloody boxes,' he says, his fork halfway to his lips, a blob of ketchup expanding as it gathers on the edge of a chip, ready to drip. 'Five bloody hours I've sat through, and nothing. You're going to have to go round there again.'

I watch as the drop of ketchup falls through the air, missing the plate, disappearing onto his lap. He doesn't notice, he's too busy eating and I wince at the noise of his teeth scraping along the prongs of the fork as he pulls off his next mouthful.

'I don't know where else to look,' I say. 'For all we know she's emptied out the boxes and put everything away. What are you so desperate to find?'

He ignores my question, scraping up the last few pieces of fish off his plate. The moisture oozes out from the whiteness of the flesh, glinting under the kitchen spotlights and I put my cutlery down on my plate, my own dinner untouched. He wipes the side of his mouth with a piece of kitchen roll, the ketchup smearing across the white tissue like blood.

'So, you'll go?' he asks, but I know it isn't a question.

'What about Buddy? He'll bark if he sees me and if Paul's in his office, he'll hear him.'

'I've thought about that,' he says. 'And I've bought something which will sort out that problem.'

You've picked me up every morning for the last two weeks. I know you get impatient when you have to sit in traffic, that you like the car temperature at nineteen degrees and you turn down the volume on the radio when I get in so it's easier for us to talk. Until I met you, I never believed there was only one person for everyone, I'd thought fate was simply a construct devised by the strongest to give hope to those who had none. But you looked at me on Friday, really looked at me and I didn't breathe until you blinked and looked away, breaking the connection between us, as fragile as a spider's thread, my stomach falling, exploding into an infinity of stars at the endless possibilities. I know you saw it too. All those things I've wanted to say for the longest time and now I know you feel exactly the same way.

SUNDAY

Jo

I'd expected to feel lighter, as if the burden of what I'd been carrying around with me for the past four weeks would somehow transfer across to my mother. I don't know how to calculate how much weight you can attribute to a life. It's not sufficient to equate it to the physical sum of skin and bones. Dad had only been ten stone when he died; a fragile paper husk compared to the person he'd been a couple of months earlier. The cancer diet isn't for the faint hearted. It had stripped him from the inside, swallowing muscle and flesh as well as fat, draining every last drop of water out of his skin in a rabid thirst, never satiated, four stone in eight weeks, always wanting more. And the guilt I'm carrying feels far heavier than that.

I'd thought the knowledge that I hadn't been responsible would act as some kind of a release but nothing has changed. I still wake up in the morning, the first couple of seconds in blissful ignorance before the shame returns, tightening around my throat. Sometimes I wish it would stop me breathing. A life for a life; it's what I deserve. I may not be technically responsible for his death but my intention was clear even if my mother had completed what I'd started. Or perhaps it's nothing to do with Dad. Perhaps it's because the guilt that is already there from lying to Paul expands to fill the space of what has been removed, a law in physics that I'd never learned.

Paul looks at his mobile phone. 'I need to go out for a bit.' His once blue eyes are now a dull grey colour, and I realise I no longer have any idea what he's thinking. I have an unfamiliar need to fill the silence between us, as if it will start to unpeel if I leave it, like flaking paint, revealing things I don't want to see. 'Are you going to be OK?' he asks.

'Fine. Why?'

He stares at me. 'You've been really quiet since you got back from your mum's on Friday.' I hesitate, wondering whether I should tell him what she's done. Whether he'd understand that taking a life that consisted of nothing but pain and was only days or perhaps even hours from being over, was a true act of love. I don't know whether he'd see it that way. Or whether he'd consider us both murderers. 'Jo?' he says, putting his arms round my shoulders and looking into my eyes. 'Are you sure you're all right? You're not feeling ill? You've barely eaten anything in the past few days.'

'I'm just a bit nauseous,' I reply. He nods, thinking he understands. He moves as if he's going to touch my stomach and I turn around so he can't, picking up the dishcloth to wipe the counter. 'Where are you going?' I ask, as he grabs his car keys out of the bowl in the hall.

He hesitates. 'We need a couple of bits of stationery. Printer paper and some ink. I won't be long.' He walks across the drive and I can see him staring at his phone screen as he opens the car door, his eyebrows drawn together.

Grace is sitting on the sofa in the snug watching television; still in her pyjamas. Last night I'd woken up disorientated, my heart racing as a loud noise had pierced the darkness. I'd staggered out of bed, across the landing into her room. She'd been fast asleep despite the racket. Buddy had been sitting on the rug beside her bed, growling at the empty chair that she'd left in the middle of her room. He'd whimpered when I'd walked in, pawing at her duvet. I'd gathered him up in my arms, his fluffy coat making him seem bigger than he actually was, and had carried him downstairs to the kitchen where he'd howled as I'd shut the door. When I'd tiptoed back into her room, Grace hadn't moved, asleep with her mouth slightly open and her hands tucked under one cheek, like she used to do when she was little. I'd picked up her chair and had pushed it back underneath her desk, wondering why she'd left it out to start with.

Her Head of Year had called to let me know she's going to speak to her and the other girls involved at school tomorrow. I hope she has more success than I did in getting to the bottom of what they'd been fighting about. Grace still won't tell me. Paul had tried to talk to her but she'd clammed up, telling him it wasn't important. The Head had suggested Grace might find it helpful to see the school counsellor and as she won't talk to us, I didn't feel I could decline her offer. Part of me hoped Grace would refuse, that she didn't need to talk to a stranger, but she'd agreed to the appointment, and the Head assured me any discussions would remain confidential. I'd understood what she had been saying. That Grace would be under no obligation to tell me what they'd talked about. More secrets that would end up being hidden between us.

Paul had said we should go and speak to Anna to get Maddie's perspective, but Grace had pleaded with us to stay out of it and I'd agreed, for the moment. She still won't tell me what Maddie had told Katie, but as I'd told Paul, interfering in these situations generally makes things worse, and I don't want Grace to be any more reluctant to go to school than she already is.

I look at my daughter now, the dark shadows under her eyes still evident, her silent reaction to the cartoon playing on the screen a noticeable contrast to Livvi's hysterical laughter. The thought of her finding out what my mother and I had done makes me shiver.

'You need to get dressed, sweetheart,' I say. 'We've got to walk Buddy.'

We cut down the path at the bottom of the road to take Buddy into the woods – there's some shade under the trees and as Livvi refuses to wear a hat I want somewhere we can get out of the sun. It's even hotter today; the glare feels uncomfortable even this early; it has an intensity like that first blast of heat when the oven door is opened. Buddy dashes ahead along the path at the side of the lake, jumping into the water as Grace throws him a stick and then leaping out, shaking the droplets of water out of his coat and all over Livvi. He turns to look at me, his tongue out, and I smile. It's almost as if he's laughing. I'm going to have a nightmare de-tangling his coat when we get back. I quicken my pace down the narrow footpath, Buddy scampering along in front of me, the girls following. The mud dries almost immediately on Livvi's face where Buddy has splashed her, leaving her covered in tiny dots that blend in with her freckles. Grace complains she's thirsty, and that her ankle is sore. I let out a small sigh of relief by the time we get home.

I tell Buddy to sit and stay on the step as I open the front door and kick off my trainers, grabbing the old towel that we keep on the coat rack, letting him inside carefully, keeping him on the mat as I wipe his feet. He struggles and barks as I tell him I'll be as quick as I can and he licks my face, still yapping when he looks in the direction of the kitchen. He wriggles so much that I let him go and he skids away from me, pushing the kitchen door open with his nose and running around the island in the middle of the room.

'What's got into him?' Grace asks. He runs back to the front door and paws at it, whining.

'Sorry, Buds, we're not going out again,' I tell him. 'You've had your walk for the day. He barks a couple more times, like he does if there's someone there. I open it again to check, holding his collar, but the driveway is empty. I rub the top of his head. 'You're such a daft thing, aren't you? There's no one here. See?'

The sun is directly overhead now and so bright that I have to squint when I look across the gravel. I pull on Buddy's collar to get him to come inside and peer at my car at the same time. There's something on the door. I screw up my eyes, but it's difficult to see properly with the sun reflecting off the paint. I slip on my shoes and walk out towards it. Someone's been here. With a spray can. I'm staring at the words *YOU OWE ME* that have been written in large white capital letters across the blue paint of the driver's door.

I retreat towards the front door, my skin prickling across the back of my neck. What if someone's in the house? I try to grab my thoughts that threaten to spiral out of control and think logically. There's no sign of a break-in. I walk into the kitchen, checking there are no broken windows as I get my phone out of my pocket and dial Paul's number. It goes straight through to voicemail and I leave a message telling him to call me. The girls have taken their drinks outside and I can hear them on the trampoline. I walk upstairs, calling Buddy to come with me, padding as carefully as I'm able to in my socks across the floorboards.

'Hello?' I call out. 'Is anybody there?' There's no reply. Buddy scoots off, barking, thinking we're playing some kind of game of hide-and-seek.

As I walk into Grace's room I shiver. Someone has been in here. It feels different. As soon as I've had the thought, I tell myself not to let my imagination run away with me. Nothing looks out of place but when I close my eyes, the air seems to tingle against my face like a weak electrical current. I check my phone again, but there's still nothing from Paul.

I head back downstairs and look out of the window, the hideous white writing still visible. The girls haven't noticed; I can hear an off-key version of 'Shotgun' coming from the back garden. A car pulls into the drive and the flutter of panic in my stomach recedes when I realise it's Paul. He gets out of the car, empty handed.

'Where's the printer paper?' I ask as he walks towards the front door.

He frowns, hesitating. 'They didn't have any.' My face hardens. 'What's the matter?' he asks.

'I've been trying to call you,' I say. 'Have you seen my car?' He shakes his head, confused, as I point at it from the safety of the doorstep. 'Someone's spray painted on the side of it.'

His eyes widen as he looks at the words scrawled across the door. 'Jesus.' He walks over to it and bends down, running his fingers over the letters which have dried quickly in the heat, now a permanent feature, not budging when he licks his finger and attempts to rub part of the 'Y' off. 'Have you called the police?' he asks.

I shake my head. 'We've only just got back from walking Buddy.' He looks pale.

'Shall I call them now?' He doesn't answer, staring down the drive. The pavement is empty. I follow his gaze, wondering if he's looking at Anna's house, something slipping in the bottom of my stomach. 'Paul! Shall I call the police?'

He mutters something I can't hear. I lift up my phone as he walks towards me.

'I don't think we should.'

'Why not?'

'They won't do anything about it and we'll have to hang around waiting for them to come out. I'd rather just get it booked into the garage.'

'But shouldn't we at least report it?'

He shrugs. 'You can if you want, but I honestly don't think it's worth the hassle. I'll call the place we got the MOT done at to see if I can drop it in first thing tomorrow. Bloody graffiti bastards.' He puts his arms around me and I stare at the words over his shoulder. They don't make any sense. I don't owe anyone anything. I think about the smashed window in my office, the two incidents happening too close together to dismiss as coincidence, feeling Paul's hand tremble as he takes mine to walk back inside.

Buddy reacts to the sound of the doorbell before I do, dashing to bark at the letterbox. I get up off the garden lounger where I've been lying for the last half an hour, the heat combined with our earlier walk making me dozy. Paul is playing swing ball with the girls, hitting the tennis ball backwards and forwards as they stand opposite him with their rackets poised; Livvi aiming in one direction and Grace the other. It's the first time I've seen him look relaxed for days and for a moment I feel a pang of envy.

I open the door to find Caroline standing on the doorstep.

'Aren't you going to ask me in?' she says.

'Yes, sorry,' I say hastily. 'I'm just surprised to see you here.' She walks into the hallway, staring at the photos above the mantelpiece. I'm trying to remember the last time she came over. The silence is broken by the sound of the girls shrieking from the garden.

'They're playing with Paul,' I say, twisting my watch round on my wrist at the thought of how Grace is going to react when she sees my sister. Caroline nods.

'I'm surprised they've got the energy in this heat. I couldn't run when it's like this.'

I laugh. 'Me neither.'

'Well, you've got a good excuse in your condition, haven't you?' She smiles as she asks the question and I turn away to walk into the kitchen. She follows me and I see Grace look at us through the open patio doors, frowning slightly as she tries to work out if it's really my sister. I forgot that she hasn't seen her with short hair. I watch as she drops her racket and heads slowly across the grass, Livvi calling after her to come back as she's ruining the game. Paul puts his hand up to shade his eyes, trying to see inside the kitchen and the fear I saw earlier returns, casting across his face like a shadow.

I brace myself for a confrontation as Grace walks over to Caroline, glancing into the hallway at the front door as if she's expecting someone. My sister looks at her and opens her arms.

'Hi, Grace. I'm sorry I upset you. Forgive me?' Grace hesitates, then hugs my sister back. I force myself to smile, wishing she hadn't let her off the hook quite so easily.

'Do you want to come and play swing ball?' Grace asks.

Caroline smiles at her. 'Not right now. I've got something to discuss with your mum. Give me a few minutes and then I'll come out, OK?' Grace doesn't get a chance to reply before Paul steps into the kitchen, his tennis racket still in his hand, the muscles in his jaw relaxing when he sees Caroline standing by the sink.

'Hi, Caroline. You all right?' She nods. 'Coming back out to play, Grace?' he asks. 'Livvi is annihilating me.'

'Sure.' Grace runs out of the door and Paul follows, pretending to swipe her with his racket but I can't help feeling that wasn't what he'd come in to say at all.

'Is he OK?' Caroline asks, watching him as he disappears into the sunshine.

'He's fine,' I say, too quickly, and she catches the tone in my voice, turning to look at me.

'He looks tired.' It feels as if she's studying my face, looking for the tiny signs that I am unaware of that will tell her what she wants to know. Things that no one else would notice but my sister can read me like a book, despite the years of being apart. I try to stop biting the inside of my cheek as she knows I do that when I'm lying, but there are too many clues that give my guilt away to hide them all. 'I thought he was going to come in and whack me with that racket,' she says.

'He's just a bit protective of me at the moment,' I reply. 'Someone graffitied my car.'

'Bloody hell,' she says.

'Look.' I pull up the blind from where I've drawn it almost all the way down to keep the sun out. Caroline peers through the glass, squinting against the brightness. 'Someone did it when we were out walking Buddy. I'm worried it's connected to what happened at the office.' Now it's my turn to study her as she turns my words over in her head but she was always better at this game than me, and if she had anything to do with this, she doesn't show it.

'You heard what the police said. They're sure it was kids,' she says. 'No note with the brick. Nothing personal.' I want to believe her but the coincidence keeps poking me, not letting me forget about it. She turns away from the window, tucking her hair behind her ear. 'You left Mum's in a hurry on Friday,' she says, changing the subject.

'I had some things I needed to do. And you turned up late.'

She doesn't reply and there's an awkward silence as she

wanders down to the other end of the kitchen and into the snug where the floor is littered with Livvi's toys.

'Mum said you hadn't made any final decisions,' Caroline says, 'about the business.'

I hesitate. 'Not yet. But I haven't heard anything that makes me think I should sell it.'

'What does Paul think you should do?' she asks, picking up a couple of soft toys off the sofa, putting them back in the box on the shelf.

'It's not Paul's decision,' I say. 'He'll support whatever I think is best.'

'But he's not against you selling it.'

'I didn't say that.' It feels as if she's using my words against me, pulling them out of my mouth like a magician does with one of those silk scarves that end up being linked to a hundred more in a row that goes on forever. I wish she hadn't come.

'I just wonder what he'd think if he knew you were lying to him,' she says. I reach out to put my hand on the back of the sofa. Please may our mother not have told her what we did. She wouldn't have. She'd have known it would destroy her as much as me.

'What do you mean?' I say, weakly.

'I know you, Jo. And I know when you're hiding something.' I can't bring myself to reply, not wanting to give her any more ammunition without realising it. 'I knew it the moment I walked into Mum's house.'

I think back, desperately trying to remember our conversation. I'd left almost as soon as she'd arrived, needing to be anywhere else after my mother's confession, feeling as if I had been submerged in ice-cold water.

NIKKI SMITH

'You'd drunk almost half a bottle of Sauvignon. We both know Mum doesn't touch the stuff. I don't think you'd have done that if you really were pregnant, would you?'

She walks over to me and hands me a couple more soft toys as I stand there, speechless, my cheeks burning as my carelessness rises up my face.

'What do you think Paul would say if he knew?' she asks quietly. I look at her and I know she can see the question that's a plea in my eyes. 'I won't say anything to him. Not yet, anyway, but you should have another think about what you want to do with the business. Perhaps this is what you needed to hear to convince you to change your mind.'

184

MONDAY

Caroline

I hadn't slept well after seeing Jo yesterday, lying still in the dark last night so as not to wake Rob. I tell myself that I didn't have a choice. What my husband will do if he doesn't get what he wants would be so much worse than anything I could say to her.

At the moment he's in the bath, an evening routine after work that normally takes him between forty-five minutes and an hour, his damp towels discarded in a pile on the floor for me to pick up after he's finished. Each one of his footsteps around the bedroom had echoed like the beat of a drum, marking the end of a temporary stay of execution. I'm praying my conversation will make Jo change her mind. If he thinks he's going to get the money he might leave her alone.

I've come out to the greenhouse at the end of our garden. We'd inherited it when we moved in, a small, metal-framed relic from the nineteen-eighties, the bottom of the panes of glass green with mould, the crazy-paving tiles it sits on chipped around the edges. He'd seen the way I'd looked at it and had said we needed to get rid of it, but after I'd shrugged my shoulders and agreed, he hadn't bothered to go to the trouble of removing it. He'd have needed to pay to get someone in and he only takes something away if he knows I want it. He doesn't know how much time I spend in here whenever he's out, even in the winter. How much I love the smell of compost, of tomato plants, of things growing. It's a small sanctuary away from the house and I'm very careful to make sure he doesn't realise how much it means to me.

If he knows I'm out here he'll stare at me through the kitchen window. He thinks he can see me, but he can't. He only sees what he wants to; his wife wearing the same T-shirt she's had for the past ten years, the one that has a hole in the sleeve and faded stains of various colours down one side. His wife whose hands tremble with a combination of excitement and fear when she opens the door to come out here, who has to triple check the kitchen is clean and tidy so there isn't a reason for her to be called back. He doesn't see the person who creates new life whilst she's in this place. The person who plants cucumber seeds in small pots and waters them, waiting until they start to grow. He doesn't see how good I am at watching over things, waiting patiently when others would have given up a long time before. I've learned that sometimes even when there appears to be no hope, things will find a way to survive against the odds.

Dad and I had used to exchange plant cuttings. Over the years I'd propagated tiny shoots from his hydrangeas, rhododendrons and azaleas which are now growing in our flowerbeds. His hydrangeas had changed colour from pink to blue when I'd planted them in our garden. He'd told me it was due to the acidity in our soil and I'd wondered if part of Rob's personality had somehow permeated into the ground itself in the years we'd lived here. I think Dad had known how much I like being out here. My little greenhouse is about a tenth of the size of his, but he'd seen I had a talent for nurturing things, for making them grow. I think he'd hoped I'd be able to do the same thing with Rob. But I'd failed. I hadn't been able to find whatever is required to make him flourish.

I don't want to admit it, but anything I'd hoped to be able to cultivate in him died a long time ago. I'm left with a handful of withered branches that will be dry and brittle inside if I snap them off; devoid of life. When I'd visited Dad in that last week, I think he'd known it, too. In those final couple of days when he'd declined so rapidly, he'd squeezed my hand, as if he'd been trying to tell me something, but Jo had leaned down first to try and hear what he was whispering and I'd missed my chance. I'd been so desperate for her to leave us on our own, just for two minutes, but she hadn't. She'd repeated his words, saying he'd asked to 'Go now, please,' but I don't think that's what he'd meant at all. He'd opened his eyes a fraction and had looked straight at me when she'd said it, as if it had been an instruction.

I glance at my watch. I've been in here twenty-five minutes. I pull off my gardening gloves and put them on the wooden rack next to the plastic flower pots. I don't want to be in here too long in case he thinks I'm enjoying myself. I slide open the door, the metal frame catching on the runners. The aluminium has corroded and brown speckled spots cover the silver surface, like lichen, nature working to reclaim its own. I walk back over the lawn to the kitchen, hesitating in the last patch of evening sun that lights up the grass, a tiny island of warmth amidst the encroaching shadows. I shut the back door into the kitchen quietly, pull off my shoes and hover at the bottom of the stairs, listening, but there's only silence.

He doesn't come downstairs until later, my greenhouse now a blurred outline in the darkness that brushes against the window. He pulls the cord to lower the Roman blinds and I have an urge to stop him, to rip them open so I can see out and breathe, but I hold myself back, feeling my stomach get heavier as the material descends inch by inch, trapping me inside the room. He pours himself a large whisky and stands in front of me, running his hand over his beard. The anticipation of what he's going to say is so intense I can almost see it shimmering above his glass. I turn away from him to open a cupboard, pulling out a tumbler that I fill with water, swallowing it in large gulps.

'You really think Jo's going to agree to sell?' he asks.

I hesitate. 'Yes.'

'Why the sudden change of heart?' He narrows his eyes as he looks at me.

'Paul thinks she should.'

'So, no need for me to visit?'

I'm not sure how to answer, whether this is a trick question and I'll end up with the contents of his glass in my eyes, the sting of alcohol mixing with my tears. 'No,' I reply.

'One of us needs to go at some point,' he says.

'Why?' I ask. 'So you can graffiti her car again? Threatening her isn't going to make her sell it any quicker.'

He frowns. 'What are you talking about?'

'Someone spray-painted the side of her car.'

'I haven't been near her car.' He stares at me, a muscle on his cheek twitching. I know immediately from his reaction that I've said the wrong thing and wish I could retract it. Stuff the words back inside my mouth and swallow them, even if they make me choke. He swills his glass round, the ice clinking against the side, and I brace myself. 'Don't ever tell me what to do,' he adds quietly.

I shiver, trying to keep very still, hoping I'll provoke him less if I don't move.

He walks up to me and stands with his face a couple of centimetres away from mine, so close I can smell the whisky on his breath, before he reaches out and tries to tuck a piece of my hair behind my ear, but it hasn't grown back long enough. I flinch, instinctively, and he runs one finger over my chin and smiles, his Adam's apple moving up and down as he swallows, weighing up his options. 'I make the decisions, Caroline. What's best for both of us.' He's finding it harder to hide his animosity; it rises to the surface like bubbles in water. I stay completely silent, knowing better than to answer. It's a game he plays, waiting for me to make the next move, revelling in the fact that he knows he's physically stronger than me and I have nowhere to hide.

He traces round my jawline with one finger. 'I wonder why your father didn't leave the business to your mother? Or to you?' The way he asks the question makes me realise he already knows the answer and I feel sick.

Rob puts his glass down on the counter and picks up the bottle to refill it, holding it underneath as he twists the cap off and empties in the last of the amber liquid. It's the same thing Adam does, a habit he'd inherited from his father without even realising, and I wonder how many other things he's picked up over the years. Whether he'll ever be able to forget some of the things he's witnessed.

'Let's hope Jo doesn't need too much time to think it over.' He smiles as he leans over and kisses me, the whisky tasting sour on my lips, before walking off into the sitting room. I stand very still as I hear him switch on the television until I'm quite sure he's not coming back. Then I refill the ice cube tray that he's left on the counter with water and carry it over to the freezer, being careful not to spill it as I shut it inside.

I pick up the empty bottle and open the cupboard to put it in the bin. Talisker. His favourite brand, unchanged from when I'd met him twenty years ago. My husband rarely changes his habits. Jo said he'd been drinking whisky that night, too. That she could smell it on him when he'd reached over and tried to slide his hand under the blanket she'd tucked around her legs as she'd sat on the sofa. She'd been ill then, so pitifully thin that she'd begun to resemble an old woman, her body shrinking in on itself, her eyes hollow, her collar bones jutting out from beneath her skin. She had repulsed me.

I'd thought she'd done it to recapture our attention that had no longer focused on her every mouthful, snippets of time we'd grabbed hold of to try to establish some normality in our lives, discovering it was impossible to spend years in a heightened state of terror. I'd assumed she'd lied, invented falsehoods that had burned like a bonfire, so bright that no one could have failed to look anywhere other than in her direction. I'd told her I hadn't believed her, but I wish she knew how many days since then I've wondered about what would have happened if I had.

I saw you today. You were coming out of Sainsbury's just as I was going inside. I almost didn't recognise you. At first, I didn't think you'd seen me as you turned your face away, headed in the opposite direction, but I called out and you looked round, my voice carrying across the asphalt, above the sound of the cars in the car park. I smiled and you walked over. You talked about work and I listened to the words come out of your mouth, each one holding my attention to begin with, as light as whipped cream, wishing I was on my own so you'd be like how you are when we're in your car. But the more you talked, the heavier your words became, as if they'd been caught in a rainstorm, weighed down, soggy and unattractive. You talked about what you were doing over the weekend with your family, that the weather was going to be too hot and you didn't look at me properly, not once. Your eyes slid away whenever mine tried to reach you. And in the way that happens when things fall apart, I suddenly saw the imperfections I hadn't noticed before. The tiny yellow stain on the collar of your shirt. The way you couldn't keep still, putting your hand in the back of your jeans as you looked across the car park, desperately searching for the first pause in the conversation to use as an opportunity to get away. Your sharp canines, too white and shiny as you smiled when my dad thanked you for giving me a lift in the morning, while you replied it was the least you could do. Then you said you had to leave, and my heart shrunk. I felt more invisible than if you'd never seen me at all.

TUESDAY

Jo

I run my hand over my stomach this morning as I lie in bed, remembering the flutters that had started like butterflies' wings beneath my skin when I'd discovered I was pregnant with Livvi and Grace, pretending the gurgles I can feel now are the same thing. I know they aren't, but if I shut my eyes, I can almost convince myself, like a child at Christmas, believing that shape beneath the wrapping paper is exactly what I want it to be.

I know I'm going to have to tell Paul and the longer I leave it, the harder it's going to be. Part of me wonders if it's the only thing that's keeping him here, whether as soon as I tell him it'll cut the fragile thread that's holding us together, giving him the reason he's been looking for to walk away. But more than that, I know a confession will turn the printed black words in the letter that's been sitting for over a week in my jacket pocket, the ones I've reread multiple times, into a permanent reality. Premature ovarian failure. Something I'm refusing to admit to myself. I'd been ambivalent about having another child, despite Paul's enthusiasm, until I'd been told that I couldn't have one. And even now, I live in futile hope that my body is still able to do something that the doctor has told me it can't, an unwillingness to accept the truth.

Now Caroline knows I'm not pregnant, I don't have a choice. Perhaps it's a good thing she found out. Her threat forces me to admit it now rather than wait for Paul to find out, the failure of my stomach to fill out into a familiar bump a giveaway sign that things aren't as they should be. I thought over the past couple of years my sister and I had grown closer, but I was naive. She's still the same person I grew up with. The one who has inherited my mother's genes, a need to create the illusion of perfection. I presume that's why she wants me to sell the business. The money will simply add to the pile she and Rob already have. Another car. A new Aga. I should have asked her what's next on the list. And whether the loss of our complicated relationship is worth it.

Paul is already up, despite the early hour. He says he's got a lot to do, but I don't know if I believe anything he says anymore. I'd felt him get out of bed several times last night; our mattress rising and then sinking again each time, careful not to stray into the cool area of sheet between us. I hear the tap turn on in the bathroom, the sound of running water tells me he's cleaning his teeth, habits ingrained into familiarity over the many years we've been together. I roll over and press the screen of his phone that he's left lying on his bedside table. The message from the unknown number has been deleted but he's posted something in his calendar for today: *Meeting. 1 p.m.*

I walk out of the office, telling Alice I'm going to see a client, disappearing before she has a chance to tell me I haven't finished the budget figures I'd promised to get to her earlier for the monthly reports. I run my hand over the paint as I close the driver's door of my car. It feels smooth under my fingertips, no rough edges betraying where the patch has been resprayed. I wonder how they've managed to do that – seamlessly blending the old and the new, no trace left of what was there before. I bend down to look at it from different angles, convinced I'll still be able to see an outline of the letters that are imprinted permanently in my head, but there's nothing apart from a plain blue panel in front of me.

I stop at a set of traffic lights in town as the green man flashes; a girl who looks like Grace did when she was younger crosses the road in front of me holding her mother's hand, her blonde hair cascading down the back of her T-shirt from beneath a sun hat. We've found her sleepwalking twice in the last week. The first time I'd woken to find her standing at the bottom of our bed, staring at me. I'd let out a shriek before realising she wasn't actually awake. Last night Paul said he'd discovered her in the kitchen again, her hands pressed up against the back door, staring out silently into the darkness through the glass. He told me he'd taken the key out of the lock, hanging it up on a hook on the wall out of her reach. I'd asked her about it at breakfast but she'd said she didn't remember. She's got her first session with the counsellor today and I hope it helps resolve whatever is bothering her more successfully than either Paul or I have managed to. She hadn't mentioned it when I'd dropped her off at school. I don't think she'd realised I'd got an email to tell me it was happening.

I turn into our road and drive past our house, checking

his car is in the drive before pulling into a space by the kerb; close enough to be able to see the entrance to our driveway. I switch off the engine after winding down the passenger window in an attempt to let in some air but outside is just as hot. I check my watch. Twelve forty-five. I tell myself it's better to know. The constant wondering makes me feel like a hamster running round on a wheel, never getting anywhere. I turn off the radio, not able to bear listening to the presenter's inane chatter on top of the thoughts whirling around inside my head.

At twelve-fifty I watch as Anna walks out of her driveway and steps onto the pavement, hesitating as she looks across at our house. The air around me tightens, the heat wrapping itself around my face so I can't breathe. Something in my chest falls away and I have to hold myself back from getting out of the car. I imagine putting my hands round her throat, her eyes widening, the fine lines at the corners wrinkling into deep creases as I squeeze.

She crosses the road, making no attempt to hurry, and I stare at her so intently that I can't believe she doesn't feel me watching her. She suddenly turns to her right, away from our house, heading down the road to where I can now see Andy's car is parked, gets inside and drives away. I let out my breath that I hadn't realised I'd been holding up until that moment. My stomach feels heavy, filled with an unexpected weight, and I wonder if part of me had been hoping she'd been going to meet Paul. At least then I'd have had an excuse to justify my behaviour.

I fish around in my handbag to find a tissue to clean my sunglasses before I head back to the office. As I look up, I catch a glimpse of a man in jeans and a white T-shirt disappearing into our driveway. I hesitate for a moment, unsure whether to follow him, but tell myself I'm being paranoid. Paul is entitled to some privacy to see his clients. It's me that can't be trusted. As I turn the engine back on and pull away, I try to ignore the voice that tells me I can't remember the last time Paul had a client visit him at home, he always goes to them. It's not until I'm sitting back at my desk, Alice listing off the things I'm supposed to be doing this afternoon, that I realise the man seemed vaguely familiar.

I finish work later than usual; Alice has already left by the time I'm ready to go. I glance through the open door of Caroline's room; she hasn't been in today and I wonder if she's really ill, as she'd claimed when she'd spoken to Alice, or whether she just hadn't wanted to face me. I unlock Dad's office and turn on the light. His bookcase is empty now; everything packed away into boxes that have been put away in the storage cupboard here or taken home, shoved onto the shelves in Paul's office until he gets a chance to put them in the loft. I'm struck by how small it feels, almost as if it expanded to fit his things and his personality, shrinking when it realised he was no longer coming back.

I run my hand over the back of his chair, asking him silently what he thinks I should do. I remember him bringing me here when I was about eight, my feet not touching the floor when he sat me at his desk, giving me some pens and paper to draw with whilst he talked to a client. I always assumed I'd come and work with him, but after Caroline and Rob's hastily arranged wedding, I didn't have any choice but to leave. I only came back because Dad had begged me to. I'd thought I could step in as a saviour, not just for the business, but for him; the man I'd idolised since I was small, the person I'd assumed was invincible. Yet when I'd seen him in that bed, swallowed up by the duvet, an emaciated pile of skin and bones, it had made me realise that the only thing I could do for him was the one thing he was asking for – the one thing I'd failed to save him from. I lock his door as I leave, putting the key back in Alice's drawer. Another thing I'm going to have to discuss with Caroline. There's no point in keeping it empty forever.

I pick up my handbag off the floor in my office, putting my finger on the new pane of glass – the glazier has polished it so well that it almost looks as if it isn't there at all; I could actually be standing on the pavement with the people walking past on their way home. They don't even glance in my direction, the window an invisible barrier, unable to see what is right in front of them. I text Paul as I leave.

Need to go and see Mum quickly on way home. Girls OK?

My mobile buzzes almost immediately.

All fine.

I pause by my car, leaning against it and then flinching away as the heat from the metal scorches my skin.

Good day?

I'm inside, seat-belt fastened before he replies.

Yup. Nothing exciting to report.

I turn on the engine, holding my breath whilst the first blast of hot air passes, waiting for the air-conditioning to kick in, weighing up how to ask my next question.

Any new clients?

I push my mobile into the holder on the dashboard whilst I wait for his answer and pull out of the small car park, driving towards Dad's house, or Mum's house as it is now, my brain having to correct the thought that rises up unconsciously. The route is so familiar I wonder if I could do it with my eyes shut. I glance at my phone periodically throughout the short journey but there's no reply until I pull up in the driveway.

No. Quiet day.

I don't reply as I get out of the car, switching my phone off as I leave it on the seat, my vision blurring as I blink back tears. I put the keys Dad gave me in my pocket, lifting the heavy brass handle and knocking sharply on the wood instead. I can hear my mother's footsteps as she comes towards the door, the click of her shoes across the floorboards. She's one of the only people I know who wears heels in the house when she's alone, refusing to succumb to a pair of slippers or bare feet. 'It's the start of a slippery slope, Joanna.' Words she repeats so often that if I cut myself open, I think I would find them engraved beneath my skin.

She opens the door with the chain on, one of the only visible signs that things have changed in the house since Dad died.

'Joanna.'

'Mum.' For a moment I wonder if she's going to leave me on the step, but then she opens the door and moves so that I can come inside.

'I wasn't expecting you.'

'I know. I won't stay long. I just needed to talk to you after – after the other day.'

She ushers me into the kitchen and I sit down at the table.

'Can I get you anything to drink? Cup of tea? Glass of wine?'

I watch her carefully as she speaks, wondering if she's spoken to Caroline yet, whether my sister has told her what she's told me.

I shake my head. 'I'm fine, honestly.'

She shrugs, as if my refusal is in some way a personal snub, and stands awkwardly, picking up a cloth to wipe the already-clean counter, needing something to occupy her hands.

'Why do you want me to sell the business, Mum?'

She hesitates, pausing the cloth on the upwards arc of one of its circles before turning to me. 'Because I think it's the best thing to do for all of us.'

'Do you need the money?' I ask. Her body stiffens, as if my words physically pass through her like an electric shock. 'If you're struggling, then I'll sell it.' She continues to wipe the counter as if she hasn't even heard what I've said. 'Mum?'

'You always were so close,' she says. 'You and your father. You used to follow him around when he came home from work when you were little. Do you remember?' I shake my head. 'Literally kept a couple of steps behind him as he walked around the kitchen. Insisted on always sitting next to him when we ate dinner. It was almost as if Caroline and I didn't exist.'

I look at her but she keeps her eyes on the counter, avoiding my gaze. I've never understood how we could have lived together in the same house, experienced the same events and yet seen them completely differently. Almost as if we'd never been looking at the same things at all.

'It wasn't like that,' I say.

She turns towards me and I watch as her eyes well up, her face changing into someone I barely recognise. She suddenly looks old, her lip trembling almost imperceptibly as I realise she's fighting back tears. I stiffen, a physical reaction to her unfamiliar display of emotion, and wonder if I've made a mistake coming here.

'I'll organise to get some valuations done,' I offer. 'I know Dad wouldn't have wanted to sell the business but he wouldn't have wanted you to sell the house.'

'Your father was a complicated person, Joanna. He wasn't the idol you set him up to be.' I shift uncomfortably in my chair, trying to ignore the memories of doing the same thing at this table whilst I avoided eating whatever meal she'd put in front of me.

'It felt like he was the only one who cared about me.' My voice is shaky.

'Not enough to stop him having an affair.' I look at her and something crumples inside me as I see she's telling the truth. 'I'm only saying this now because I want you to know he wasn't perfect. None of us are. You think you owe him something, but you don't. He should never have asked you to do what you did. It wasn't your responsibility. But he knew how much he meant to you and he exploited that. He asked me when he realised the cancer was terminal and I refused. So, he stopped asking me and begged you to come back to help him with the business instead. But I always knew that was just an excuse. He wanted you to be here because he knew you wouldn't say no to him like I did. For such a strong man, he was a coward at the end.'

My whole body feels numb. 'That's not true.'

'I wouldn't say it if it wasn't.'

'I want to sell the business because every time I think about it it reminds me of him, and of what I've done. Surely you can understand that?' Her voice trembles. 'We both know how it feels to think that you've taken someone else's life. It changes you in a way that no one else will ever understand. I only did what he asked because I didn't want you to have to come back the next day and do it all over again. I wanted to protect you from the horror of that, at least.'

I can see she's telling the truth; her words an acknowledgement of the maternal instinct that she'd never let burn brightly but had let smoulder, impossible to extinguish completely. I suddenly have a vague memory of when she used to read me a story at night; the time when I had her all to myself, transfixed by her story as I snuggled up to her, breathing in the smell of her perfume, watching the way her chest rose and fell as she spoke the words out loud. I'd forgotten we'd ever been that close.

'Why didn't you tell me?' I ask.

'I didn't want you to feel like a failure,' she says quietly. 'I know how close you and your dad were, and I wanted you to believe you'd given him what he wanted.'

'Does Caroline know?' I ask.

She shakes her head. 'You and your sister are very different people, but we both care about you. We used to spend hours with you, trying to get you to eat something. Caroline could have been out with her friends but she chose to stay here, with you. She used to sit next to you whilst you watched TV, trying to get you to eat three pieces of popcorn. Do you remember that?'

The image of a velour mustard-yellow sofa springs into my head. I remember feeling uncomfortable, constantly needing to shift position, stuffing cushions underneath my bottom to stop my bones digging into my skin.

I bite my lip, not allowing myself to reply.

She shakes her head. 'You seem to hate me and I'm just trying to do my best. Don't hate your sister too, you need each other.'

'I don't hate her.'

My mother stares at me for a moment, not speaking, before turning round, picking up the cloth to wash it out in the sink.

'You moved away just before Adam was born,' she says accusingly. 'Caroline thought you'd come back, but you never did. You barely even visited us.'

I shut my eyes, blocking out a memory that I refuse to think about at the moment. She's emotionally blackmailing me, twisting the past into unfamiliar shapes that don't fit in the way I remember. I don't like thinking about when I was ill. All those days in bed and on the sofa merge together into one blur interspersed by flashes of cutlery and tiny pieces of cut-up pieces of cheddar and my mouth full of stomach acid, the desire to feel empty superseding all others, even the urge to breathe.

'Me moving away didn't have anything to do with Caroline.'

'Rubbish. You never liked Rob but you never made an effort to get to know him properly.'

I want to ask her how she can be so naive. She doesn't know him at all. Rob is dangerous when he doesn't get what he wants, I know that from experience.

WEDNESDAY

Caroline

Rob's desperation for me to go round to Jo's again sits between us like an unwanted birthday present. He keeps trying to unwrap it and I want to put it away in a cupboard, desperate to forget about it. As her sister, he thinks I have the perfect excuse to be there if anyone happens to see me. He says it'll kill two birds with one stone; I can find out where she has put the boxes and also retrieve the recording device he'd had to leave behind when he'd left in a rush.

He doesn't know that I've already tried again to find them, looking for them when I visited on Sunday. I hadn't spotted them then, so I'm not sure another visit will help. The more he'd talked about it, the more I'd realised what he'd actually been asking, the meaning of his words seeping in slowly through the pores of my skin, and I'd felt something slide in my stomach. I'd thought of Adam and repeated the distance of seven thousand, seven hundred and ninety miles to myself in my head, grateful for every single last one of them. I know what Rob's capable of if I refuse, but his one piece of leverage is too far away for him to get to easily, and certainly not by the end of the day, which at the moment is as far ahead as I can focus.

I could tell him my sister has lied about being pregnant, that if he uses the information judiciously it'll get him what he wants. But I'm not going to, not yet. Our interests may be aligned, but the eventual outcome might not be what he thinks it will be. His eagerness for Jo to sell the business has become an obsession, but then everything is with him. I was once. In a way I still am, but over the years his desire for me has twisted into something so much darker.

When he'd suggested picking me up at lunchtime to go round there again, I'd changed the subject and he'd walked out of the room. I'd heard the car revving as he drove off to work, leaving me alone in the kitchen. He knows the waiting is almost worse than the inevitable confrontation as my imagination is capable of conjuring up scenarios that wouldn't even occur to him. I look out of the window at our empty driveway; the sky a brilliant blue colour; an abnormally blank canvas. It's been the same for days now, no sign of the clouds that skid across it like plumes of smoke, almost as if it's waiting for someone to decide what to paint, the future uncertain. I wrap my arms around myself, rubbing the goosebumps that have risen on my skin. Usually, I unfurl as it gets warmer, like a new leaf, knowing I'll get to spend more time in my greenhouse, but at the moment I shiver at the thought of what is to come.

I shut my eyes and imagine the temperature in Bali. It's probably around eighty degrees at the moment; I'd researched it before Adam left. I'm hoping he will send me something soon – I'm not sure how much longer I can wait. I'd been the patient one when Rob and I had first met; he'd been the one who had wanted us to move in together immediately, the one who had declared he couldn't live without me. Now it's me who wants time to go faster. I open the drawer under the kitchen counter and take out the neat stack of tea towels, sorting them into piles of different colours to distract me from going upstairs and looking at what I've hidden under the mattress. He could come back at any moment. Sometimes he does, just to check on me, leaving the car on the road so I don't see it, the first sign of his presence being the sound of his keys in the front door. I stay in the kitchen, imagining myself in Adam's old room instead, sitting on the bed with the duvet thrown back, my hand pressed against the sheet, reassuring what's underneath that I'm still here. That I haven't forgotten.

His car pulls into the drive later than usual after I get home from work. I edge over to the window to look out. He hasn't got anything in either hand as he opens the door and steps out, and I let out the breath I'm holding, but a small voice in my head tells me that sometimes it's better to know what's coming. I glance over the kitchen surfaces as his key turns in the lock, checking everything has been tidied away, that his cup of tea in his blue mug is waiting on the counter, struggling to contain my sense of rising panic as he walks into the room.

'Good day?' I ask. If I pretend everything is normal, sometimes I can persuade myself it is.

He doesn't answer. I walk over to the fridge and open it, staring at what's in front of me, trying to decide what to make for dinner. He comes to stand next to me and pushes it shut, the noise of the seal sounding louder than it should in the silence.

'I don't think you really want anything, do you?' he asks.

206

I know it's not a question and don't reply. He'd cleared out the entire fridge and cupboards after Adam left, leaving me without any food for two days and had refused to let me leave the house. I'd been so hungry I'd picked the leaves off the sweet violet plant in the sitting room and eaten them, chewing each one for as long as I could, hoping the nutty flavour would ease the cramps in my stomach.

'Did your father say anything to you, you know, towards the end?' he asks. I glance at him as I make myself a coffee, not adding my usual spoonful of sugar to the hot liquid as he doesn't like me having any.

'What do you mean?'

'I just wondered if he'd explained why he decided to leave Jo the business.' He narrows his eyes as he looks at me, trying to work out if I'm hiding something. I focus on the brown granules dissolving as I stir them.

'I'm not sure he really knew I was even there.' He continues to stare at me, unsure if I'm telling the truth. I focus on the image of a man with an oxygen mask over his face, not allowing any other thoughts to creep into my head.

'Those boxes,' he says, and my heart sinks. 'I think something of mine might be in them.' He's still watching me. A cold feeling spreads across my chest, like a shadow passing across the sun.

'What?' I ask.

'I gave your father some of the plans of the site to look over a few months ago and he never returned them.' We both know he's lying.

'Jo would have found them when she cleared out Dad's office,' I say.

'She wouldn't have realised what they were. I checked the boxes she put into storage when I came into the office to take you out to lunch – they're not in there, so she must have taken them home. That's why I need you to find out where she's put them.' He smiles at me, as if he's given me something valuable by sharing this secret and I'm supposed to respond with gratitude.

'Why don't I just ask her?' I say, watching his reaction.

He hesitates. 'I don't want her to know she's got them. If she sees the price those houses will be worth after the site's developed, she's never going to sell. She won't want you investing in something that benefits me in any way. You know your sister and I have never exactly seen eye to eye.'

'Jo can't tell me what to do with my share of the company.'

'Are you saying you won't go?' he asks. He stands behind me, sliding his hands inside my T-shirt and across the front of my bra, a gesture that once used to end up with us both upstairs, but that was so long ago my body can't remember. It recoils, an automatic gesture I have no control over and I don't look up, concentrating on trying not to move as he holds onto me more tightly. 'Even if I ask nicely?' he says, burying his head in what's left of my hair. I wonder if I should bother getting some milk, or whether crossing the kitchen at this moment is too risky, like walking across a frozen lake, waiting for the ice to crack.

'I'd rather not,' I say.

He takes his hands away, scraping my skin, stung by my rejection. As I turn around, I see he's gripping the edge of the counter so hard his knuckles have turned white.

'Have it your own way,' he says and walks out of the room,

leaving his cup on the counter and the scent of coffee bitter in my nostrils.

I wake up when it's still dark, confused at what has disturbed me, but am instantly alert as soon as I realise Rob's not in bed beside to me. There's a noise I don't recognise. A high-pitched whistling. It's coming from over by my chest of drawers. I turn my head. No, I'm mistaken. It's under the bed. I reach out my hand to switch on my lamp but there's a sudden shrill burst next to my ear and I freeze, unsure what to do. I keep very still and am conscious of a faint rustling that seems to be coming from in front of me, like a multitude of tiny whispering voices, and then something touches the back of my hand. A feather-light tap, but enough to make me flinch. I reach for the switch on my lamp at the same time as something crawls across my head and drops down onto my shoulder, sending an involuntary shudder down my back.

I press the switch and light floods the room but it takes a few seconds for my eyes to adjust and take in the full horror in front of me. Without my contact lenses in, everything is slightly out of focus, but I can see my white duvet cover is moving – a swarming brown sea of insects. I throw it back and hurl myself off the bed and across the room, away from their chirping noises, feeling them twitch as I crush them beneath my feet. I run my hands over my hair and pyjamas, shaking every limb to dislodge any creatures that are still hanging on. I can still feel them even when they aren't there. My body continues to jerk despite my instructions, an automatic response that I have no control over.

Crickets. He knows they're the one thing I have a phobia

about ever since one had got stuck in my hair when I was little. I pull on the handle of the bedroom door in desperation but he's shoved something under it on the other side so I can't get out. I try shouting his name, but my voice comes out in a whisper. There's no answer. The crickets hop around over the carpet and on the chair, fuzzy blurs of movement, and even though I push myself into the corner of the room next to the door, making myself as small as possible, I can't avoid them.

I swallow huge gulps of air, gasping for breath, and try lifting one foot up at a time to KEEP THEM AWAY FROM ME. The words fill every inch of space in my head but come out of my mouth as a small squeak, barely audible above their chirruping noises. I'm too terrified to open my lips more than a few millimetres in case one of them tries to hop inside, its thin feelers twitching as it crawls down my throat. I run my fingers over my face, scratching my eyelids and cheeks with my nails, needing to be absolutely certain I haven't got any still attached to me.

Their chirping merges together into one high-pitched song and I put my hands over my ears to block it out. Blood pounds to a crescendo in my head and I watch as the floor below me turns from cream to grey, coming closer and closer towards my face, rising up off the floor to meet me. Now I can only hear a faint high-pitched humming, and I wonder whether the crickets have gone, or whether I have; the sensation of the carpet under my cheek oddly familiar as I slip quietly into oblivion and everything turns black.

We looked at photos this afternoon, you and I. It was as if our encounter at the weekend had never happened. I tried to keep my distance from you whilst you took them, but I could feel your breath on the back of my neck as you leaned over behind me to check the shot. Not photos that you'd put in a family album. Not like the pictures of people that I've seen on your phone with their heads back, laughing. Someone blowing out candles on a birthday cake in the dark, the flames lighting up their disembodied face, small legs pedalling bicycles, someone lying on the grass with her eyes shut, her hair fanning out like a wave. Not like the ones on my phone either. I don't take any of people. Not anymore. Mine are of trees. Taken at the bottom of the trunk looking up at the branches above. Thick canopies of green through which I glimpse fragments of a cerulean blue sky. A view into infinity and nature's attempt to reach it. The shots today were practical. Black and white images of open laptops, pencils arranged artistically in a pot, someone's hands looking like they're pointing at something when they're not. That's the problem with photographs. They only capture one moment in time. An infinitesimally tiny fraction of a second when people are usually pretending to be something they're not. Smiling for the camera, not smiling because they want to. And then we look back and remember a reality that never existed in the first place. A futile attempt to capture perfection. I used to think you were perfect and it's only now I can see I couldn't have been more wrong.

THURSDAY

Jo

I glance at the clock on the kitchen wall and shout to the girls to come downstairs as we're late for school. If we don't leave soon, we'll get caught in traffic and then it'll take me forever to get to the office after I've dropped them off. Grace appears at the top of the stairs, holding onto the bannister, bumping down one step at time, dragging out the process as long as possible.

'Shoes on. Now, please. Where's your sister?' I hear the toilet flush and Livvi skips out, catching up with Grace on the way down. I walk into the kitchen whilst they finish getting ready, reaching for my handbag that's lying on the kitchen counter.

'Did you hear Grace last night?' Paul asks, deliberately keeping his voice low so the girls can't hear.

'No?' I look at him as he says the words, the one subject that we appear, for the moment, to be united upon.

'I found her standing by the back door again.' I frown. 'It's fine,' he continues, 'she can't reach the key now I've put it up on the hook. She was staring out across the lawn, same as last time. She scared the living daylights out of me when she came into the kitchen. We need to get a stairgate. I'm worried she's going to hurt herself wandering around in the middle of the night. Those stairs are steep.'

I nod. 'I don't want to make a big thing about it, though. It might make her feel worse than she already does. Now she's seeing the counsellor I'm hoping she might stop doing it.'

He raises his eyebrows, leaving me feeling I'm being naive to place my faith in someone we've never even met. Grace won't tell me anything about her counsellor other than that she's a woman, and she's younger than me. I don't even know her name – I think she'd been worried I'd look her up online and try to contact her.

Paul tips what's left of his tea into the sink and walks into the hall where he plants a kiss on top of Livvi's head. She giggles and squirms away from him.

'All ready, girls?' He turns back towards me. 'You're OK to pick them up from school tonight? You don't need to bother with any dinner for me.'

'Why?' I ask. 'What are you doing?'

'I told you. I've got a meeting with a client that's probably going to run late.'

I search through my scrambled thoughts but don't remember him mentioning it. It feels as if he's barely been at home long enough for us to have a conversation, going back out to his office to work after we've eaten and not returning until after I've gone to bed, climbing in silently beside me as I pretend to be asleep, unsure if I want to hear the answers to the questions I know I should ask.

I swallow my disappointment as he opens the front door,

not wanting the girls to see us argue, part of me relieved that I'm not going to have to spend another evening avoiding certain topics of conversation about scans and dates. 'I mean, what are you doing now?' I say.

'Putting the bins out.' I'd forgotten they were collected today.

'I can keep something in the oven for you, if you want?' I say.

He shakes his head. 'Don't worry about it. I'll probably need to work when I get back.' He walks out, his face redder than usual and I wonder how much time he's been spending in the garden rather than his office.

I pick my car keys up off the hall console.

'Are you sure you've got everything?' I look at Grace as I say the words. She's the one who forgot her flute yesterday, which meant we'd had to turn back when we were already halfway to school, a detour that meant I'd ended up being forty minutes late for work. I'd wondered if she'd done it deliberately, trying to extend the minutes she's not at school for as long as she can. She's been reluctant to go in ever since the fight with Maddie. I watch out of the open door as Paul passes us, dragging the bins down to the end of the drive. My husband is slipping away from me and I'm not sure how to stop him. Grace shrugs, pulling her rucksack onto her shoulder. 'Well, can you double check before we leave, please?' I ask.

She looks inside her bag before I usher her outside, expecting to see Paul walking back in, but he's at the bottom of the drive, leaning against one of the bins, chatting to Anna. He's laughing at whatever she's saying and it grates against my skin, like someone rubbing me with sandpaper. I don't notice Grace is watching him until Livvi pulls on my top.

'Can I go and say hello to Jess?'

I shake my head. 'Go and get in the car, I'm just going to have a word with Dad.' I hand the keys to Grace who visibly relaxes once she realises she's not going to have to risk seeing Maddie whilst Livvi stomps off in a huff.

Anna looks up to see me approaching, the sound of the gravel crunching beneath my feet. She smiles briefly, but I strain to hear what she's saying as she lowers her voice and by the time I reach them, they both stop talking.

'Hi, Jo,' Anna says, her greeting an attempt to cover the silence. 'I was just saying to Paul he's so lucky to work at home when it's like this. Never known it so hot for so long.' I nod, noticing she's done her hair and put on her make-up before tackling the school run.

'Can you remember to feed Buddy before you start work?' I ask Paul.

He glances at Anna. 'Sure. I'd better get back to it.'

'See you later,' Anna says as he heads back into the house and I wonder if that's just a turn of phrase or whether she means it literally.

'I've been meaning to come and speak to you,' I say. 'Please don't tell Maddie I've spoken to you, but I heard the girls got into a bit of trouble last Friday at school.'

Anna frowns. 'I don't know what Grace has told you, but –'

I interrupt her before she can finish. 'Grace hasn't told me anything. The school nurse explained what happened when I was called in to collect her.' Anna looks back across the road to where I can see Maddie and Jess getting into their car. 'Has Maddie said anything to you that I should know about? The girls used to get on so well, I can't believe they've fallen out. Or that it turned physical.'

Anna looks down at the gravel, avoiding my gaze. 'Grace just fell over.'

I hesitate, weighing up in my head whether I'm angry with her over what Maddie has done or whether this has nothing to do with my daughter and everything to do with Paul. Ever since Dad's death, I can't seem to get a proper grip on things that used to feel as solid as concrete. My husband, my daughter, my friendships; they all seem to be sliding away from beneath my fingers.

'It's really affected Grace. She doesn't want to go to school anymore,' I tell her.

'And you think that's all Maddie's fault?' Anna straightens herself up, as if she's preparing herself to go into battle.

'I don't know. You tell me.'

Anna stares at me and I can tell she's debating whether to say something. 'Perhaps you need to look a bit closer to home, Jo. Grace hasn't been happy for a while and that has nothing to do with Maddie.' She turns around and walks across the road before I have a chance to ask her anything else. I have a horrible feeling that she's right and Grace hasn't told me something I should really know about.

Alice knocks on my door just before lunchtime to ask me if I know where Caroline is. I hadn't even realised she wasn't here; I've been avoiding her this week, deliberately shutting myself away in my office. I know she's going to want to know if I've made a decision about what to do with the business and I don't want to give her the opportunity to ask the question. At the moment I'm tempted to give her what she wants. To sell up, take the money and move away from here, back to Bristol where Grace wasn't sleepwalking and I didn't wonder what Paul was hiding from me. The only thing stopping me is the reluctance to give up something I've put so many hours into to make a success, the feeling that if I give it up, the move to come back here that I pushed for will have been a complete waste of time. I used to think I owed it to Dad, but the conversation with my mother a couple of days ago has tainted those memories too, like someone scribbling over a picture I'd spent ages drawing, ruining it forever.

I tell Alice that I don't know where Caroline is, that she's probably out on a viewing, but she tells me there's nothing in her diary. I try calling her, but her mobile goes straight to voicemail and there's no answer on her home phone so I send her a text, asking her to message me to let me know where she is. She's probably off sick again. She's been off a lot recently; I think it's an excuse for her not to have to spend time with me. But she usually calls Alice to let her know she's not going to be in and I feel a flicker of concern, despite myself.

She knows she's supposed to put all viewings in the diary; it's basic safety procedure. The thought briefly crosses my mind whether to call Rob to check she's all right before I dismiss it. I try to think about Rob as little as possible. He might be my sister's husband but I can't forget what he did. Sometimes I manage to dull down its intensity so it's like a song playing at low volume in the background, but it never fades away completely. I can always hear it. He pretends it never happened; although sometimes I catch him looking at me and I know he knows it did. His hand sliding under the blanket on the sofa where I was lying that afternoon. The sharp smell of the cut-up apple lying on the plate on the table in front of me, three quarters of it still uneaten, the edges turning a soft brown colour. I'd pushed him away, too scared even to ask what he thought he was doing, the words I wanted to say expanding in my mouth, stopping me speaking. I'd scrabbled off the sofa and onto the floor with the small amount of energy I still had left, knocking over the glass of milk that my mother refilled at every opportunity, the white liquid spilling over the coffee table and dripping over the sides onto the carpet.

She'd come in at that point, alerted by the noise of breaking glass, helping me back onto the sofa, my body too weak to resist her efforts as she'd tucked the blanket back around my legs whilst Rob had sat on the other side of me, smiling at her, offering to get a cloth to clear up the mess.

Caroline hadn't believed me when I'd told her later. She'd said I must have been mistaken, that I'd misinterpreted what he'd done, that he'd just been trying to comfort me, that I was saying it to get attention. I always wondered whether things would have been different if my eating disorder hadn't swallowed up so much of the spotlight that should have belonged to her. He'd been the reason I'd moved away; not trusting anyone else with my shameful secret and over the years the memory had blurred, the feeling of his hand on my thigh, sliding it upwards until his fingers reached my knickers, pulling the elastic to get at what was underneath becoming less distinct until sometimes when I wake up in the night, my duvet twisted around me, I wonder whether it had ever been there at all.

The girls jostle to find a spot in the shade by the front door once we get home from school whilst I try to get my key into the lock, bracing myself for Buddy to run out. I hadn't shut him in the utility room before we left and Paul had said he wouldn't have time to walk him today, so I thought he'd be going crazy. They kick off their school shoes, leaving their rucksacks and cardigans in a pile on the mat before bundling out of the back door. Livvi had managed to emotionally blackmail me into having Jess back to play; standing in the playground hand in hand with her when I'd arrived. I'd proffered a few feeble excuses, my embarrassment growing at a rate equivalent to Anna's, who was attempting to say something similar to Jess. Finally, I'd given in, not wanting to make a scene in front of the other parents, telling Anna I'd drop Jess back before tea, watching Maddie pretend to be engrossed in conversation with Katie whilst Grace stared silently at the asphalt.

I hear Livvi and Jess squeal as they climb onto the trampoline, but Grace comes back into the hall, frowning.

'Where's Buddy?' she asks.

'I don't know, sweetheart. Probably in his bed?'

She shakes her head. 'He's not, I've looked.'

'Well, go and have a hunt around for him.'

She disappears and I can hear her calling his name as I pick up their bags off the floor, waiting for him to scamper out, but there's silence as I walk into the kitchen and Grace stares at me, her eyes wide.

'He's not here, Mum.'

'Go and have a look upstairs.'

She walks off, and I go to get a glass of water but don't want to run the tap whilst I'm trying to listen to Grace. I can hear her footsteps as she comes back downstairs again, appearing from behind the door with a furry bundle in her arms.

'He was asleep on my rug.' She smiles. 'I must have left my bedroom door open.' I take a deep breath as I fill the kettle. I don't know what she'd do without him at the moment.

Livvi looks so devastated when I tell her Jess has to go home that I almost relent, giving them the extra half an hour they're pleading for, but then I catch a glimpse of Anna's house out of the window and change my mind, walking Jess back over the road and standing at the bottom of her drive by the gate as Anna opens the door to let her in. She waves at me and I lift my hand in response against the velvety blue sky, still cloudless, an uneasy truce.

I walk back into our house, past the dark red peonies that appear almost black in this light, their floral scent overpowering, my stomach growling in protest, mistaking the smell for food. There are toys strewn all over the floor of the snug and I shout to Livvi who has disappeared up to her room to come back downstairs and help tidy up. There's no answer so I call out again, my irritation rising.

'If you want to have your friends over, then you're responsible for clearing up the mess afterwards,' I say, my head beginning to throb. 'Grace, can you help too, please?'

She swings her feet off the couch, staring reluctantly at the mess in front of her. 'Don't just expect me to do it. I want everything picked up off the floor and put away.' I march into the middle of the room and pick up a teddy, some felt-tip pens and a colouring book off the carpet.

'Who had these out last?' I ask.

'I was doing colouring,' Livvi says. I hand her the book and pens and wave the teddy at Grace.

'This must be yours, then?' It doesn't look familiar, but the girls have so many soft toys stuffed into boxes in there that I can't remember every single one.

She shakes her head.

'No? So, neither of you are claiming it? I'm pretty sure it's not mine.' I can't hide the sarcasm in my voice as I start to lose my temper, and I can see the girls staring at me hesitantly, aware this is a situation where, if they say or do the wrong thing, I'm likely to explode. The pain that has been sitting in my head, waiting patiently, reaches its fingers around my brain and begins to squeeze, and I screw up my eyes in agony.

Both girls remain silent. 'It really doesn't have an owner?' I shout. 'Well, it can go to the charity shop, then.' The small black eyes in the teddy bear's face stare back at me, a tartan ribbon tied neatly in a bow round its neck. It's heavier than I expect. I look at it more closely, running my fingers across its nose, feeling the shape of the plastic. Is it plastic? I tap it. It's not plastic. It's glass. And under my fingertip it feels smooth, a perfect hemisphere. I squint at it. Although I thought it was black, it's not completely opaque; I can see a miniature version of my face reflected in it.

I turn it over in my hands, looking at a small gap in the

seam of its fur, and put my finger into the space. There's a familiar ripping sound as the Velcro pulls apart. I expect to see stuffing underneath, but instead I'm looking at a grey metal solid panel. My headache is now so bad that I have to sit down on the sofa as a series of flashing black-and-white dots appear on the outer edges of my vision. I try to take a couple of deep breaths. I think I'm getting a migraine. It's the first time I've had one for years.

'Livvi, can you get me a glass of water, please? And Grace, can you bring me that packet of ibuprofen that's in the kitchen drawer?' They slink off, relieved they can no longer hear the anger in my voice. I look at the teddy. There's a small slit in the middle of the metal panel in its back. I stare at it, a realisation of what I'm holding in my hands slowly dawning.

I stand up, my legs wobbly, ignoring Grace as she holds out a blister pack of tablets, and walk through our utility room to the back door, holding the bear by one ear. I don't bother to stop and put my shoes on as I take it outside, feeling the heat of the paving stones under my bare feet, dumping the lump of metal and fur in the black dustbin.

I run back inside and lock the door behind me, jamming the bolt across the top of the frame. I call Paul, but his phone goes to voicemail so I leave a message telling him he needs to come home immediately. Someone has been in our house. Watching us.

FRIDAY

Caroline

I wake up in bed with a jolt, frantically searching the duvet cover for anything moving in front of me, my breathing only slowing once I've convinced myself I can't see anything on the white cotton. I glance at my alarm clock. He must have already left for work and not woken me. Or maybe he's downstairs, waiting to see what I'll do when I get up. He's watched every move I've made these past few days, but hasn't asked me to go around to their house again. The anticipation is like stretching an elastic band – I know it will only extend so far before it snaps. He won't even let me go to work; taking my car keys, mobile and the home phone with him when he leaves in the morning, saying he'll call the office to let Alice know I won't be in. The bruise across my cheekbone from where I fell is fading, but it's still livid enough to suggest our perfect lives aren't as perfect as they seem.

He'd assumed what he'd done would break me. It almost had. I flinch whenever anything touches my skin and I think I must have damaged the nerve under one of my eyes when my face hit the carpet as it hasn't stopped flickering. I feel it constantly, like the flutter of an insect's wings, but when I stand in front of a mirror it's barely noticeable. He smiles when he sees it, and I feel betrayed by own body, my distress revealing itself without permission.

I think of Adam lying on a beach, the sand shifting beneath him to fit the outline of his body, and I remember what's under his mattress. These two things have got me through the past week. Rob must have picked up all the crickets whilst I'd been passed out on the floor. When I'd woken up, he hadn't mentioned it, like so many other incidents that happen in our house and are then never spoken about again, the horror sinking into the floors and walls, contaminating them. I'd wondered whether I'd imagined the whole thing, unable to stop myself flinching each time I thought I'd heard something rustle. It had only been when I'd gone to bed last night and had moved my alarm clock to find an insect lying underneath it that I'd been certain it had really happened. I hadn't been able to see it was dead without my contact lenses in, and had held my breath, swallowing a scream, narrowing my eyes until they could focus enough to see the tiny desiccated body, one of its wings detached. I'd lowered my clock back down on top of it and had pushed it very slowly over to the other side of my bedside table. Rob had been lying with his back to me, oblivious to the shudder that ran involuntarily across my skin.

I get up, squinting as I go into the bathroom to put my contact lenses in before pulling on the same pair of shorts and T-shirt I'd left on the end of the bed last night. I hesitate at the top of the stairs, listening intently, but can't hear him. I come down slowly, one step at a time, but when I reach the bottom there's only a heavy silence. His study door is open; the room is empty and he's not in the kitchen. His car isn't in the drive. He's gone.

After so many hours of having him near me, my body refuses to relax. I take deep breaths and lower my shoulders as I make myself a cup of tea, staring out of the window into the early sunshine where the trees at one side of our garden cast dark shadows across the lawn. Holding my cup in one hand I open the back door, breathing in the fresh air. I can feel the heat already; it remains in the earth overnight, warming it like a blanket. He'd run the mower over the grass yesterday evening, and I can smell the leafy green scent that's a chemical reaction released by the grass as a result of being in distress. I walk down to my greenhouse, stopping on the path to bend down and touch the lawn, the short blades tougher under my fingers than I'd expected. People underestimate grass. It's one of the most resilient plants in the garden and one of the most unappreciated. Continuously chopped down it always regenerates, surviving even in the harshest conditions.

I slide open the door of my greenhouse, the aluminium frame squeaking in protest. The air in here is even warmer and I inhale the distinctive scent of tomato plants and compost. I've stacked up the few canes that aren't being utilised in a growbag in one corner, leaning them against one of the panes of glass, and I watch now as a small spider climbs across its web from one stick to another, the strands heavy with moisture. I run my hand across the wooden counter, brushing dust and pieces of dry earth onto the ground between the slats, realising for the first time in days that my eye is no longer twitching. I only keep essential items in here, so if he looks inside, he won't see I've made any kind of an effort. There's a rusty trowel next to a black plastic tray in which I've planted radish seeds and a few flowerpots, the various sizes all stacked inside one another like Russian dolls. In the top one are the white labels that I write on in pencil each year to remind me what I've planted when the pot resembles nothing but a pile of earth. I pull one out. I can still see the faded grey letters. Pak Choi. Something I'd tried to grow for the first time last year, but probably won't again; it has a tendency to bolt. It's another reason he lets me come down here – I tell him I'm saving money by growing our own vegetables. I get a tissue out of my pocket and lick it – wiping it on the narrow stick to remove any trace of the letters until it's a blank surface again; the potential to be anything, and a flicker of excitement runs through me.

I bend down under the counter to look at the one small patch of bare soil on the ground beneath. It's only shallow – not deep enough to cultivate carrots or tomatoes. I'd attempted to grow them the first year we moved in, when I knew nothing about gardening. I couldn't understand why they didn't thrive until Dad told me their roots needed more space. I dig down a few inches. The soil is loose and dry as it hasn't had anything in it for months and is easy to move with my hands. I stop when my fingertips touch plastic and pull out a small box, wiping my hands on my shorts until the only bit of blackness that remains is a narrow line underneath my nails.

I open the lid and carefully take out a tiny pair of pink bootees. It's the only thing of hers I still have, the only thing I'd had a chance to buy. I'd lost her at six weeks, just after I'd told him I was pregnant. He hadn't been pleased, like he had when I'd told him about Adam. That first time he'd thought having a baby at twenty would tie me closer to him, make it harder for me to leave. It had in many ways, but having a son had changed our relationship in a way he hadn't expected. I had developed a bond with my baby that was stronger than the one I had with my husband, and Rob knew it. Just as he knew another child would be an additional drain on his finances and something that would take my already divided attention even further away from him.

I'll never know if he caused it or whether it would have happened anyway. He'd muttered that it must have been something I'd eaten when he'd found me on the bathroom floor that morning, but we'd both had the same meal the night before. I'd asked him to call a doctor but he'd ignored me, lifting me back into bed, tucking the duvet in tightly around me, holding me in place. He'd stroked my damp hair and told me I mustn't worry, that he'd look after me. That perhaps it was a virus I'd caught off Adam. I'd seen him frown as I'd moaned in pain, grabbing his hand. He'd stared into my eyes, searching for something, handing me tissues each time I'd been violently sick. Looking back, I'm still convinced his concern had been genuine. I'm just not sure it was for me.

I touch the woollen bootees with my fingertips. I don't know if she actually had been a girl, but that's how I'd imagined her on the day I'd found out. I'd always wanted a little girl. A baby sister for Adam. Someone whose hair I could tie up in those pretty clips I'd seen Jo use on Livvi a couple of years ago. Seeing how Rob is with her opens up a series of what ifs, like looking at a mirror in a mirror, infinite possibilities. Perhaps he would have been different if I hadn't lost her. Perhaps we could have been a normal family. I can torture myself with the lives I never had. As I put the tiny shoes back into their box, I tell myself it had been better this way. It had taken all my energy to save Adam. I only need to look at what's under the mattress in the spare room to know I wouldn't have been able to save her too.

He'd told me we could try again but I'd come home from dropping Adam at school a few months later to find a letter from the local surgery tucked into the back pocket of his jeans confirming the tests following his vasectomy showed he was sterile. I'd waited for him to tell me but had realised after a while he never would. He'd stopped looking me in the eyes, had spent more and more time in the office, and had begun a competition with his own son for my affection, one that he'd lost before he'd even started.

I lower the box back into the small hole in the soil and cover it up with parched earth. I'm not sure if I'll be coming in here to dig it up again. As soon as I've heard from Adam once more, I can do what needs to be done.

I've realised appearances are so deceptive. I used to want to be one of those people who seem as if they're having the best time, the ones who post the most photos on Facebook with their friends, so many different friends, always laughing. The ones I used to see on the train. They used to make me feel inadequate, as if I had something missing. Not an arm or a leg but something they were born with that I could never have; an innate sense of how to be. The ones who have the largest number of contacts on their phone. The ones who are always the centre of attention at a party, the ones who drink the most and shine the brightest. The ones everyone else thinks they want to be. And I could have been one of them. You would have been my pass in. But now I don't want to be them at all. I just want you to leave me alone but I think it's too late. You're not going to stop. And I can't make you. I've tried telling you I don't want a lift anymore but you still insist on picking me up. Pulling up beside me in the car and waiting for me to get in. And now I understand that those people I used to envy are actually the ones we should watch the most. They have the furthest to fall and the ground is always so much harder when they do.

SATURDAY

Jo

'I'm taking the girls out to the supermarket,' Paul says. I'm sitting eating breakfast on the patio and he puts a cup of coffee down on a mat on the small wicker table next to my seat. 'Give you a bit of time to yourself.'

I nod briefly but keep my eyes on my laptop, ignoring him. His gesture is designed to placate me but I can't hide the fact that I'm still furious.

He hovers, waiting for me to respond, but I say nothing, not wanting to start a conversation in case it ends up in an argument, my guilt and fear metamorphosing into insults that will leave me feeling worse than I did before. The girls flit in and out of the kitchen and I don't want them as witnesses while we shout at each other, feeling obliged to pick a side.

'Fine. See you later.' He leans down to kiss me but I turn my head away before he can reach my cheek, leaving the feel of his dry lips on the side of my forehead. He hesitates briefly, almost long enough for my outer layer of anger to thaw, struck by a sudden fear over what is happening to us, before he walks away and the moment vanishes. Livvi runs over to me and throws her arms round my neck to say goodbye, telling me she'll make sure she puts some dark chocolate digestives in the trolley as she knows they're my favourite. I'm relieved I've got my sunglasses on so she can't see my eyes well up.

I hear the door shut and the noise of the car reversing over the gravel before I get up and walk into the kitchen, looking out of the window to check they've gone. Anna's car is still in her drive; I can't see any signs of movement as I stare at her house across the road. Buddy whines, annoyed that he's been left here, but I need to do this first so he'll have to wait for me to walk him.

Paul had come home on Thursday night to find me awake in bed with the girls asleep beside me. He'd said his meeting with a new client had ended up with him going on for a few drinks and he hadn't checked his phone to see my frantic messages until he was on his way back. The relief as I'd heard his key in the door had quickly been replaced by a fury that had filled my insides and whose embers were still burning two days later. I'd told him to sleep downstairs in the snug; the scent of stale beer and perspiration mixed with something I couldn't quite put my finger on emanating from his skin.

I'd showed him the teddy the next morning whilst the girls were cleaning their teeth before we left for school. We'd stood outside the back door as he'd turned it over in his hands, ignoring the rancid smell on its fur from being in the dustbin overnight. He'd insisted he recognised it, that Livvi had bought it from the local charity shop a few months ago, something she'd paid for with her pocket money. He hadn't realised it was a camera. If that's even what it was. I'd told him Livvi had denied it was hers and he'd laughed, telling me she had so many soft toys in the snug he wasn't surprised she couldn't remember all of them. He'd said I was overreacting; that even if it had ever been a recording device, it probably didn't work and there was no SD card in it now, so it clearly wasn't being used.

I'd almost believed him, but something in his eyes as he'd dumped it back into the dustbin had made me feel as if I had been looking at a reflection of myself, the mirror image of someone trying desperately to hide something. A pair of icy hands had wrapped themselves round my heart. I hadn't been overreacting. Livvi hadn't recognised it and she always remembers everything she's bought in that shop. So many toys that have seen better days with bits hanging off them that she's had to soak in Milton overnight before being allowed to play with them. This one had looked brand new before I'd thrown it away.

I walk outside, over the patio across the grass to his office; unlocking the door with the spare key. The bottom sticks as I pull it open, the wood has warped in the heat. It's quiet once I get inside, the faint hum of the traffic from the road and the birds are silenced when I push the door shut behind me. I can see our house from the small window above his desk. I hope he'll be out shopping long enough for me to do what I need to. I walk past the shelves that he's screwed to the wall; Dad's boxes sitting amongst his files. I need to sort them out but I can't face doing it at the moment. I open Paul's laptop, the screensaver springing into life; a photo of us all in a restaurant in France a couple of years ago, experiencing a stab of anguish. It had been the last holiday when we'd been blissfully unaware of the seriousness of Dad's cancer.

The box asking for a password flashes, and I have no idea what it is. I try our birthdays, Paul's favourite football club and our wedding anniversary but the box remains red, refusing to let me in. I don't know how many times it will allow me to guess, but it's pointless to continue trying. I have no idea what it could be. I flick through the various papers lying on his desk and pinned to his noticeboard. Invoices to clients, various half-finished draft proposals, hand-drawn flowcharts full of computer-related jargon that are all meaningless to me.

I'm about to give up when I open the A4 pad that he's been leaning on. There's nothing written on the first couple of sheets but as I lift it up, a folded piece of plain paper falls out of the back. Three words have been written on it in red felt-tip pen in large capital letters: *YOU OWE ME*. I drop it on the floor in shock before fumbling to stuff it back into the pad and rearrange the desk so it looks as if I've never been here. Did he write it? Or did someone send this to him? He must know why the same words were written on the side of my car.

I've only been back in the house for five minutes, contemplating whether there is anything else I can search through whilst he's not here, when the doorbell goes. I open it to find Anna standing outside.

'I wondered if you had a minute.' She fiddles with her bracelet. 'I saw Paul take the girls out earlier and I thought it would be an ideal opportunity for us to talk.'

'I'm actually right in the middle of something at the moment,' I say.

'Please?' She stares at me, ignoring my feeble excuse. 'It won't take long.'

I let her inside reluctantly, shutting the door behind her. Buddy looks up briefly as she walks into the kitchen and then lies back down in his basket, his hopes of a walk extinguished.

'Cup of tea?' I ask, hoping she'll refuse.

'No thanks. I can't stay. I just wanted to talk to you about Grace.'

My body stiffens as I refill Buddy's water bowl that he seems to have finished for the second time today already.

'Maddie told me why they've been arguing.'

I pull out a chair, indicating that she should sit down, not wanting to admit that my daughter has refused to confide in me about it.

'Why?' I ask.

'Grace thinks she's seen a ghost,' she says.

'*What?*' My reply comes out louder than I expected. Livvi's comment about Grace seeing a man on her chair a couple of weeks ago echoes in my head. Anna looks at me, her cheeks flushed.

'I don't know how else to put it. She told Maddie and asked her to keep it a secret, but Maddie told Katie. Grace got upset as Katie was laughing about it and they ended up pushing each other and Grace fell over.' I stare at her. 'And yes, before you ask, I've had a chat with Maddie about the need for trust between friends and keeping things confidential. She's going to apologise, but swears that Grace falling over was an accident.'

'A ghost?' I say the word again in the hope it will make more sense the second time. Anna nods. 'Grace would have told me.'

The flush on Anna's cheeks deepens. 'She thinks your dad

is visiting her, Jo. That's why she hasn't said anything. She doesn't want to upset you.'

The memory of Grace's face as Caroline and I shouted at each other across Dad's bed flashes into my head. I know how upset she'd been to see us fighting. But that had been between Caroline and I; nothing to do with Dad. And she'd seemed fine with Caroline when she'd come over the other day.

A shiver runs down my back. What if Grace had seen what I'd tried to do to Dad? I've refused to let myself think about it, locking it away in a box in my head that I've told myself I will never open. My mother's confession hasn't helped to ease my guilt – she only finished what I'd started. I repeat a mantra to myself on a daily basis that it was what he'd wanted. What he'd begged me to do until I'd finally relented, knowing he'd have done the same for me. And most of the time it helps. I no longer see the image of his face as I'd lowered the pillow every night before I go to sleep, his eyes black, sunk so far into his wrinkled skin they had almost disappeared.

Anna puts her hand on top of mine and I jump. I hadn't realised my breathing had speeded up and I can see her looking at me, concerned.

'I just thought you should know, Jo.'

The memories of that day are blurry, my brain keeping them behind a filter as if it knows I won't be able to deal with the sharpened version, but Grace wasn't there, I repeat to myself. She'd gone home with Paul earlier in the day. There is no way she could have seen what happened.

'Grace is seeing the school counsellor,' I blurt out, needing

235

to change the subject, to shut the box and nail the lid on so tightly it never comes off.

Anna nods, her hand still on top of mine. 'That's good. I hope it'll help. Sometimes it's easier to talk to someone who isn't so close to the issue, you know, to give a bit of perspective.'

'Don't say anything about it to Maddie, please,' I add. 'I'm not sure if Grace has told her.'

'Course not.' Anna moves her hand away and stands up. 'I'd better get back.' She leans forward to give me a hug, something that would have come naturally only a few weeks ago but now feels slightly awkward, both our bodies more tense than usual, unable to relax into the gesture.

'Thanks for telling me,' I say.

'I wasn't going to say anything. But then I thought, if it was Maddie, I'd want to know. It's better to get these things out in the open.' She looks at me, hesitating, and I wonder if she's still talking about the girls.

'You do know Paul asked me to bring the girls home from school a couple of weeks ago, don't you?'

I nod, crossing my arms as protection against what she's about to tell me.

'I don't mind doing it at all,' she continues, 'but when I dropped them off, he asked me not to say anything to you. Said he was supposed to collect them and that you'd be annoyed. I agreed, but I don't feel very comfortable about it. I'm not sure what's going on between you two, but I'd rather not get stuck in the middle of it.'

I step forward and hug her back, embarrassed at my earlier suspicions. 'I'm sorry he asked,' I reply. 'I'll talk to him.'

★

Paul gets back with the girls just before lunchtime and I unpack the multiple bags that he lifts onto the counter in silence. He's bought so many things that I haven't put on the list, clearly acquiescing to the girls' requests, wanting an easy life. I watch him as he opens the fridge to put away the yoghurts, acknowledging I don't know this man as well as I thought I did, even after twelve years together.

We empty the last bag, the girls' squeals of laughter from outside emphasising our muteness. Paul's mobile bleeps in his pocket and he glances at it.

'I need to go out for a bit,' he says as he puts it back in his shorts.

'Why?' I ask.

'One of my clients has got an issue with his router.'

I stare at him. 'It's a Saturday. And I didn't think you did routine support at the weekend.'

'I don't normally, but I get a lot of work off them and they're desperate. I need to keep them happy as I can't afford to lose them too. They're not far away. I'll only be half an hour. An hour at the most.'

I contemplate saying something now; asking why he's got a piece of paper in his office with the same words that were written on the side of my car, but Livvi appears in the doorway, dripping, asking for a towel. Paul picks up his car keys and has disappeared by the time I get back.

I retrieve my phone from the table outside and open up the FindMyFriends app, clicking on Paul's name, and watch as the small circle containing his face moves slowly down our road. It stops before it gets to the main junction, but I know the app isn't totally accurate; sometimes it takes a few seconds to catch up. I wait, looking at the screen as I listen to Grace shouting at Livvi to stop spraying her on the trampoline. The circle hasn't moved. It should turn left or right at the junction to the main road but it's stationary. I refresh the app but the circle appears on the screen in the same place, no more than a couple of hundred metres away.

I walk over to the patio door where I can see the girls' figures bouncing inside the trampoline net.

'Grace? Livvi?' I shout. 'I'm just nipping out. Dad's forgotten something. I'll be ten minutes. Don't answer the door and be careful on that thing. OK?'

'Yes,' they reply in chorus, not paying any attention. I walk out of the house and along the pavement, not able to stop myself peering into Anna's driveway on the other side of the road. Her car is still parked where it was this morning.

I look at the app I have open on my phone. His car still hasn't moved. Our road is relatively straight once I'm past our next-door neighbour's house, and I squint into the distance to where it joins the main road. I can see Paul's car just before the junction. He's stopped beside the kerb. I stand by the hedge, feeling like an idiot, tempted to just call him to ask him what he's doing. Perhaps he's broken down. Or run out of petrol. I clasp at straws and watch as another car pulls up behind him and a man steps out, walking round to the passenger side of Paul's car where he opens the door before getting inside. He looks like the same man who walked into our house the other day; the same man who had stood next to Livvi and talked to her about the china figurines when we visited Parkstone Losey House.

I'm about to walk over to confront him when Grace runs out of our driveway, shouting for me. She's crying and I can't understand what she's saying as she pulls me back towards the house. I run into the kitchen to find Livvi squatting on the floor in front of Buddy's basket, her hand on his fur.

'There's something wrong with him, Mummy.' I kneel down beside her as Grace backs herself up against the door frame, wrapping her arms around herself. I put my hand on Buddy's head but he doesn't move. I try picking him up but he's floppy in my arms and won't open his eyes. Grace has crouched down on the floor, pulling herself into a ball. Livvi stares at me. There's a trail of vomit that leads from the side of Buddy's basket across the tiles. I stand there, helpless, holding him against my chest.

'You've got to do something, Mummy,' Livvi whispers, lifting up her hand to stroke his paw. 'Has he got the bug Daddy's got? He said he had a headache when we were at the shops.' I can't speak, the lump in my throat too big to swallow, an emptiness in my stomach that I haven't felt since Dad's funeral. I tell the girls to grab a blanket out of the snug and stick something on over their swimming costumes as I pick up my keys and we get into the car, lifting Buddy onto the back seat.

As I pull out of the drive, I'm vaguely aware of Grace saying something over and over to herself, but I can't hear her properly and Livvi is silent, one hand holding Grace's, the other on Buddy, tears running down her face. The vet's surgery is a couple of miles away and I wish Paul was here, despite everything, as I don't know how to cope with this on my own.

I drive into the car park and stop, ignoring the designated spaces, tucking the blanket around Buddy as I lift him off the seat, the girls running ahead of me to open the door. Livvi gabbles to the receptionist as the vet comes out of his treatment room and they both try to take Buddy off me, telling me I have to let go of him, but I don't want to as I know that when I do, they'll tell me what I can't bear to hear. A lady sitting in reception stares at me sympathetically but I just want to keep holding him and I know my tears are making his fur wet but I can't stop crying and Grace is pulling at his blanket telling me I need to let go.

I try to tell the vet he was fine this morning and ask if I could have done something if I'd noticed earlier and he shakes his head, but there's no reassurance in his gesture and I know he's only doing it so he can separate us. My arms are so empty and light without him and I can't breathe as Grace reaches for my hand and the receptionist puts her arm round Livvi as she takes her behind the reception desk.

I can see the vet as he hasn't pushed his treatment-room door shut properly and Buddy isn't moving. I want to ask them to cover him up with his blanket as he might get cold and the vet must be able to read my thoughts as he does, and my heart leaps, until I see him let his stethoscope drop and he rubs his forehead. He catches my eye, his hopelessness evident even through the narrow gap.

SUNDAY
Caroline

Ever since we visited my mother a couple of weeks ago, Rob has been dropping suggestions as to what Jo may have done with my dad's belongings; where she might have taken the boxes. He mutters about me going back to visit Jo's house when they're out, telling me he'll sit outside in the car in case they came back. I feel as if I'm teetering on the edge of a precipice every time he speaks, bracing myself for the inevitable fall that could come at any moment. I can't avoid him forever. The tension has escalated into a humming noise in my head, shrieking like a metal detector whenever he comes near.

Yesterday evening, he'd come through the front door with a Chinese from the small takeaway in the village, whistling, a noise he's been making ever since he locked me in our bedroom. I'd divided up the portions from the plastic tubs between us, watching him swallow a forkful of lemon chicken before I'd dared to take a mouthful, keeping the conversation firmly on how the building work was going at the site to distract him from any thoughts of Jo or boxes.

The same meal used to be a regular Friday-night treat when

I'd been growing up. I'd been so excited to hear my dad's key in the door before he'd appeared in our kitchen, handing me a paper bag of prawn crackers and I'd stuck my hand inside, licking the grease and spiky crumbs off my fingers. Mum had opened up the plastic boxes to dish up the food onto the plates we'd put in the oven half an hour earlier to warm up, pouring something orange and gelatinous out of a small polystyrene tub over the pieces of chicken. Jo's portion had decreased in size as her weight had plummeted, until eventually Dad had stopped bringing home a takeaway at all.

When Rob had come into my father's estate agency about a vacant property for sale, I'd felt he was the first person to notice me in as long as I could remember. The weather had been hot then, too, I remember we'd propped the door open with a fire extinguisher in the hope of getting a breeze, but the air hadn't moved, thick with expectation. Dad had sat me behind a desk at reception. My exam results had been a disappointment my mother had assured me we were putting behind us, but the reality had hit me every day I walked into the office – somewhere I'd never wanted to end up but the only place that would take me.

For as long as I could remember, everything had been about Jo – whether she was eating, how much she was eating; star charts Blu-tacked on the wall to record the times she gained a pound, the squares printed on the pieces of paper horribly blank; a testimony that reflected all our failures.

Rob had stared at me, filling the emptiness I'd felt inside in a way no one had done before. He'd smiled when he'd seen me blush, my father oblivious to our silent dialogue. I'd hovered by the office door as he'd walked back to his car, his keys jangling, his phone number scribbled on a piece of paper in my pocket.

He'd begged me to move in with him when I'd found out I was pregnant eighteen months later and I'd jumped at the chance, flattered by the intensity of his passion, desperate to be in the limelight for once. I'd ignored what Jo had told me, refusing to believe her accusations, persuading myself I'd glimpsed a vulnerability that Rob had hidden behind his designer suit and his new car, something he'd chosen to reveal to me and me alone, despite the ten-year age gap. I thought I loved him enough to make it work.

It had only taken until a few months after Adam was born before I first began to understand it was impossible to live up to Rob's expectations. He'd elevated me onto a pedestal in the centre of his world and I'd teetered, then fallen, becoming a source of constant disappointment, my hopes and desires detracting from his idea of perfection. I used to think that if I tried hard enough, I could mould myself into what he wanted, but that person has always been a figment of his imagination. He's never actually seen me at all. I no longer exist except as a mirror, reflecting as best I can what he wants to see, portraying emotions that I haven't felt for so long that I've forgotten what they feel like. I have no idea who I actually am underneath this façade at all.

I'd dreamt about Adam last night, running about at the edge of the waves on the beach. He'd been about five, his feet leaving tiny imprints in the sand that had been swallowed up as soon as the water had washed over them. He'd put his hand in mine and told me it would be all right and I'd shut my eyes and believed him, the sun so bright it had burned white flashes on the inside of my eyelids that I could still see when I'd woken up.

His postcard had arrived yesterday after Rob had left to visit the site. A photo of a set of dark wooden outdoor furniture on a patio overlooking a lawn with a small swimming pool, surrounded by Nipa Palm trees. I'd turned it over in my hands.

Dear Mum & Dad,
Had a very exciting afternoon fishing (lol!) at the famous Otan river. Unhooked several catches and still have water all inside trainers. It's not great as they're probably (obviously!) spoiled. Took outstanding freediving film in caves. Epic!
Love, Adam

My gorgeous boy. When I'd tried to imagine him jumping into a river it was difficult to hold him in my head all at once. I'd seen him as a little boy, white skinny arms and legs with armbands, but at the same time, he was nineteen, with a tanned physique, a leather bracelet round his wrist that he took off whenever Rob was around. Years that had stretched on for so long I'd thought they were never going to end had merged together in a fraction of a second that flashed by in an instant, a bittersweet blur. I'd gripped his card between my fingers, staring for several minutes at what he'd written before I'd taken it upstairs and put it under the spare-room mattress.

I haven't heard from Jo since I confronted her last Sunday. Seven days should have given her enough time to put things in motion. I'm not sure if she's going to. Maybe she's already told Paul she made a mistake, or that she lied, and if she has, my one piece of leverage has gone, I won't be able to stop Rob doing whatever he's contemplating.

The shrill of the home phone interrupts my thoughts. I walk upstairs to where Rob has left it on top of a small melamine tray on his bedside table, along with his empty coffee cup. I glance at the screen. It's my mother. One of Rob's approved callers.

'Caroline?' Her voice is frailer than I expect.

'Hi, Mum.'

'I'm looking for a present for Livvi's birthday. Have you any idea what she might like? I can't get hold of Jo to ask her.'

'I'm not sure. We got her a Sylvanian family set.' I catch a glimpse of myself in my full-length mirror as I'm speaking, the bruise under my eye now a murky yellow colour, faded enough to hopefully disguise with foundation. I don't tell her I haven't spoken to Jo all week.

'I might pop into town on Wednesday for something. I could come and see you both in the office. Check if there's anything in particular Livvi wants. Are you and Rob going to go over to Jo's on Friday? Give her your presents? You know Livvi would love to see you both. She idolises your husband.'

I mumble something non-committal.

'And it'll give me a chance to talk to Jo about the business,' my mother adds. 'I think she's coming around to the idea of selling it. Rob will be relieved, won't he?' I trace my fingers along the edge of my cheekbone where a sprinkling of tiny red bloodspots have blossomed under my skin. If I didn't know better, they could almost be mistaken for freckles.

'He will. We can talk about it when I see you, then,' I say, wanting to end the conversation, realising I don't have an excuse to put off what I need to do any longer. I hesitate after she hangs up, not sure whether I'm ready.

I pick up the tray and walk into Adam's old room, the carpet thick beneath my feet. It absorbs the sound so it feels as if I'm walking silently, my presence invisible. I don't belong in this house; it's his territory. I've tried to do what I promised I would. I've kept my son safe. I repeat the words over and over as I go into his room. I'm conscious I've failed him, and others, in so many ways, and the guilt sits heavy in my stomach. At least I know he's happy now, somewhere on the other side of the world, and the relief is so intense that I lose my concentration and stumble over the leg of the bed, letting go of the tray that falls onto the duvet, catching hold of the edge of the mattress to break my fall.

As I pull myself up, I hear footsteps on the stairs and freeze at the thought of what Rob will do if he finds me in here. I can't believe I didn't hear his car on the drive, or the door opening. Perhaps he came in round the back. His footsteps reach the landing. I hold my breath, looking around the room, desperate to find a reason to be in here. I pray he'll go into our bedroom but I hear him start to walk in the opposite direction; straight towards me. My fingers tingle with adrenaline, readying myself for the confrontation.

'Caroline?' he says, his body blocking the light as he stands in the doorway. 'What are you doing in here?' I pull shut the window that I'd opened a couple of seconds earlier, my hand shaking as I grip the handle for support.

'Letting out a wasp,' I say as I turn towards him. 'I could hear it buzzing from the hallway. They're so aggressive at this time of year.' His eyes flicker over the duvet cover, trying to find a reason to doubt me. 'You're home early?' I say, picking up the tray and upended mug to keep my hands occupied. 'I thought you said you were meeting Simon to run over expenditure on the site?'

He walks towards me, hesitating as he reaches the bed and I force myself to keep my eyes on his face as he sits down, the duvet that gathers around him revealing the sheet underneath. My breath catches in my throat as he adjusts his weight, exposing a narrow gap at the edge of the mattress. Acid rises up my throat from my stomach and I swallow, praying I've pushed everything in far enough underneath so as not to be visible. He leans back, picking a couple of pieces of fluff off the duvet cover.

'I thought you'd want to know I've been round to Jo's house and done what was needed,' he says, pausing briefly to let his words sink in as I look at him, not wanting to believe what I think he's done. 'One of us had to.' The tray suddenly feels so much heavier in my hands, as if the weight of a small animal has been placed on it and handed to me to carry.

Smell is the most evocative of senses. I learned that in A-level biology. Just one sniff and millions of olfactory neurons that sit in an area the size of a postage stamp tell your brain which one out of a trillion different fragrances you are breathing in, transporting you to places that you visited years before. I read that male lunar moths can track females from five miles away just by their scent and I wonder if the same thing is possible with humans, whether you can follow me from place to place, recognising my presence from the molecules I leave behind, invisible to everyone else. I know whether you are in a room before I look up to see if you are there. And it's not because of the particular deodorant you wear. I can feel you watching me. I wonder if you can smell the acrid bitterness that lingers on my clothes after you've been near me; I think it attracts you more than my conversation ever did. The odour of fear. I wash it off each night but it comes back the next day, more pungent than ever.

MONDAY

Jo

I tiptoe downstairs, unable to sleep, leaving the girls curled up in my bed where they've ended up for the past two nights, needing them to hold the reality of death at a distance. I try to avoid looking at the empty hook on the wall in the hallway where Buddy's lead used to hang as I walk into the kitchen.

The house echoes with an unfamiliar silence; the only discernible noise the quiet humming of the dishwasher finishing a cycle. It seems to have been more reliable since the plumber came out to fix it, although I'm not sure what he actually did for a hundred and fifty pounds. I know Buddy's gone, but as I make myself a cup of tea, I imagine I can hear his paws scrabbling on the travertine tiles and whip around, a bubble of expectation in my chest which bursts when I see there is nothing there.

The vet had told us afterwards he was sure antifreeze had been responsible. Lethal to dogs, even in very small quantities, and Buddy was the second labradoodle this year he'd seen poisoned by it. He'd said the first dog had got hold of a bottle that had been left in a cupboard by his owners and had chewed through the plastic cap. He'd sowed the seeds of implication gently, seeing how distressed the girls were, and I think he'd been trying to absolve my guilt. I'd told him it was impossible for Buddy to have done that. We didn't have any antifreeze. The vet had nodded sympathetically, hearing the defiance in my voice, and had suggested perhaps he had come into contact with it on one of our walks. Or on our driveway. The poison must have been in his system for a while and would explain why he'd been so thirsty before he collapsed; his kidneys had already been starting to fail.

I'd stared at Paul who'd met us at the surgery, the question of whether something could have been slowly leaking from our car since the garage had returned it hung in the air between us, unspoken. Neither of us had voiced what we'd both been thinking as he'd lifted Livvi up into his arms, muffling her sobs. Grace had refused to leave, staring at the door of the room where we'd left Buddy which the vet had finally closed. I'd sat with her until the receptionist had come over and whispered that she needed to lock up for the night, promising we could come and collect his body the next day so we could bury him. Grace had finally let me put my arm around her and I ushered her out to the car, her limbs unnaturally stiff as we'd walked across the asphalt.

'We need to talk.' I'd mouthed the words silently at Paul as soon as we'd got home and he'd frowned, a look of confusion on his face as he'd opened his mouth to say something. 'Not now,' I'd added quietly. The repercussions of his deception from a few hours earlier had continued to smoulder, flames lighting other flames, consuming me, my body a burnt-out shell walking around the kitchen on autopilot.

We hadn't had a chance to speak before he'd finally gone to sleep downstairs on the sofa in the snug, unable to fit into our bed when the girls had crawled in beside me, refusing to leave my side. I'd been relieved, whispering the lie that I hadn't wanted to wake them up when they'd finally fallen asleep. I'd wondered if this was how it would be going forward – me with them in one place and him somewhere else. Physical walls between us rather than just the ones we'd created in our heads. I'd barely slept, pulling back the curtains to look outside when I'd heard him go downstairs and open the front door, watching as he'd got on his hands and knees on the driveway with a torch, searching under my car for any signs of a leak. He'd glanced up and had shaken his head when he'd seen me, but I'd let the curtain drop, ignoring him.

Grace hadn't left my side for the whole of the next day; reaching for my hand when I'd tried to slide quietly out of bed in the morning, getting up and following me if I left the room. She'd insisted on coming with me to the vets to pick up Buddy's body, bringing it back with us to bury in the garden. Paul had dug the hole, an excuse to pretend he wasn't avoiding me, both of us unwilling to step onto that first rung of the conversation that would lead us somewhere from which there was no way back, our relationship too fragile to survive the fall.

The kitchen door creaks as Grace walks in, her hair matted on one side where she's been lying on it. She looks so tired that for a moment I wonder if I should keep her off school but I hope the normality of routine might help to keep her mind off what has happened. She sits down beside me and I look at where she's bitten the skin around her cuticles, tiny scabs marking the edges of her nails.

'Are you OK?'

She shrugs and I recognise her need not to speak for fear of crying.

'I'm worried about you, sweetheart. And not just because of what's happened with Buddy. Ever since Grandpa died, you've been . . .' I notice a tear run down her cheek. 'It's OK to miss him, you know. I miss him too.' She shakes her head, wiping her face on her hand. 'What is it, then?' I ask. 'Why have you and Maddie not been getting on? I can't help unless you talk to me.'

She stares at me, her eyes wide. 'Have you ever done something you wish you hadn't, Mum?'

I frown. The image of a pillow floats into my head and I push it away. 'Like what?'

'Like something you didn't realise you weren't supposed to do, but you got into trouble for?' She fiddles with the tablecloth, picking at the edge so the threads come loose.

I hesitate. 'Everyone makes mistakes, Grace. That's just life. You just have to apologise and try and move on.'

'But what if you can't?' she asks.

'What if you can't what?'

'Apologise.' She lowers her voice to a whisper, not looking at me.

I swallow. 'What d'you mean?'

'I did something bad and I think Grandpa is still angry with me.'

I stare at her, understanding her words as they settle in my head but finding they make no sense. 'What did you do?'

She doesn't answer and I wonder if I've asked the question too quickly, an accusation that has backed her into a corner. I force myself to wait for her to speak but she stays silent, pulling at the tiny pieces of cotton. 'Is this what you and Maddie have been fighting about?' I ask, finally.

She hesitates, then nods. 'I told her about it and then she told Katie. She promised me she wouldn't say anything to anyone.'

'What did you tell her about?'

'That sometimes I feel like Grandpa is here . . . in my room. He moves things. I put them down and when I come back, they aren't where I've left them. I wake up in the night and – and it feels like he's there, sitting on my chair, watching me.' She stutters as she struggles to get the words out and I can see how much she's suffering but a small part of me is relieved. She hadn't seen me with him at the end. Or what I'd tried to do. At least I'm spared that.

'Sweetheart, Grandpa isn't here. And you don't have to tell me what you did if you don't want to, but I know whatever it was, Grandpa wouldn't be angry with you.' I reach across for her hand. 'He loved you very much, Grace. You know how close you were. Do you think he'd want you to feel scared like this? Of him?'

She shakes her head. 'You don't understand. You think I'm imagining things. Just like Maddie and my counsellor.'

I try not to think of Dad when I last saw him, focusing instead on memories of him with Grace and how he used to smile when she walked into the room. 'Grandpa wouldn't hold a grudge. He wasn't that kind of a person,' I say.

'I can prove it,' she replies.

I frown. 'How?'

'He sent a message to me on Dad's phone. When I came downstairs the other night, it flashed up on his mobile just as I walked past. It was lying on the counter and I picked it up and saw it.'

I swallow. 'What did it say?'

She looks at me. 'It said *I'm watching you*. And so I know he is.' Something slips in my chest as there's a loud click from the latch on the kitchen door as Paul walks in. Grace stands up, our conversation over. Livvi appears behind him and starts to make breakfast, none of us commenting on the half-empty packet of dog biscuits beside the cereal boxes in the cupboard.

I hand Grace the car keys and tell both girls to go outside and get into the car, Livvi refusing to leave without Buddy's blanket – rolling it up and squashing it into her school bag. I listen for the bleep to tell me they've unlocked the doors before walking back into the kitchen where Paul is standing by the toaster.

'We need to talk,' I say to him and the tone of my voice makes him look up. 'I wanted to say something before but I thought I should wait until the girls weren't around. I know you didn't go to see a client on Saturday. I saw you parked at the end of the road.'

His face drops and something tears inside me – the last few threads holding us together; my hope that somehow I'd been wrong, that there had been a simple explanation for his behaviour.

'Who was that man who got into your car?'

He doesn't reply, holding out an empty plate in front of him as if he thinks the answer is going to magically appear on top of it.

'Was he here the other day, too?' I can almost see his thoughts as they pass by in front of his eyes, his brain desperately trying to sort them into some kind of order that will explain all of this. There's a sudden tap on the kitchen window and he spins round to see Livvi pointing at me.

'Are you coming, Mummy? We're going to be late.'

I nod. 'I'll drop the girls at school,' I say to him, 'but then I'm coming straight back and you can tell me what the hell is going on.' I walk out, wishing I hadn't seen the look on his face that confirmed his guilt without him needing to open his mouth.

Both girls sit in the back of the car and don't speak a word for the entire journey. I switch on the car radio, but every upbeat note of the pop song grates painfully against the tense atmosphere and I turn it off again. I keep checking on them in the rear-view mirror; Grace motionless, staring out of the side window and I have to swallow hard when I see her reach across and link her hand with Livvi's, their fingers entwined tightly in a small ball.

I walk into the kitchen when I get back and see Buddy's water bowl lying on the floor as I call out Paul's name, but he doesn't answer. I frown as I pick up the metal container, tipping out the last few drops of liquid over the sink before bending down and stuffing it into the cupboard underneath as far as I can reach.

As I stand up, I hear a loud thud.

'Paul?' I shout into the silence, my voice echoing off the kitchen tiles. There's no reply. I press the handle down on the back door but it's locked. I reach up to get the key down off the wall and walk out across the grass to his office, but that door is shut too, the padlock fastened over the bolt, and when I peer through the window, I can see it's empty.

Something slippery slides around at the bottom of my stomach as I come back into the kitchen and hear the noise again. Louder this time. A thump. Like something falling on the floor. I stand quite still, listening closely. I'm sure it came from upstairs. I slip off my shoes and put one foot on the stairs, trying to be as quiet as I can, and climb them slowly, one at a time, holding onto the bannister. The landing looks exactly as I'd expect as I tread softly across it and into Livvi's room. Her bed's unmade and I smooth out her pink duvet over the bed whilst I'm in here, a delaying tactic to avoid going into Grace's room. *He moves things.* Her words hover, unwanted, in my head.

I brace myself, forcing myself to take the few steps needed to get through her doorway. She hasn't bothered to draw her curtains this morning which is unlike her, and the room is full of shadows in the half-light. I pull them open, needing to feel the sunshine. Her chair is pushed neatly under her desk, her dressing gown lying on the bottom of her bed. There's nothing out of place. Maybe the noise came from the loft. One of the many things we've stored up there falling over. I could get Paul to look if I knew where he was. I walk back across the landing into our bedroom. It's empty, and there's nothing on the floor in here or in our en suite when I poke my head round the door.

I sit down on our bed, my legs shaky, and call Paul's number but it goes straight to voicemail. Where is he? I hang up without leaving a message, staring at the duvet cover where a few dog hairs are stuck to the duck-egg-blue throw. My eyes fill unexpectedly with tears and I don't bother to try to stop them as they fall. I want to stay here, to bury myself under the covers and not come out. Memories of Buddy lying on the bed run through my head and I press my face into my pillow as there's a loud crash from the other end of the corridor. I sit up in shock.

Grabbing my phone, I try to ignore the panic that flutters in my chest. 'Paul?' I call out his name again, hoping that he just didn't hear me the first time, but my instinct tells me he's not in the house. Perhaps Grace left her window open and it's slammed shut. *I drew her curtains. I would have noticed.* I stand up, keeping my phone in one hand and walk slowly across the landing until I'm hovering in her doorway.

A quick glance across her carpet tells me nothing has fallen on the floor. Her window is shut but there's a faint smell that wasn't here before. I frown and turn to walk out when I notice something blue sticking out of her wardrobe door. The panic scrambles further up my body, leaving my stomach ice-cold. I don't remember seeing that when I was in here before.

I walk towards her wardrobe. The right-hand door is shut, the sleeve of one of Grace's sweatshirts trapped between it and the frame, dangling at an odd angle, like a broken arm. I pull on the door which swings open and the whole garment slides off its hanger into my arms. I step backwards in shock. A shiver runs down the back of my neck. The rows of

257

wooden hangers which are normally spread out evenly across the hanging rail have been pushed to each end, leaving a large gap in the middle, one that's the perfect size for someone to fit into.

The smell is stronger here. A stale muskiness. Something foreign and out of place in this room. As I peer in more closely, sliding the hangers back into place, I hear the unmistakable sound of the front door slamming. I drop Grace's top on the floor and run across the landing, down the stairs, throwing open the door to stare out over the gravel. The driveway is empty. I'm shaking. I dig my nails into my palm as I lean against the wall, trying to persuade myself I'm imagining things. I can't bring myself to contemplate the alternative. That someone has been in my house, hiding inside my daughter's wardrobe.

TUESDAY
Caroline

My heart had shrunk as I'd absorbed his words as he'd sat on Adam's old bed on Sunday evening, each one slicing off a piece of me until there had been nothing left. I'd known early on in our marriage that he could be cruel, but until that moment, I hadn't thought he was capable of going so far. Perhaps I had always known and hadn't wanted to admit it to myself. The thought that he'd been less than a few inches away from what was under the mattress flashes into my head.

His forehead had shone with a layer of sweat and I'd wondered whether it had been from the heat or his eagerness to impart the information that had seemed to spill out through every pore.

'Did you find what you were looking for?' I'd asked.

'No. I ran out of time. I searched everywhere in the house, so it must be outside in Paul's office. At least now I can get in and out without having to worry about the bloody dog.'

I can't bring myself to meet his eyes this morning, concentrating instead on where his hair is beginning to thin at the front, revealing his skin, as pale as bone. I can't see any resemblance to the man I married and wonder how long he's

259

been like this. Whether the line he's stepped over has made me see how far he's prepared to go, or whether he's been like this for years, and I've chosen not to notice, focusing instead on keeping Adam safe.

'Has your sister called the solicitor?' he asks.

'What d'you mean?'

'You said she'd changed her mind.'

'I don't –' I start to say.

He takes a couple of strides towards me across the kitchen. 'She's your bloody sister. You work with her. You must have some idea what she's doing about it. Hasn't she said anything?' I glance at the pot of kitchen utensils on the granite counter; the handle of the scissors within reaching distance. He follows my gaze and smiles. 'I don't think we want to go there, do we?' he asks, his face so close to mine I can feel his breath on my skin. My heart beats faster, and I hope the flush of adrenaline isn't obvious on my cheeks. He reaches out and grabs hold of my wrist with one hand, clasping it firmly, wrapping his fingers round my forefinger with the other. I stay very still.

'Just remember, Caroline, that I keep you safe. Don't ever think about doing anything to jeopardise that. And I don't have unlimited patience. If Jo isn't going to change her mind then she might need a bit of gentle persuasion. Agreed?' I nod, the pressure on my finger insistent enough to be uncomfortable. He hesitates, and I can almost feel the idea drop into his head. 'And if I can't find what I'm looking for, then we need to make sure no one else does. I'll sort it this afternoon.' He lets go of my hand and turns to walk out of the kitchen.

'What do you mean?' I ask after him.

He doesn't answer. 'I need to get to work. I've got a meeting with Simon about the site. Don't you need to go as well?'

'I'm going in late. I'm going to do some paperwork here first. Finish writing some details for a property we've got a viewing on later.'

He nods, but I can tell he's already lost interest. I watch him through the window after he shuts the front door. Instead of getting straight into the car, he goes into our garage and reappears a minute later, holding something that looks like a watering can, but without my lenses in, I can't see it properly. He lifts up the lid of the boot, puts it inside, shuts it again and drives off.

I stand by the window for a few minutes, waiting for my heartbeat to slow, checking he doesn't reappear, but the driveway remains empty. He won't want to miss his meeting. I make myself a coffee, the jar of granules one of the few things in the cupboard that I don't have to ask permission to use, running over his last words in my head. They keep floating back to the surface, like empty plastic bottles, rubbish that I can't get rid of. I should get ready for work but I'm in no hurry to see Jo. I'm going to have to get her to call the solicitor. And the more I push the issue, the more she's going to hate me. She won't believe I'm trying to help her. As I finish my coffee the bruise on my face throbs underneath my thick layer of foundation and I realise with a jolt what Rob had been carrying as he walked to the car. I know what he's going to do.

I glance at my list of reminders I've written on the pad I keep on the counter; Rob's company logo imprinted on the top of each page. I don't need to write down the most important thing. I won't forget that one, however hard I try. I was hoping I'd never have to do it. That somehow, I'd be able to leave it undisturbed, or throw it away like I've almost done so many times before, but it's too late to back out now; I'd made a promise.

I open the fridge to get out what I need to prepare dinner for this evening. I could do it when I get home but it's another way to delay going upstairs. He said he wants chicken curry. He calls it curry but, really, it's chicken in a sauce that doesn't really taste of anything. He doesn't like anything too spicy or hot as it gives him heartburn. I chop the onions and blink away tears. I should have put my lenses in before I started. I tip everything into a pan with some olive oil, being careful not to turn the gas up too high, and turn out two chicken breasts from their plastic packaging onto a chopping board, slicing them into pieces, the slimy raw flesh under my fingers making me cringe. I block out any thoughts of animals, leaving everything in the pan to cook for a few minutes before pouring in a jar of the sauce Rob likes. It's a bland beige colour that smells vaguely of something artificially sweet and I have to turn the overhead fan on to get rid of the smell.

I leave it to cook for fifteen minutes whilst checking the weather app on my phone to see what it's like in Bali today. Twenty-six degrees with sunshine all afternoon and a couple of showers this morning. Hotter than it is here today. Adam must be so tanned by now. I turn off the gas and take the lid off the pan, holding my hand over the contents, the heat almost burning my skin. This is what he must feel. If I shut my eyes, I can almost imagine I'm there with him.

I walk upstairs slowly, hearing his voice in my head. I tell him I don't want to do this, that I need to go to work, but he says it's time. No more delays.

I go into his old room and put my hand under the mattress, pulling out his postcards together with the notebook they're resting on. I put the cards to one side and sit down on the bed on the indent Rob left, holding the notebook in my hand. It's brown leather, with 'Ideas and Thoughts' in black writing printed on the front cover, each letter debossed in the material so I can feel the grooves when I run my finger over the words. The leather isn't as smooth now as it was when it arrived, cracks have appeared over the years it's been under the mattress, like wrinkles in aged skin. There's a dark stain on the back where I'd dropped it in the dustbin when I'd first opened it after it had landed on my doormat, retrieving it a few hours later and hiding it away in here.

It seems a lifetime ago. Adam had still been a teenager and I'd refused to do anything that could jeopardise his safety. I hope she understands, wherever she is. I had no choice. And now he's the same age as she was then, and he still seems so young. 'I'm so sorry I couldn't help you,' I whisper as I open the cover to reveal the same words I'd glanced at briefly three years ago, wanting to erase them from my memory the minute I'd read them:

Private Property of Lauren Taylor. Keep your nose OUT.

'I hadn't forgotten. I had to wait for the right time,' I say, propping up the pillows behind me on the bed, settling back on them as I'd used to do when Adam was younger, my arm curled around his shoulders as he'd nestled into me whilst

I'd read him a bedtime story. This time he's not with me and it's her presence I feel instead as I draw my knees up in front of me and open the book. The spine bends and creaks, like someone whose joints are stiff from being stuck in one position for a long time, and I wonder if it's me or her who lets out a sigh as I begin to read.

There are only a finite number of ways to say no. And I've tried every one that I can think of, but you don't seem to understand. Words are not solid enough. I know they mean different things to different people and the tone you say them in matters just as much as the actual things themselves. But I need more options than the English language currently provides me with. Like how in Inuit there are fifty different ways of saying snow. I need something definitive, something more impenetrable than Rapunzel's tower, something that doesn't leave any possibility for maybes to creep in through the gaps, long fingers scraping away the cement between the bricks, reaching inside to touch my skin. I need something that will bite back, something as real as scissors or a knife, something sharp and deadly that wounds you if you don't take any notice, like shards of glass that will slice through one of your arteries, leaving you bleeding out all over the floor.

265

WEDNESDAY

Jo

Where the fuck is he? Photos of him with the girls scroll round on the screensaver on my office computer in front of me; I've given up trying to do any work. I call his mobile again, the three seconds before his voicemail kicks in now so familiar, I can time them more accurately than a stop watch. I haven't heard anything from him since Monday morning. Two whole nights. No phone calls, no texts, no emails. I've never been out of contact with him for this long since we got married. And I've always known where he was. At least, I thought I had.

I can't trace him on my FindMyFriends app as he's stopped sharing his location and I can't tell if he's actually looked at any of the dozens of text messages I've left. Every one shows up on my phone as 'delivered' rather than 'read'. I keep telling myself he could have viewed them on his home screen and never actually opened them, but I know it's just another way of delaying the panic that keeps trying to climb up my body, shaking my brain so my thoughts end up in a tangled mess.

How long do I leave it before I call the police? On Monday

night I vowed I'd call them if I hadn't heard from him in twenty-four hours, telling myself he'd be home before then, that he just needed a night away to sort his head out. But that deadline had come and gone and now over forty-eight hours has passed. They'll ask me why I waited. I'll have to explain how I'd seen some bloke I think I'd met once, briefly, getting into his car. That I'd confronted him about it. And then he'd disappeared. I can imagine what they're going to say. I've run through it all in my head already. Probing questions asking me how well I really knew my husband with a few knowing glances that will destroy an already-fragile marriage.

What have you done, Paul? What's so bad that you've had to take off without talking to me first?

I know he never really wanted to move back here, but I thought he'd accepted it, assumed he'd settled into the new routine we'd established for ourselves. I know he's been quiet for the last couple of months but I never thought he'd do something like this. Perhaps I've been kidding myself; shutting my eyes to the signs that he's never been completely happy. I keep replaying the memory of the way that man had looked at Livvi when we'd seen him at Parkstone Losey House. Like he'd wanted to know all about her. And how keen Paul had been to get us all away from him. Has he left us for him? Wouldn't I have noticed if he felt that way in the twelve years we've been married?

I've told the girls he's gone away camping with some friends from university – a reunion to celebrate a birthday and they've accepted it along with the fact that it's somewhere so remote he doesn't have Wi-Fi or 4G access so can't call them. I've kept his return date vague, but they're going to start asking more questions and I'm at a loss as to what to say. None of his friends have seen him – the non-specific texts I've sent to those who we're still in touch with in Bristol asking if they've heard from him have all proved a waste of time, and he hasn't got that many friends around here to ask.

He's taken his car – I'd checked the garage after I'd assumed it was parked in there on Monday. Finding it gone had made me feel better initially, a confirmation that he'd left of his own free will, but then it had struck me that this meant he couldn't have been the person I'd heard in Grace's bedroom which made me feel worse than I had before.

I've moved both girls into my bedroom with me for now; they think it's a special sleepover treat whilst he's away, the three of us in separate sleeping bags on top of the duvet so we don't wake up if Livvi wriggles too much. That's what I've told them, anyway. They don't know I've kept the zip of mine open so I'm ready to jump out at any moment.

I survived yesterday on caffeine, having spent hours lying awake in the darkness listening to every noise and creak that seemed so much louder than they had done in the day. I'd double-locked all the doors before going to bed, sliding the bolts across to make sure there was no way anyone could get in. I'd made sure the stairgate Paul had bought was shut tightly once we'd all cleaned our teeth, telling Grace it was so she didn't wander down in the middle of the night, but that had just been an excuse. I'd wanted the extra reassurance that I'd hear it opening if anyone came up the stairs.

I glance at my phone, debating whether to call Anna. Paul and Andy aren't exactly best friends but they get on well enough. I dial her number, nothing left to lose.

'Jo?' Her voice is warm, friendly.

'Hi, Anna.' I swallow, not sure I've thought this through properly, wondering if she can hear the beat of hesitation.

'Everything OK?'

'Yes, fine. I just wondered if you or Andy had spoken to Paul today.'

She pauses – or is that my imagination?

'No. Why?'

'I'm just trying to sort out who's picking the girls up from school and can't seem to get hold of him.'

'Oh.' She doesn't seem to think it's odd that I'm asking. Would I be able to tell if she was hiding the fact that she knew he'd left us? 'I'm collecting Maddie and Jess later; I can get the girls as well if you need me to? I mean, if Grace is happy to come back with us.'

I'm grateful she's trying to build bridges, unsure whether Grace would want me to reciprocate.

'Thanks for the offer. Can I let you know?'

'Sure, no problem. Paul's probably just turned his phone off whilst he's working. Andy does that. Says he needs to concentrate. Can't multi-task to save his life.' Is she telling me that she knows his phone is off? I didn't tell her that. Only that I couldn't get hold of him. Perhaps she's just trying to be sympathetic and my lack of sleep is making me paranoid.

'Yes, you're probably right.'

'If I see him, I'll let him know you're looking for him,' she says as she hangs up. I don't tell her that I'm a hundred per cent sure he knows this already.

I have no one left to call. Paul's an only child, his parents had died years ago and they were never close. It had been one of the things that had first attracted us together – both of us had missing pieces; unfinished jigsaws where we needed the other person to fill in the gaps. I set another deadline for tonight in my head; extending my self-imposed cut-off from lunchtime, an attempt to delay the inevitable. I tell myself I'm doing it for the girls, wanting to save them from what I know could lie ahead.

Yesterday, when they'd been getting ready for bed, I'd gone outside into our garden, needing a few minutes outside alone in the dusk, the deep-blue sky tinged with smoky orange towards the horizon. I'd walked past the freshly dug earth in one of our flower beds that now had a large terracotta pot on top of it. Grace had said she wanted to plant an apple tree in the space. She'd thought it would be a good way to remember Buddy as he'd always tried to eat the ones that had fallen onto Dad's grass. Paul hadn't told her what the vet had said. That we needed to put something solid on top of where we buried him to stop the foxes digging up his body. I'd shuddered and had walked back inside, making sure I'd double locked the patio doors, hanging the key back on the wall out of Grace's reach.

I put my phone down on my desk as I hear my mother's voice coming from the direction of Caroline's office. It irritates me that she always goes in there first. She has to walk past mine to get to Caroline's but my sister still seems to possess a greater appeal. The secret we now share, the horror that has been wrapped up in pillow cases and sheets that stops me breathing if I think about it, doesn't seem to have brought us any closer together.

I walk into reception and hover in Caroline's doorway,

watching as my mother bends down to kiss the air either side of my sister's cheeks, not making contact with her skin, afraid to get too close. She sees me and smiles.

'Joanna.' I smile back, neither of us making the effort to cross the small floor area between us, the few carpet tiles an insurmountable obstacle.

'Mum.'

'I just came in to see if Livvi wanted anything specific for her birthday. I did try to call you at the weekend but I couldn't get hold of you.' It's an accusation. My fault if I'm not available whenever she wants something. I take a deep breath. I feel as if I'm meeting a stranger for the first time when I see her; any warmth that we've managed to establish in our last encounter is wiped out and we have to start all over again.

'She mentioned a camera,' I say. 'I think you can get V-Tech ones that are pretty indestructible.' And can you get her dad to come home, I ask silently in my head. Just bring him back and she won't need anything else.

'I'll have a look in John Lewis,' my mother says. 'Adam used to take some brilliant photos, didn't he, Caroline? Has he sent you any recently?'

My sister smiles briefly. 'A few,' she says, glancing at her computer screen before she has to expand any further. Normally the way my mother manages to manipulate the conversation around to Adam whenever Grace or Livvi are mentioned would make me prickle, but today it barely registers. I have more important things to worry about.

'I hope he's making the most of it,' my mother continues. 'I still don't understand why he left when he did. It would have been better for him to have a gap year after university.' It's so unusual to hear her criticise Adam that I glance across at Caroline who stares at her for a couple of seconds before looking at me.

'Is Livvi having a party?' she asks, as if she hasn't heard what Mum said at all.

'No. She wants to go indoor skydiving so we're taking her to a place that does it at the weekend.'

'Isn't that dangerous?' Mum asks.

'We went a few years ago,' Caroline says. 'It was brilliant fun.' A small balloon of joy floats up inside me as I think she's defending me for once. 'It's perfectly safe,' she continues. 'As long as you don't do it if you're pregnant or anything.' She stares at me, and I look back, a flush spreading across my cheeks. She's not going to do this now, surely. I glare at her and shake my head slightly, enough so that it's obvious. She tilts her head slightly to one side and I know what she's asking. Am I going to give her what she wants? Fine, I think. She can have it. I don't care anymore. Sell the business. Take the money. I just want my family back together. I nod tightly and blink to stop my eyes welling up as her mouth turns up at the corners, her smile almost imperceptible if you weren't looking for it.

'Joanna, are you OK?' my mother frowns.

'Not really,' I say, wiping under one eye with my finger. 'Buddy died.'

'Oh, I'm so sorry,' my mother says. For a moment it looks as if she's going to move towards me but then I see her foot stop, mid-step, and she fiddles with the pendant on the end of her necklace with one hand instead.

'The girls are in pieces about it. Livvi doesn't want to let go of his blanket. She packed it in her bag this morning and would have taken it into school with her if I hadn't told her she had to leave it in the car.' I dig my nails into my palm. 'I can't bear to get rid of it.'

'What happened?' my mother asks.

'The vet thinks he was poisoned. Antifreeze.'

'I am sorry.' Caroline is staring at me, her face paler than usual. I can't even tell if she means it.

'I'm going to ask the solicitor to proceed with the sale of the business if that other firm you mentioned are still interested.' I look at my mother, who finally steps towards me, putting her hand on my shoulder.

'It's the right thing, Joanna.'

'Is it?' I don't know anymore, but I'm certain I don't want to stay here any longer. I want to take the girls somewhere where we'll feel safe.

My mother moves her hand away, stung by my comment as Caroline continues to stare at me.

'If it all goes smoothly,' I say, 'it shouldn't take long to sort out.' I smile at them both in the silence that follows. 'Oh, and I hope you're both going to come to Livvi's birthday on Friday. It'll be the last one she has here before we move.'

I call Paul's mobile once more whilst I'm waiting for the girls in the school playground at pick-up, silently making all kinds of promises to a higher power about what I'll do if he answers, but his voicemail kicks in again, and I slide my phone into my pocket as Grace comes out of her classroom.

'Grandma said she might come over to drop your present

off on Friday,' I say to Livvi as she gets into the back of the car, her arms clasped tightly around her schoolbag that she refuses to put on the floor. 'And Auntie Caroline might pop in, too.' I look at Grace in the mirror and notice her sit up a bit straighter.

Livvi leans forward. 'What about Uncle Rob?'

'Possibly, sweetheart. We'll see.'

'He always gets me good presents.' She hesitates. 'Dad will be back, won't he?'

'Course he will,' I say, my voice artificially bright, not allowing the possibility of Paul failing to be home by Friday to seep like water through the cracks in my façade, spilling into the lake that's growing ever deeper in the pit of my stomach.

'Is he coming home tonight?' Grace asks. I hesitate as I feel her eyes on the back of my head, trying to read my thoughts. Don't go there, I think. There are things that you don't want to see.

'Not sure, sweetheart. I think it depends how the camping goes. Have you got much homework tonight?' Her eyes narrow as I glance at her again in the mirror, wondering if she realises how much I hate lying to her.

'I get a birthday wish, don't I?' Livvi asks. 'When I blow out my candles?' I nod. 'Can I ask for Buddy to come back?' she asks.

I swallow. 'We all wish that, darling, but I'm afraid he can't. I'm so sorry.' The lack of sleep I've had for the past couple of nights suddenly hits me and it takes all my willpower not to let my eyes shut for a moment, to drift into the rhythmic hum of the engine, the seat warm against my back. I turn up the air-conditioning to its highest setting, needing the blast of cold air on my face, switching on the radio to keep us all distracted. I turn into our driveway and am praying so hard for his car to be there, that I wonder if I'm imagining it when I see that it is.

'Daddy!' Livvi flings open her door before I've even switched off the engine, running across the gravel still carrying her schoolbag, Grace following closely behind. I lean my head against the steering wheel and squeeze my eyes shut, refusing to let myself cry. Anger rushes in like a tidal wave, obliterating any earlier feelings of worry. My hands tremble as I walk across the driveway. The front door is already open, and I can hear the girls' voices inside.

'Hi, Jo.' He looks at me as I walk into the kitchen and I stare at him, a mixture of relief and hate and anger and exhaustion all churned into one.

'Hi.' I can't bring myself to say anything else as I put my car keys down on the counter, my fingers shaking, and pick up the kettle to fill it under the tap.

'Did you have fun?' Livvi asks him and Paul looks at me, his eyes asking how he should respond. I hesitate, wondering whether to say nothing, to let Livvi realise my excuses to cover his absence have been a lie and leave him to explain why he decided to disappear for three days without bothering to let any of us know where he was.

'She means in the tent. Camping,' I say finally, throwing him a lifeline, not to save him but to protect the girls from having to face anything else at the moment. 'For Ben's birthday.' I can see he's grateful, but if he thinks it opens up the possibility of forgiveness he's mistaken. 'Why don't you take a drink and a biscuit outside, girls? I've got some things I need to talk to Dad about.'

'About my birthday?' Livvi smiles as she takes a couple of chocolate digestives out of the tin.

'I can't possibly tell you that,' I say. She follows me over to the patio doors which I open, taking the key down off the wall. The girls walk out onto the lawn as I watch, not wanting to look at him.

'I'm sorry, Jo,' he says, 'I needed to get away.'

I turn around and walk back towards him, keeping my voice down only because I don't want the girls to hear. 'You've been gone for three days without so much as a text to let me know you were OK. Where the fuck have you been?' I hurl the words at him like knives, the urge to physically hurt him so strong I have to force myself not to get too close.

'I've been staying in Travelodge in Brighton,' he says.

'Brighton?' I repeat.

'On my own,' he adds, anticipating my next question. 'I just needed some time to think.'

'And you didn't consider letting me know where you were? Or even that you were safe? Have you any idea how worried I've been?' He doesn't answer. 'No, of course you haven't, have you. Because you're a *fucking selfish prick*.' I step towards him, pushing my hands against his chest, forcing him to step backwards. He doesn't attempt to defend himself and I notice his scruffy stubble and red-rimmed eyes. He looks almost as knackered as I do.

'I wasn't going to come back at all but I couldn't do it. I missed you all too much.'

He says it quietly and for a moment I can see something in

his face that hints at his anguish but it's swallowed by the fire that's raging inside me.

'I have to tell you something,' he continues. I brace myself, waiting for him to tell me he's seeing someone else. 'About why I left. There isn't an easy way to say it so I'm just going to come out with it. I've got myself into debt.'

I frown, confused. 'What?'

'A couple of months ago I lost quite a bit of money betting online, so I borrowed some more to cover it up, but I ended up losing that too. And now the people I borrowed it from want it back.' I'm looking at him, but his words don't make any sense. He doesn't gamble. I swallow. 'How much?' I ask.

'Twenty thousand pounds.' He looks down at the floor as he says it.

'Twenty thousand?' I repeat his words, wondering if I've misheard.

'And I can't afford to pay it back. I tried selling things and hoped you wouldn't notice – I pawned my watch and the jewellery your mother gave the girls last year, but it wasn't enough and now they keep adding on interest.' I think back to the earring I'd picked up off the floorboards on the landing, realising where it had come from. The heirlooms she'd wanted the girls to have. Images start to slot themselves into place in my head. 'I was desperate, Jo. I've wanted to tell you for ages, but I didn't know how to. And then we had the funeral and I couldn't –'

'Are you saying this is my fault?'

'No, no – I didn't mean that. I just didn't want to worry you, and then you told me about the baby and I – I just didn't know what to do.' I stare at him blankly.

'The people you borrowed the money from, they're the ones who vandalised my car, aren't they?' I ask, remembering the words written in large white letters and he nods, slowly.

'They've been here? To our house?'

He glances at me as we hear a shriek of laughter from the garden. He swallows. 'Only once. They insisted on meeting to talk about how I planned to pay them back. They didn't come inside. They stayed in my office. The other times we met at different places in my car. It was their phone charger you found.'

I put my hand on the counter to steady myself. 'You let them know where you live? Where your family lives?'

'I didn't have a choice, Jo. They weren't here for long. Ten minutes at the most.' The memory of seeing the empty space between the hangers in Grace's wardrobe makes me livid. Somebody touching her things. I can't believe he's been so stupid.

'No, Paul. They haven't only been here once. After you decided to leave on Monday, they came back, into our home. Into Grace's bedroom where they hid inside your daughter's wardrobe.'

'What?' His face is ashen.

'Inside Grace's wardrobe. I heard a noise in her room and when I went to look, I could see someone had been hiding inside it.'

'They couldn't have. I didn't give them a key to the house. How did they get in?'

'I don't know. Perhaps you left the back door open. They ran out before I had a chance to have a conversation with them.'

He stumbles over to the table and sinks down into one of the kitchen chairs, putting his face in his hands. I think he's crying but I'm too numb to care.

'I'm so sorry, Jo. I never meant this to happen.' He looks up at me. 'Are you and the baby OK?'

I stare at him. 'There is no baby, Paul. There never was.'

THURSDAY
Caroline

It had taken me an hour on Tuesday to read her entire note-book, and I'd been concentrating so hard I hadn't moved from my position on the bed. When, finally, I'd put it down, I'd realised my legs had gone to sleep; a numbness that had given way to tingling and prickles of pain as I'd stretched them out, wincing as I'd wiggled my toes. I'd closed the cover, trapping her between the pages, and had put my hand up to my face to catch the tears that fell, hot and heavy, on my skin.

I'd cried for the life Lauren could have had, the things she'd missed out on. I'd cried because she'd deserved so much better. I'd known who she was from the photo they'd printed in our local paper after it happened. A photo of her at her sixth-form college, her smile hiding the issues they'd said had been all in her head. Rob had seen me reading the article and had told me he'd worked with her. He'd hired her as an intern at his building firm. She'd only been there three months. He said he hadn't known her that well, that she'd kept herself to herself, but he'd organised flowers and a card to be sent to her funeral from the whole company. She'd been the same age as Adam is now. Her mother had used to shop in our local Tesco before it happened; I never saw her afterwards. Tragedy often swallows families whole.

I'd made a choice when this had dropped through my letterbox onto the hall floor, its plain brown paper packaging disguising the bomb inside. I'd chosen my son. I don't regret my decision. A mother's instinct is always to protect her child. I wish I could have taken care of her too. But I couldn't do both. I'd had to put this away under this mattress where it's ticked silently, all this time, waiting for me to be ready.

I had opened it when it had arrived, almost three years ago. I'd peeled off the paper, seen her name on the front cover, and hadn't been able to move. It had been Halloween and Adam had been planning to go out trick or treating with some of his friends. He'd come downstairs to show me his Scream mask and had pulled it off as soon as he'd seen my face, worried he'd terrified me. He hadn't realised my reaction had been nothing to do with his costume. I'd still been holding the notebook, offering it out like a poisoned chalice, hoping he'd demand to look at it, that I'd be forced to show him, that I wouldn't be the one with the responsibility to have to decide. But he hadn't. He'd held up his mask, telling me that all his friends were wearing something similar, and had disappeared into the kitchen to grab something to eat.

I'd watched as he'd walked away, my legs finally obeying my instructions to move, and had taken the package upstairs, putting it in the airing cupboard under a towel, the first place I could think of, returning to it after Adam had gone to meet his friends, carrying it outside, intending to put it in the dustbin. But I hadn't been able to bring myself to throw it away. I'd known keeping it would be more dangerous than letting it go, but I couldn't stop thinking how her mother would feel, and it had become my burden to carry. To hold onto as a constant reminder.

Under Adam's mattress was one of the only places Rob wouldn't look. Anywhere in my room and he'd have discovered it on one of his expeditions to hunt for things he thought I shouldn't have. I slide it back under there now, the cover catching on the sheet, a sign of resistance against returning into the dark, but I stroke it reassuringly. It won't have to stay under there for long.

Two hours to go until Rob gets home. I've had viewings all day today and hadn't gone back to the office after the last one; I hadn't wanted to face Jo. I would never have told Paul that she's pretending to be pregnant but my sister doesn't know that and I can't tell her. She forwarded me the email she's written to the solicitor; I showed Rob last night. It'll keep him away from her for now, long enough for me to do what I need to do.

I empty the dishwasher that's finished its cycle and fold the washing that's been hanging on the clothes rail to dry. I iron three of Rob's shirts – I need to look as if I'm carrying on as normal. I tidy the house, running the hoover over the hallway and sitting room and dust the already clean surfaces. I carry the washing basket upstairs, lifting the pile of clothes into the airing cupboard, an arm of his shirt falling out as I push the door shut, as if he's still trying to grab hold of me even when he's not here. I look around our bedroom, adjust the books on my bedside table into a neat stack and put

Rob's reading glasses into the jacket pocket of a suit that's hanging in his wardrobe.

I squirt bleach round the rim of the toilet in our bathroom, spraying the sink with Cif and wipe it with a cloth until the porcelain gleams bright white. Opening the bathroom cabinet, I sort through the various tubes and packets, throwing out anything that's exceeded its expiry date, tidying the shelves so I can see exactly what's on them. I empty all the bins in every room, stick the rubbish into a black liner and take it outside to throw it away. I drag the heavy dustbin down to the bottom of the driveway – the bin men will collect it tomorrow morning.

Walking out of the house into the back garden, I can't resist going into my greenhouse once more. The stillness inside trembles with anticipation. I look around quickly, checking nothing is out of place, picking up the watering can that has fallen onto its side and propping it up against one of the glass panes before pulling the door shut, the screech of metal against metal cutting into the silence.

I turn the oven onto its lowest setting and dish out the sausages and mash I've cooked onto two plates, covering them with saucepan lids so they'll still be warm when he gets home. On one of our first dates, he'd cooked me the same meal, I remember sitting in his flat and eating it off my knees as he didn't have a proper dining-room table. He hadn't touched his food, saying he wasn't hungry, not taking his eyes off me as he watched me eat mine, and I'd smiled, not wanting to offend him, swallowing forkful after forkful even though I hadn't wanted to finish such a large portion. He'd said I needed spoiling. That I deserved someone who would put

NIKKI SMITH

my needs above their own and keep me safe. I'd remembered his words a couple of years later when I'd burned a pair of his trousers whilst ironing them and he'd pressed one of my fingertips onto the metal plate to show me how hot it was. I'd heard the sizzling my skin had made before I'd felt the pain, a blinding light which had filled my head until I'd cried out, unable to help myself, and he'd let go.

I walk around each room one last time, checking everything is where it should be.

I want to leave the house looking perfect.

I was taught diaphragmatic breathing when I went to counselling as a way of dealing with stress. I'm supposed to shut my eyes, put one hand on my tummy and the other on my chest, inhaling deeply through my nose and then out through my mouth, concentrating on the feeling of my stomach rising and falling. It used to help shrivel the balloon of anxiety that expanded beneath my ribs. I'm trying the technique now, in my bedroom, but it isn't working. I don't think anything will after what you did yesterday. I should never have gone with you when you asked. You acted surprised when we arrived at the house and no one answered the door, but now I realise you'd known all along there wouldn't be anyone there. You let us in with the vendor's keys we'd collected from the estate agent, smiling at me, already an expectation you were going to get what you wanted before you even opened the door. I have to keep stopping as I write this, sticking the top of my biro into the palm of my hand so I can focus on the pain instead of the images in my head. At some point between stepping over the threshold and feeling your hot coffee breath on my lips you turned into a monster. I push the biro point into my skin again, watching a red dot rise up in a perfect hemisphere, swallowing the blue ink, trying to block out the memory of the frayed hem on the bottom of the curtain next to my head, loose threads splayed over the carpet like dead spiders' legs. I hold my pillow over my face, the familiar scent of my mum's fabric softener the only thing that stops the smell of you that has impregnated my nostrils, despite the number of times I've showered. You wrote what you did all over my skin, indelibly marking me so you'll be part of me forever, no matter where I am, or who I'm with.

FRIDAY
Jo

I've made Paul spend the last two nights on the sofa since he got back. This morning he sneaks back into our bedroom just before I wake the girls up, a whispered prior arrangement so he can give Livvi her birthday presents. I don't want to ruin her day. They are still oblivious as to what he's done, my desire to blurt it out outweighed by my unwillingness to hurt them. He puts a cup of tea down on my bedside table; another peace offering I refuse to touch.

He says the people he owes money to won't come back. That they've given him a week to come up with a plan, but I don't believe anything he says anymore. He'd double locked the back door when I'd come downstairs yesterday morning and has been sleeping with the key next him on the sofa. I haven't told him I'm selling the business – I'm sure it's only a matter of time before he suggests it; I know it's the only possibility he has of getting the amount of money he needs. I want him to ask me, to give me another reason to stay angry, to bolster my courage to push him further away, out of the house completely. I want to ask him how he can have been so stupid, but whatever he says won't help me to understand; his assurances that he'll never do anything like this again already slipping through my fingers.

He's angry with me too; I'd told him about the baby deliberately, wanting to hurt him. I'd seen the bewilderment on his face and could tell he hadn't believed me until I'd fetched the letter out of my jacket upstairs and had thrust the crumpled piece of paper into his hand, watching whilst he read the doctor's diagnosis of early menopause. A single tear had slid down his face as he'd absorbed the information and something inside my chest had turned cold, as if a fire that had previously been burning out of control had been extinguished.

I'd wished, too late, that I could take it back. I hadn't set out to hurt him. I'd hit back because he'd hurt me.

'I'm so sorry,' he'd said but I hadn't asked if he was saying it to me or to himself.

Livvi appears at the end of our bed, followed by Grace; the excitement of her birthday enough to camouflage the silence between Paul and me as she opens her presents. If I strip off his skin I'm not sure whether I'll find the person I married underneath, or whether I'll keep peeling away layers until there is nothing left and I'll realise he never existed in the first place; the man lying beside me a stranger dressed in a set of pyjama bottoms my husband used to wear. I wish we could go back, but I realise now this is how marriages end – not in a raging argument, but in the slipping apart of lives that once ran parallel, a failure to realise it's too late to find a way back to reach one another.

He watches Livvi as she pulls the wrapping paper off a parcel and I can see he's wondering if it will be the last time he'll be here to see this, whether next year she'll be opening one set of gifts with me, and another set with him somewhere else. There's a silent pause after she unwraps the last one, and I know what we're all remembering as we look at the mountain of discarded paper and ribbon. Buddy would have dived into the middle of it as he had done on the morning of Grace's birthday last year, grabbing a mouthful of blue tissue paper; Paul had chased him around the room in order to retrieve it.

I get up, gathering all the rubbish in my arms before the memory has time to solidify into something that will taint the atmosphere.

'School,' I say. 'You girls need to get ready.'

I put my head round Grace's door on the way downstairs, checking she's got her uniform on as, recently, she's disappeared in here and got lost in other more important activities, but today she's dressed and is busy doing her hair.

'I can do that if you want,' I say to her as she pulls it up into a ponytail.

'No, it's fine, Mum.' I feel the invisible rope between us loosen a fraction and it makes me want to grab on to it more tightly, pulling it back in for just a few more months, even though I know that's impossible.

'Grandma and Auntie Caroline might pop over this evening to give Livvi their presents.' I watch as she visibly stiffens in front of the mirror, briefly pausing her hairbrush before beginning the rhythmic strokes again. 'Are you OK with that?' She nods, a black band between her teeth. 'Are you sure? You still seem a bit off whenever I mention Auntie

Caroline's name.' She takes the band out of her mouth and stretches it with her fingers to the point I'm convinced it's going to snap.

'No, I'm not.'

'Because I can tell her she can't come if you don't want her to?' I grit my teeth, hoping it will give me an excuse not to have her in the house.

'It's fine, Mum. You know how much Livvi adores her and Uncle Rob and I really want this to be a nice birthday for her.' She tucks a few loose strands behind her ear as she looks in the mirror. 'I don't have a problem with Auntie Caroline. It's Uncle Rob.'

A cold feeling presses on my chest. 'What d'you mean?' She turns towards me and I think she's listening to see if anyone else can hear her, but Livvi and Paul are both downstairs. I push her bedroom door shut just in case. 'What about Rob? Has he done something to you?' I can barely get the words out. She shakes her head.

'Not to me.' I swallow to get rid of the sharp taste of apples in my mouth. Grace sits down on her bed and I walk over to her, taking her hand in mine.

'What then?'

'He's the reason Grandpa got angry with me. He was on a video and Grandpa was watching him.'

I frown. 'What kind of video?'

'A video that Grandpa had up on his computer screen when I went into his study. I didn't know he didn't want me to see it. He got so cross. I'd never heard him shout like that before.'

'Grandpa shouted at you?'

289

'Yes.'

'When was this? Why didn't you tell me?'

'A few weeks before he died. He told me not to tell you and I said I wouldn't and then he got really ill and I didn't think it was right to say anything. I think that's why he's come back, Mum. Because he's still angry with me. I shouldn't have gone into his study. I was only trying to find him to get him to play Patience with me.'

I swallow. 'What did you actually see?'

'The screen was a bit fuzzy and there wasn't any sound but this girl came out of a house and Uncle Rob was following her. She was running and he was running after her. When he caught up with her, he put his arm around her shoulders and it looked like she was trying to get away from him and then Grandpa saw me watching by the door so I didn't see anything else.'

'Did you recognise the girl who Uncle Rob was with?'

'No. But it wasn't Auntie Caroline. She was much younger. About the same age as Adam.'

I wait in the car for the girls to say goodbye to Paul before leaving for school, not wanting to be in the same room as him unless I absolutely have to, but my mind keeps slipping back to what Grace said. *About the same age as Adam.* Nineteen? Younger? I'd been fifteen when he'd slipped his hand under the blanket that covered my legs on the sofa. *Stop it. Get the girls to school first and then you can think about it.*

My leg trembles as I press down on the accelerator and I force myself to smile as Grace and Livvi clamber into the back, fixing a grin onto my face like I did all those years ago whenever anyone asked me if I was OK. Fine, I always said. I'm completely fine. And they'd believed me. They hadn't been able to see that I was drowning, legs kicking frantically in the blackness, face upturned to the sky, my nose the only thing still above water, about to go under at any second.

I'm aware Livvi is talking to me as I pull up opposite the school gates, but I have to ask her to repeat what she's said, reassuring her that I have remembered the Tupperware box full of shop-bought cupcakes that she wants to take in to hand out to her class. I pass them to her through the passenger window as she stands on the pavement, her hands so full she can't manage to take Buddy's blanket off the back seat and bring it into school, as she has done every other day this week.

As she shuts the door, I feel myself gasping for breath, as if I can't get enough oxygen into my lungs. I force myself to concentrate on the road ahead as I drive away, making my mind as blank as the tarmac that I can hear humming beneath the car wheels.

I open the door to Caroline's office as soon as I arrive but it's empty and Alice shakes her head.

'She's out. Got a couple of viewings this morning.'

I sit down at my desk, keeping my office door open so I can see when she walks past. *It wasn't Auntie Caroline.* Maybe Grace had been mistaken. Maybe it had been a really old video when they'd both been younger. Caroline had only been nineteen when they'd got together. I know I'm trying to convince myself and the excuses balance precariously in my head, ready to tip over at the slightest touch. My mobile screen lights up. A message from Paul.

We need to talk.

I text back.

I have nothing to say.

There's a brief pause when my screen goes black before it lights up again.

Can you collect the girls from school this afternoon? I won't be around as am trying to sort stuff out.

I don't reply.

There's a noise in reception and I call out to Caroline as she walks past.

'Can I borrow you for a minute?' She pauses in the door-way, her face expectant. She thinks I'm going to tell her something about the sale of the business. That the solicitor has been in touch. 'Come in,' I say. 'And shut the door.'

She walks inside, putting a paper bag down on my desk in front of her. 'Almond croissants,' she says. 'I haven't had any breakfast. Want one?' I shake my head. The thought of any food at the moment makes me nauseous. Old habits die hard; my determination not to eat had always been strongest when I'd been stressed. She sits down, tears off a piece and my stomach grumbles in protest.

'Grace told me something this morning that I need to ask you about,' I say. She nods, her fingers covered in flakes. 'She said a couple of months ago she saw Dad watching a video of Rob.' Caroline continues to look at me, a slight crease between her eyebrows, but otherwise giving no sign that she's heard this information before. 'He got really cross when he realised she was watching it,' I say carefully.

'And?' She pulls off another piece of croissant, brushing something off her cheek as she puts it into her mouth. 'Are you sure you don't want some of this?'

I nod, swallowing the saliva that fills my mouth.

'Grace said there was someone with Rob in the video.' I point at her cheek. 'You've got a bit on your face.'

'Who?' She pulls a folded paper napkin out of the bag and licks the corner of it before rubbing her skin. 'Better?'

I nod without really looking, needing to get out what I'm going to say, already feeling as if I shouldn't have started this conversation. He's her husband. She's not going to tell me anything.

'Grace didn't recognise them, but she said it was a girl, about the same age as Adam.' I stare at my sister, who looks back at me, her posture suddenly rigid. 'You've still got some flakes on your cheek,' I add, lifting up my hand to brush them off but she flinches when my fingertips touch her skin. I realise they aren't flakes at all. The yellow I can see is discoloured skin and there's a line of purple running along the edge where she's smudged her foundation with the napkin.

She covers her cheek with one hand, looking down at my desk.

'What happened to you?' I ask. She hesitates and in the second before she tells me that she caught it on her utility-room door, I realise I don't need her to explain. The tiny fraction of time is enough for me to see what she's living with. How Rob hadn't ever changed from the person who'd sat beside me on that sofa, one hand under that blanket, his fingers marking my flesh. What had aroused him most wasn't where he'd touched me, it had been seeing the fear in my eyes and although he hadn't come near me again, I'd known he wouldn't be able to hide that desire for long. The bruise on her face tells me I was right. She waits for me to nod, another person to add to the list of people who have swallowed her excuses, not wanting to get involved.

Neither of us speak, the silence settling around us, covering up the past. I reach for the paper bag on the desk, raising my eyebrows in a question and she nods, just once. I tear off a piece of croissant and put it in my mouth, an unspoken message to let her know if I can take this step, she can too.

'Do you want to stay with him?' I ask. Her eyes well up as she shakes her head. 'Is he at work?' She nods. 'Why don't you go and pick up some of your things? You can stay at ours.'

She doesn't move for so long I'm about to repeat the question, but then she speaks so quietly it's almost imperceptible.

'The business,' she says. 'I wouldn't have made you sell it.'

I interrupt before she can finish. 'It doesn't matter.'

'You don't understand,' she says. 'Rob wanted the money. He's trying to buy another site that he wants to develop.'

'Let's focus on one thing at a time,' I say. 'Go home and grab what you need for a few days.'

She takes a deep breath. 'Can you come with me?' she asks.

I hesitate. 'I need to check someone can pick up the girls,' I say. 'I'll meet you outside.' She nods again, and I put the remainder of the almond croissant in my mouth. I start to dial Anna's number as Caroline gets to her feet. 'Would you mind driving?' my sister asks. 'I can't face it.'

'Sure,' I say. I fish around in my handbag for my car keys and push them across the desk. She picks them up and glides out, as sleek as ever, shoulders back. If I hadn't seen the bruise, I'd have assumed her life was perfect.

'Hi, Jo,' Anna answers.

'Hi. I just – I just wondered if you'd be able to do me a favour and collect the girls from school this afternoon? I'm sorry to ask but Paul isn't around.'

'It's honestly not a problem. It might give Grace and Maddie the opportunity to make up.'

'Thanks so much. I should be home by three-thirty.' I walk out of reception, squinting in the brightness. Caroline's already standing by my car, the passenger door open, fiddling with my keys. As I head towards her, she shuts the door, pressing the keys to lock the vehicle.

'I've changed my mind,' she says. 'I think it might be better if I went by myself.'

'Are you sure? I'm happy to come with you if you want.'

She shakes her head. 'Rob won't even be there. He'll still be at work.' She looks at me. 'And if he does come back, it's better if I'm on my own.' She swallows. 'Can you do me a favour and cover my two-thirty appointment?'

I nod. Anna's collecting the girls for me so I don't need to rush back. 'I really think you should have someone with you,' I say.

She looks at me and smiles, briefly. 'Trust me, Jo. I need to deal with this by myself.' She doesn't look worried, but the faint outline of the bruise on her face tells me she should be.

'I don't think you should go on your own,' I tell her again.

She presses my car keys back into my hand. 'I'll be fine, Jo. I'll meet you back at yours. Thanks for offering to let me stay.'

I frown at her rejection of my offer of help and watch as she walks away across the car park, her handbag over one shoulder. As she reaches her car, the sun disappears momentarily behind a cloud, the only one I can see in the entire sky. The temperature drops and goosebumps rise up on my arms. I feel like I did almost twenty years ago when I'd left her to fend for herself, telling myself it was her choice to stay with him as I'd headed to Bristol University to get away from both of them and hadn't come back. I have a sudden urge to rush after her, to insist she lets me go with her, but she's already started her engine and is pulling away.

I arrive at Caroline's two-thirty appointment and experience a flicker of annoyance as I realise the property she's supposed to be photographing is vacant. We could have come at any time. I finish the job quickly, anxious to get back, hoping Anna has remembered to pick up the girls, and it's not until I get in my car to drive home that I notice Buddy's blanket is missing off the back seat.

FRIDAY
Caroline

I pull Buddy's blanket out of my handbag as I walk through my front door, struggling to free it as I've stuffed it inside so tightly, not wanting Jo to notice I'd taken it. I rub the soft material over the towel in the cloakroom, covering every inch, the smell of something unfamiliar hanging in the air for a few seconds, as if it's contemplating whether it wants to be there, before it decides to blend in with the other thousands of molecules and disappears.

I open the bin and find the remains of the onion I'd chopped up yesterday, brushing it with my fingers and then touching my eyes, blinking as the tears run down my face. I take the blanket upstairs and do the same thing to Rob's T-shirt and trousers that are hanging over the end of the bed, making sure I press it inside every crease before folding it up and hiding it under my pillow. I check my watch; three-twenty. He'll be back any minute.

My stomach doesn't turn over at the sound of his key in the lock like it usually does. I check my face in the bathroom mirror. My eyes are still red and there are tear-streaks down my cheeks. I listen as he follows his usual routine, going straight into the downstairs cloakroom to wash his hands before he comes upstairs. I sit up against the pillows on the bed as he comes in, a pile of crumpled toilet-roll on the duvet in front of me. He pulls off his trousers and shirt, a faint smell of petrol clinging to his skin, before grabbing the clothes he was wearing yesterday off the end of the bed.

'What a bloody nightmare,' he says and I notice his hands are shaking as he pulls on his jeans. 'The card payment system at the garage failed so I had to queue at the dispenser to get cash out and then . . .' He trails off as he sees my face. 'What's the matter?'

I let out a choked sob. 'Jo just called.'

He frowns and coughs, clearing his throat before he speaks. 'What did she want?'

I stare at him, not attempting to hold back the tears that slide down my cheeks. 'She called to say there's been a fire.'

I don't know your name as he never talks about you, but you weren't what I expected. I came to your house and saw you through the window. You had such lovely long, red hair. I've always wanted red hair, ever since I was little. All the strongest women seem to have that colour; from Pippi Longstocking to Sansa Stark; the ones who burn brightest with a core of steel. I was going to ring the bell, to tell you what your husband, my boss, was capable of. But then he walked into the room with you and I realised you already knew and you couldn't get away from him either. I saw the way you looked at him. I look at him like that now too. He's killing us both, slowly, as effectively as if he was strangling us with his bare hands. I haven't said anything to anyone; they won't believe me. They'll see my counselling sessions and think I'm making it up, that it's all in my head. He cut me open and tore out my insides so there's nothing of me left, just an empty shell. When I first met him, three months ago, he made me feel special. I bet he made you feel like that too. He agreed to hire me when so many others wouldn't, my exam results and medical history providing a perfect get-out clause. He had a way of getting me to reveal things I wouldn't normally show people, unravelling them all like a ball of wool, winding them around his fingers until he had too much of a grip for me to ever get away. You're the only one who understands, the only one who has seen through the mask he wears to what lies beneath. Which is why I'm leaving you this. I couldn't save myself, but perhaps I can save you.

FRIDAY

Jo

I pull into our driveway with my phone on the seat beside me, the photos of the rental property ready to be uploaded when I get to work tomorrow. I walk across the road to Anna's house, my top sticking to my skin in the humidity, the sun's rays lighting up the edges of the dark clouds that have been absent for weeks. The weather forecast on the radio said there'd be a storm this evening, the first time it'll have rained in over a month. The garden needs it; even the grass is beginning to die off in brown patches. I knock twice before she answers.

She smiles. 'Hi, Jo.'

'Sorry I'm late. My appointment took a bit longer than I thought it would.'

'No worries. It's probably a good thing. Gave the girls a chance to chat. Do you want to take Grace's stuff? They brought their PE bags home today so it's going to be a fun weekend of washing.' She hands me a large blue kit bag.

'Great. Do you want to give me Livvi's as well?'

Anna tilts her head as if she hasn't heard me properly. 'Sorry?'

'Livvi's things?'

The crease in Anna's forehead deepens. 'I don't have her bags, Jo. Livvi isn't here. Her form teacher said she'd already been picked up. I presumed Paul had collected her.'

'What?' We're both staring at each other as if we're speaking different languages. Acid rises up in my throat. I fish around in my handbag, trying to find my mobile, not sure what it's going to tell me. I glance at my screen which doesn't show any missed calls and dial Paul's number but there's no answer as it goes straight to voicemail.

'He's not answering,' I say, my voice sounding as if it doesn't belong to me. My legs start to tremble and I have to hold onto Anna's front door for support. Grace appears in the hallway; she's overheard our conversation.

'Where's Livvi, Mum?'

'I don't know, Grace, just let me think.' The man's face from Parkstone Losey House swims into my vision. Please not that. Please don't let him have found out where she goes to school.

'Andy!' Anna shouts in the direction of her kitchen as she slips on her shoes. 'Can you look after Maddie and Jess for a minute? I'm just going over the road with Jo.'

She holds my arm as I stumble down her drive. 'It's probably just a misunderstanding, Jo. We'll sort it out.' I can't breathe properly, the acid now burning in my chest. What was it he'd said when they'd been looking at those china figures? Something about how fragile they were? We get to the front door as Paul pulls into the drive, the colour draining from his face when he sees me.

'Where's Livvi?' I shriek, but I can already see his backseat is empty and the way he grips his keys, his knuckles white, confirms he has no idea where she is either. Grace slumps down onto the stairs by the coat rack, her face white.

'We'll find her,' Paul says, putting his hand on my shoulder. 'There must have been some kind of mix up.'

'Really, Paul? Or is this down to you?' Grace and Anna stare at me, taken aback by my tone. Paul rubs his face.

'We need to check she's not in the house,' he says. I know logically he's right; it's the first thing the police will ask, but Livvi has never used the spare key to let herself in; I'm not even sure she knows where we keep it. Grace starts to cry and I look at Paul, his eyes wide, realising in that moment his agony mirrors my own and no matter what his faults, there will always be a connection between us. I pray to an entity I don't believe in to bring her back safely, not to punish her for the things Paul or I have done.

Paul notices it first. I'm too busy darting from one room to another trying to find her, anxiety expanding in my chest like a balloon, making it hard to breathe. She isn't in the kitchen or the lounge. Or behind the sofa in the snug, although, with the various toys lying discarded on the floor and felt-tip pens and colouring books littering every surface, I have to look twice to double check. I run upstairs, two at a time, my heart pumping, and throw open her bedroom door. The room is empty. Dropping down on my hands and knees, I peer under her bed.

'Livvi?' My voice wavers and I clear my throat. There's no answer and nothing to see on the cream carpet apart from a thin layer of dust, the grey fluff forming thick circles round the bottom of each wooden leg, as if attracted by a magnet.

I stand up and wince, biting my lip as a burning pain shoots through my toe. I've caught it on the edge of her chest of drawers. Cursing, I hobble into Grace's room, pulling open her white-painted wardrobe doors covered in half-torn Disney *Frozen* stickers that she's tried to peel off now she's outgrown them. The rows of clothes hang motionless, no pairs of small legs protruding underneath.

'Livvi? It's Mummy,' I shout into the silence, trying to ignore the throbbing in my foot. 'You need to come out if you're hiding. I promise I won't be cross.' I listen intently, praying for the sound of a creaking floorboard, a muffled giggle, footsteps scuttling across the carpet. Nothing.

Our bedroom is at the other end of the hall where our duck-egg-blue throw lies undisturbed on top of the duvet, in exactly the same position I'd left it this morning. There's no sign of any obvious tell-tale lumps that I pretend not to spot during one of our games of hide-and-seek. Oh God, where is she? Our wardrobe is locked. The bathroom's empty. I wince as I swallow the metallic taste where I've bitten the inside of my cheek, running back down the stairs to the kitchen.

'She's not upstairs. I've searched everywhere,' I say. Paul glances over my shoulder whilst I'm speaking, staring out through the patio doors across our lawn. He's not listening to me. I grab his arm to get his attention, wondering if he can feel the same ice-cold fingers that are squeezing my lungs, the same weight that has sunk to the bottom of my stomach like an anchor, preventing me from moving. 'What are you looking at?' I ask, trying not to shout. 'We've already checked outside.' I can't keep the edge of hysteria out of my voice as I pull on the sleeve of his shirt, urging him to do something, anything, to find her. He shakes my hand off roughly, pushing me aside as he twists the door handle and realises it's locked, his gaze still fixed on the bottom of the garden.

'What? What is it?' I screw up my eyes against the brightness and blink away the tears that blur my vision. 'She's not out there, Paul.' Two swings dangle limply beneath a metal frame and the trampoline is empty, the canvas mat stretched tight, waiting expectantly for the next jumper.

'Get out of the way,' he yells. I stagger backwards, shocked by his unexpected aggression. 'Are you blind, Jo?' He jabs his finger repeatedly towards the end of the garden as he struggles to get the key off its hook on the wall and into the lock. I can't see what he's pointing at. 'There!' he shouts. 'Look!' I can hear the panic in his voice as he fights to open the door. At first all I can discern through the faint patterns of small handprints smeared on the pane of glass is his office at the end of the garden, the timber structure silhouetted against the evening sun. He finally manages to turn the key before I notice the faint haze around the bottom of the building that is spreading slowly across the grass. It drifts in swirls and the smell hits me the moment Paul flings open the patio door. Smoke.

'Have you searched in there?' He glances at me and I don't need to answer. He sprints across the lawn, screaming her name, as I sink down onto the tiled floor, unable to move as I watch the flames appear. Their red and orange tongues are initially hesitant, contemplating the taste, but once they realise it's a meal to be savoured, they rise up and devour the whole building in a matter of minutes.

FRIDAY
Caroline

'What do you mean, a fire?' Rob struggles to get his T-shirt over his head. He likes them to fit snugly. He thinks it shows off his figure.

'Jo said Paul's office caught fire.'

He hesitates. 'Was there much damage?'

I watch as he rubs his hand across his beard, wondering if he's going to admit what he's done.

'It's Livvi,' I say. He coughs again, a couple of times, and I hear his breath catch in his throat. Tiny beads of sweat appear along his receding hairline, the first sign his body is in distress.

'What about Livvi?' His forehead creases.

'She was inside the office when it caught fire.'

'What?' He steadies himself on the bedrail, the colour draining from his face.

'Livvi was in Paul's office,' I say. 'She was playing in there after she got back from school.'

'Christ.' His breathing is more laboured and his knuckles turn white as he grips the rail. 'Is she OK?'

I stare at him and slowly shake my head. 'The fire-brigade pulled out her body.'

He staggers onto the bed, his body crumpling as he sits down. 'Oh, God. Fuck. What the hell was she doing in there? I checked . . . when I smashed the window there wasn't anyone . . . I don't understand how . . .' He's gasping for breath now, grabbing handfuls of the duvet in a vain attempt to anchor himself to the reality that is unravelling around him.

'She must have been hiding,' I say. 'I'm so sorry. I know how much she meant to you.'

He points frantically at the bathroom. 'Inhaler.' The word comes out as a wheeze, difficult to make out.

'What?' I ask. 'Are you OK?'

He grabs my hand and squeezes it, staring into my eyes.

'In –haler. Or Epi – Epipen.'

I can barely hear him as he fights to get the words out.

'You want me to get your inhaler?' I climb off the bed and walk over to where he's dropped his trousers, taking his phone out of his pocket and entering his pin. I dial my own number, picking my mobile up off the bedside table and letting it go to voicemail when it rings, before hanging up.

I walk slowly to the bathroom, taking his blue inhaler out of the cabinet where I'd left it yesterday, having pressed it two hundred times whilst I'd sorted out all the labels for the flowerpots in my greenhouse, counting each puff of white gas as it had disappeared into the air. He turns his head towards me, his eyes wide, watching as I open his bedside drawer, unable to move as he struggles for breath.

'I can't seem to find your Epipen,' I say, handing him the inhaler. 'I know you asked me to put it in here when we were clearing out your old car, but it doesn't seem to be there now.' I think of it sitting in the kitchen cupboard downstairs where I'd put it earlier, wondering if an epinephrine shot at this stage would be enough to save him. It's possible.

He scrabbles to put his inhaler in his mouth, pressing the button over and over as he waits for it to dispense relief that never arrives. He lets go of it, eventually, realising it isn't helping, and shuts his eyes, focusing what little energy he has left on getting the increasingly small amount of oxygen into his lungs as he falls sideways onto the bed, the noises coming out of his mouth reminding me of a new-born puppy.

I lift his head, taking Buddy's blanket from under my pillow and sliding it underneath him, his eyes fluttering helplessly. Watching my bedroom clock, I wait for the second hand to pass twelve; once, twice, three times.

I lie down on the duvet so we're facing each other. 'You deserve this,' I say. 'Do you remember Lauren, Rob? I never met her, but I know what you did to her. We were away the weekend she took her own life. You took me to that hotel in the New Forest. It was so out of character for you to take me anywhere, but I naively hoped you were trying to make an effort with our marriage.' He brings one hand towards my face but I push it away, putting it back by his side. 'Now I realise it had nothing to do with us. It was because you felt guilty about what you'd done.

'When they found her that morning, I thought something about it didn't quite make sense. The fact that she worked for you and was found in one of the vacant properties you were interested in buying. What did you do to her?' I look down at him but his eyes are shut and I don't think he's capable of telling me, even if he wanted to. 'My dad knew as well, didn't he? That's why he left the business to Jo. He knew that if he'd left it to Mum or me you'd have found a way to get your hands on it.' I tap his face and his eyelids flicker, briefly. 'Dad found something that proved what you did and you can't find it. You thought it must be in the files that Jo took home and if you burned down Paul's office, you'd get rid of it for good.'

Rob's making very few noises now and doesn't put up any resistance as I remove Buddy's blanket and roll it up whilst I look at him, his left hand clenched into a fist, his wedding ring just visible above the faint white scar where he'd told me he'd fallen off his bike when he was little.

I feel as if I'm standing outside reality, in a space where I can see what we might have had if things had been different. 'I don't know how Dad found out, Rob, but he wasn't the only one. I know too. And you might have burned down Paul's office, but a secret always finds a way to come out in the end. It's been here all this time.' I touch his hand, wanting him to know I'm saying goodbye, but he doesn't respond. I pick up the pieces of toilet roll off the bed and flush them down the loo as I walk out, catching a whiff of smoke from his jacket that's hanging over the bannisters as I shut the front door.

I lift up the lid of the boot, stuffing Buddy's blanket into a carrier bag before opening the driver's door, pulling out carefully past Rob's car so as not to scrape the paintwork. Just like he always told me to.

FRIDAY

Jo

My mother arrives outside our house at the same time as my sister, and I hurtle across the driveway to embrace Livvi as she steps out of the car. Paul is standing on the doorstep, his face an ashen-grey colour.

'What the hell do you think you're doing?' I shout.

My mother frowns. 'What are you talking about?'

'Do you know how worried we've been? We had a fire in Paul's office and we had no idea where Livvi was.'

My mother steps out of the car. 'I thought I could smell smoke. I just wanted to take my granddaughter out for a birthday treat. I did tell her teacher when I picked her up.'

'Her teacher probably thought I'd given you permission to collect her. Why didn't you call me and let me know where you were?'

'I did let you know. I left you a message on your home phone.'

'You didn't, Mum. There's nothing on the answerphone. I've checked.'

'Well, I left a message.' She sounds indignant but fiddles with her handbag, a sign she's flustered. I hug my daughter again, not wanting to let her go. She kisses me, her lips sticky from the ice cream my mother has treated her to.

'You should have tried my mobile. You gave us such a fright. I was just about to call the police.' I'm not sure whether I'm talking to Livvi or my mother, the sense of relief making my legs feel as though they might buckle beneath me.

Paul steps outside and I let go of Livvi reluctantly, knowing how worried he's been too. He looks at me, grateful, swinging his daughter up into his arms, but I can't forgive him for what he's done to us. Not yet. He carries her over to where Grace is standing in the hall and my mother trails behind, keen to get away from my stony glances.

Caroline gets out of her car as they go inside and walks over to me.

'Everything OK?' she asks.

'Fine. Now. Mum collected Livvi from school and didn't bother telling me,' I say. 'And there was a fire in Paul's office. He managed to put it out, but the whole place is completely wrecked. Did you pick up your things from your house OK?'

She shakes her head and hands me a carrier bag and the spare key to our house that I'd given her in case of emergencies months earlier.

'These belong to you,' she says. I take them, looking at her, confused.

'I need to ask you something, Jo. I need you to say that I was with you this afternoon. At the appointment. It's important.' She hesitates and I glance back at the house where I can hear Grace laughing.

'Why? What happened? Was Rob there?' I ask her.

She doesn't answer.

'Perhaps it's better that I don't know,' I reply, staring at the key, the implications sinking in like a lead weight as I slip it into my trousers. 'I tried telling you what he was capable of, but I should have tried harder. And I shouldn't have left all those years ago without making sure you were safe. We need to look after each other.' She nods, and I can see something in her eyes that wasn't there before. Fear? Relief? I can't tell.

'It was him, wasn't it?' I say, glancing at what's inside the bag. 'Rob took your key, let himself into our house and poisoned Buddy, didn't he?

She doesn't reply.

'Oh God, he's been watching us, hasn't he? It was him hiding in Grace's wardrobe.'

Caroline touches my arm. 'You should go. Be with your family.' The sound of Livvi giggling escapes through the open door and I turn my head.

'I think Paul and I are going to spend a bit of time apart,' I tell her. 'He's got some issues he needs to sort out and I need to be on my own for a while.'

Caroline nods slowly. She stands very still, almost as if her body is unwilling to move but I can see her hands are trembling.

'Why don't you come in?' I ask.

She shakes her head, as if my question has forced her to make a decision, but still doesn't try to leave. I put the carrier bag down by my feet and envelop her in an embrace. 'I already told Alice before I left the office that I was meeting you at the property,' I say in a low voice. 'I said we'd be there all afternoon. And we were.' I fish in my pocket and hand her a set of keys. 'If anyone asks, I left you there to lock up. You said you were going to hang around to finish some paperwork.'

She smiles and wipes her eyes. 'The police might call you,' she says.

I nod. 'Are you OK going back there on your own?' I ask.

Caroline smiles, sadly. 'I've been through worse.'

'Call me if you need anything,' I add.

I walk over to my car and open the boot, putting the bag inside. My sister heads back down the drive and starts her engine before I run after her and tap on the window. She lowers it.

'I have to know,' I say. 'That video of Rob – do you know who he was with?' I look into her eyes and can't tell if she's lying to me as she shakes her head.

'I've no idea, Jo. Sometimes it's just better not to ask.'

Epilogue

Ten Weeks Later

Caroline

I ask for the package at the post office and the lady behind the counter hands it over, the corners of her mouth turned up in a sympathetic smile that I've seen often recently.

'It came a few weeks ago, but your son called before he sent it and asked me to put it to one side for you. He said you'd be in to collect it when you were ready. I know you've had a lot to deal with. I was so sorry to hear about –'

'Thank you.' I cut her short, not wanting to hear her condolences. 'I'm actually going on holiday for a while to see him. He's in Bali.'

'That will be nice,' she says. 'It'll do you good to get away.'

I smile as I take the package and walk out onto the street, opening the envelope and flicking through the bundle of Indonesian rupiah notes. It's cooler today, I can feel the breeze on my face; there was a storm last night which had broken the heat. I wonder how I'm going to cope out in Bali.

My suitcase is in the hallway, the house is packed up into storage boxes. I've given Jo a set of keys and asked her to organise viewings to rent it out whilst I'm away. If things go as planned, I'm not sure how long I'll be gone. I need some time alone with my son. Just the two of us.

Jo had insisted on selling the business. She said it was the best thing for all of us and will let me know when everything is completed. She's moving back to Bristol but has said she'll wait until I'm back before she goes so there's someone here to look after Mum. Paul moved back there after Rob's funeral; he's rented a flat and is trying to build up his business. Jo has agreed to clear his remaining debts; she used Mum's house as collateral until the proceeds from the sale come through, but has insisted she's not moving back in with Paul for the moment – she wants to wait and see what happens before making any final decisions. She's said I'm welcome to go with her, that she'd love to have me living nearby and I promised her I'd think about it. A new start. Away from all the memories.

The post-mortem had concluded that Rob had died of a sudden-onset asthma attack, and although it had been impossible to say what had triggered it, they suspected it had been the smoke from the fire he'd started in Paul's office; his fingerprints found on a petrol can dumped nearby. I told the police I hadn't seen him since he'd left for work on the Friday morning, but that he'd tried to call me that afternoon. I hadn't picked up as I'd been too busy – pulling together the property details with Jo. I couldn't give any explanation as to why he'd committed arson.

I'd told Adam I'd come out to Bali as soon as I could. He hadn't come home for the funeral. I'd told him I didn't want him there. We'd kept it as the four of us, close family; my mother's face paler than it had been at Dad's service a few months earlier. I'd watched Paul reach for Jo's hand during the service and had seen her squeeze it briefly, before letting it go again.

She'd put her arms around me after we'd come out of the crematorium and hadn't let go, her eyes glistening with tears as she'd stepped backwards. I know she hadn't been crying for Rob. My mother had hesitated before putting a hand on her shoulder and I'd seen a look pass between them, something I hadn't fully understood.

I still don't know for certain how Dad had found out. All his belongings that Jo had taken home from the office had been destroyed in the fire but I think he must have got hold of CCTV footage from the vacant property where Lauren's body had been found. He'd been selling it off for development when she'd died and must have been horrified to watch her trying to run away from his son-in-law. He'd thought he was protecting me and his grandson by not saying anything about it, but we'd continued to suffer whilst the family of an eighteen-year-old girl had never understood why her life had ended as it had, suspended by a dressing gown cord from a curtain rail. My husband had been responsible for more than anyone realised. Except for me, perhaps.

I pat my handbag, checking I've got everything I need; tickets, my brand-new passport, my phone and my purse. The taxi pulls into the drive, the sound of the car making my stomach clench until I see the driver through the windscreen. One step at a time, I tell myself. I shut the front door behind me, tucking a wispy strand of hair that's come loose from my ponytail behind my ear.

The driver looks at me in his mirror. 'Heathrow?' he asks.

'Yes, please. Terminal four. Would you mind stopping if you see a post box? I've got a package I need to drop off.' He glances at me in his rear-view mirror as he pulls over half a mile down the road. I open the taxi door and hesitate, momentarily feeling bereft as I look at the small rectangular parcel wrapped in brown paper, before letting it drop through the red slot. I hope it gives Mr and Mrs Taylor some answers to the questions that must have haunted them over the past three years.

I sit staring out of the window for the rest of the journey, looking at the people in the cars that slide alongside me; men, women, children; imagining lives that I'll never know anything about. When we pull off the motorway, I take the three postcards Adam had sent me out of my bag and reread each one. I don't want to leave them where someone might find them. The secrets others know about are always the ones that come back to haunt you.

My beautiful, brilliant son. In less than twenty-four hours I'll be with him. I'd come home a year ago to find him hiding behind the door of our bedroom clutching a hammer, waiting for his father to walk in. He'd said he couldn't bear it any longer. I'd managed to persuade him not to do something that would ruin the rest of his life. I wouldn't have been able to bear the guilt of losing another child. I'd promised him I'd find a way, but had told him he had to leave first. To go somewhere safe. This had all been his plan originally, I'd just changed a few of the details.

I trace over his writing on the last postcard he'd sent me with my finger, feeling the familiar indentations his biro had made in the surface.

Had a very exciting afternoon fishing (lol!) at the famous Otan river. Unhooked several catches and still have water all inside trainers. It's not great as they're probably (obviously!) spoiled. Took outstanding freediving film in caves. Epic!

I look at the initial letter of each word, putting them together to construct a sentence, smiling as I read it to myself in my head.

Have a flat for us. Cash waiting at post office.

Not just a way of us keeping in touch, but a way of him letting me know things were ready on his side, a method of communicating that Rob would never figure out. Even though I'd refused to let Adam get involved, he'd done the only thing he could by telling me a new life was waiting for me; giving me a glimmer of hope to cling to.

I read the others he'd sent me one last time in order, each one containing a different message, wondering what else he'd said in the one Rob had burned, realising that it didn't make any difference now:

Namaste! Experienced epic diving at Pulukan. Lodgings are nice. Plan on investigating surfing on Nusa – heard it's mental?!

I think Seminyak's awesome. Lovely, magnificent ocean, seen twelve turtles incubating many eggs. Baby elephants randomly emerged at dusk yesterday.

The cab pulls up outside the terminal and I get out, handing the driver three twenty-pound notes, the postcards still clasped in my hand. I walk inside the revolving doors, following the signs to 'Departures', pausing by one of the dustbins, letting his words disappear inside, severing the final connection to what we've done.

There's a tiny moment of silence, a fraction of a second in which I consider a million different outcomes, a sense of guilt settling like an anchor at the bottom of my stomach, before I hear the cards hit the bottom of the bin. I take a deep breath, reach into my bag to pull out my passport and walk towards the check-in desk.

A free woman.

Acknowledgements

Several authors far more experienced than myself warned me that writing a second novel would be difficult – they were right; and their description of it being 'a bit like a second album' didn't quite represent how tricky it would be. However, it has made me appreciate all the support I've received during the writing of this one, and, I should add, throughout 2020 and 'lockdown' during which *All In Her Head* was published – an interesting time to launch a debut novel (!)

I'd like to thank my loveliest of agents, Sophie Lambert – I know how lucky I am to have her and am so, so grateful for all her expertise.

Thanks also go to my editor Harriet Bourton whose wise suggestions have helped to keep me sane during some of the hairier moments this year, and for her brilliant ability to identify exactly what is and isn't working when I can't see the wood for the trees. Thank you also to Lucy Frederick, Francesca Pearce and everyone at Orion. You are all honestly a delight to work with and I couldn't ask for a more supportive team.

A big shout out to all my friends - I haven't seen any of

them as much as I'd have liked to this year but my life would be so much duller without them – Laura, Lauren and Zoe, my daily writing support team; all of the Ladykillers who make me laugh so often, Lynn, Ceril, Nanna, Anna & Els, and so many other local and not-so-local friends who have given me more support and encouragement than I could ever have hoped for. I should also mention the Debut 2020 group as well – in what has been 'a year' this group has provided advice, support and many giggles on a Friday evening zoom. Here's to meeting up in person in 2021.

This book is dedicated to my parents, but I'm so grateful to my whole family – close and extended – for their support in ways too numerous to mention them all here. My sister-in-law for spending hours at a BBQ discussing a tricky plot issue with me, my father-in-law for asking about my book in every bookshop he visits, my daughters who make me laugh and continually inspire me, my cat for her attempts to step all over my keyboard and destroy my book on a daily basis, and to my husband, for his love and unending patience. I feel so fortunate to have a partner who is the exact opposite to Rob in this book.

During the writing of this book, I have been privileged to hear stories from so many women who have, at some point in their lives, lived in fear of a partner. I would like to thank them for talking to me. There are many charities out there, including Women's Aid (www.womensaid.org.uk) who are working to change this, but there is still a long way to go. And finally, a huge thanks to everyone who helped champion my debut novel – other authors, booksellers, book bloggers and the team at Curtis Brown Creative. Your support has been so very much appreciated, and I am so, so grateful for your reviews and feedback.

Most importantly, thank you for reading this book. I am so grateful to each and every one of you. Without readers, stories would remain unheard, and in the words of Emily Dickinson which are perhaps more apt than ever this year, 'To travel far, there is no better ship than a book.'

Credits

Nikki Smith and Orion Fiction would like to thank everyone at Orion who worked on the publication of *Look What You Made Me Do* in the UK.

Editorial
Harriet Bourton
Lucy Frederick

Copy editor
Marian Reid

Proof reader
Linda Joyce

Audio
Paul Stark
Amber Bates

Contracts
Anne Goddard
Paul Bulos
Jake Alderson

Design
Debbie Holmes
Joanna Ridley
Nick May

Editorial Management
Charlie Panayiotou
Jane Hughes
Alice Davis

**Discover the debut thriller getting
inside *everyone's* head . . .**

ALL IN
HER
HEAD

Alison feels like she's losing her mind. She is convinced that her
ex-husband Jack is following her. She is certain she recognises the
strange woman who keeps approaching her at work.

She knows she has a good reason to be afraid. But she can't
remember why.

Then the mention of one name brings a lifetime of memories –
and the truth – crashing back . . .

'Tense and moving'
HARRIET TYCE